LAYING

RHETORIC, CULTURE, AND SOCIAL CRITIQUE

LAYING CLAIM

African American Cultural Memory and Southern Identity

Patricia G. Davis

The University of Alabama Press

Tuscaloosa

The University of Alabama Press
Tuscaloosa, Alabama 35487-0380
uapress.ua.edu

Hardcover edition published 2016.
Paperback edition published 2021.
eBook edition published 2016.

Inquiries about reproducing material from this work should be addressed to the
University of Alabama Press.

Typeface: Bembo

Cover image: Reenactors from the Third Regiment, United States Colored
Troops marcing into battle at Fort Pocahontas, Charles City County, Virginia,
May 2008; photo by Patricia G. Davis
Cover design: Gary Gore

Paperback ISBN: 978-0-8173-6025-2

A previous edition of this book has been cataloged by the Library of Congress.
ISBN: 978-0-8173-1921-2 (cloth)
E-ISBN: 978-0-8173-8999-4

Contents

Figures

Acknowledgments

What began as a sense of bewilderment at the continuing cultural and political power of the Confederate battle flag and subsequently evolved into a series of intellectual questions centered on the intersection of race, memory, and identity has now crystallized in the form of this book. As memories do not occur in a vacuum, neither do the books that detail their functioning. *Laying Claim* is the result of numerous conversations, conferences, symposia, workshops, and lectures over many years. These interactions have deepened my understanding of memory, culture, and identity.

I would like to thank Bob Hall and Luis Falcon at Northeastern University for providing me with intellectual and financial support for the research that went into this book. I would also like to thank Pat Aron for opening her home to me during my stay in Boston and for being a wonderful friend.

A fellowship in the Department of Communication Studies at the University of North Carolina, Chapel Hill enabled me to conduct additional research and further refine my ideas. The productive mix of being in an intellectually stimulating environment that was actually located *in* the South proved invaluable to the development of the book. I am especially thankful to Eric King Watts, Carole Blair, Dennis Mumford, Della Pollock, and Bill Balthrop for their mentorship and discussions.

My time at Georgia State University has been instrumental in seeing this project to fruition. I am particularly grateful to the Communication Department and the College of Arts and Sciences, as the financial support and research leave I received in 2013 and 2014 were invaluable in enabling me to travel to both old and new research sites to gather additional data, to complete the analysis of this data, and to write and revise the final product. I am very thankful to my graduate student assistants, Aron Christian, Geoffrey Henry, John Russell, and Kristen Everett, for all the work they have done to help me see the book through. I am especially appreciative of Michael Bruner, Natalie Tindall, and Mary Stuckey for reading all or portions of this work and offering me the feedback necessary in its final stages.

I am also thankful to those who, as my reenactor friends would say, "did what they did not have to do." In particular, I thank George Lipsitz for his astute and timely feedback, and Stephen Small for generously sharing the insights gleaned from many years of work studying plantation museums; I am also grateful to Alex Orailoglu for his keen editorial eye. I owe my deepest gratitude to Beth Ferholt and Rachel Kahn for their friendship, as well as for their emotional support and generosity with their time, and to Gayle Aruta for making my life manageable. *Laying Claim* would not have come to fruition without you.

I also owe a huge debt of gratitude to the many reenactors, museum professionals, online posters, and National Park Service historians, as well as the visitors to the museums I studied. It is your experiences, observations, and conversations that have provided the backbone for this book. *Laying Claim* would not be possible without your contributions.

I offer my thanks to Dan Waterman of the University of Alabama Press for his belief in the book, his patience, and his unerring support. I would also like to offer my sincere gratitude to Mark Lawrence McPhail and an anonymous reviewer for feedback that improved my analysis significantly. I am also sincerely grateful to Michael Schudson, Val Hartouni, Robert Horwitz, Michael Hanson, Stefan Tanaka, and Esra Ozyurek for their insights.

Much of the historical research for this book was conducted at a number of archives and libraries. In particular, the Virginia Historical Society, the Moorland-Spingarn Research Center at Howard University, the Southern Historical Collection at the University of North Carolina Wilson Library, the Geisel Library at UC-San Diego, the Snell Library at Northeastern, and the Pullen Library at Georgia State were valuable resources whose collections complemented my human research.

Portions of this material have been presented at numerous conferences over the years. These included meetings of: the National Communication Association, the Association for the Study of African American Life and History, the American Studies Association, the Southern American Studies Association, the Southern States Communication Association, the

International Association for Media and Communications Research, the Popular Culture/American Culture Association, and the Cultural Studies Association. Additionally, the "Public Memory and Ethnicity Conference" at Lewis & Clark College in 2007, the annual meeting of the Center for the Study of Citizenship held at Wayne State University in 2007, and the "Symposium on New Interpretations of the American Civil War" sponsored by the Center for the Study of the Civil War Era at Kennesaw State University in 2010 provided smaller, more focused venues for me to hone my ideas about African American memory, citizenship, and historical agency.

Finally, I wish to express my thanks to my daughter, Joelle Davis, who traveled with me to many of the Civil War sites I visited and absorbed this aspect of history and its reconstruction the only way a child, tween, and teenager can: with alternating fascination, bewilderment, and nonchalance. I also give thanks to my parents Simon C. and Ollie F. Spencer, whose emotional support and guidance made all of this possible.

LAYING CLAIM

Cultural Memory and African American Southern Identity

An Introduction

Over the last century and a half, it has been declared—in numerous venues and by various interlocutors—that the South will rise again. This is an assertion reliant upon a vision of the past replete with images of a beautiful bygone southern civilization, supported by narratives foregrounding principled rebellion against the threatened loss of that civilization and, ultimately, defeat in the hard-fought war that transformed it. Once a powerful rallying cry, the avowal of a southern renaissance invokes memories that have formed the contemporary basis for a regional heritage and identity initially constructed decades before the first shots were fired at Fort Sumter. These memories have functioned rhetorically as a potent binding agent, securing a sense of collective consciousness across class and gender lines. Though they have served as the dominant memories of the era, they offer stories that are partial, racially exclusionary, and dismissive of alternative experiences.

When I was a young child growing up in a small town in southern Virginia, the inevitability of that oft-quoted prediction appeared fairly certain to me. The region's most vaunted and recognizable symbol, the Confederate battle flag, maintained a steady and ubiquitous presence in my hometown, being displayed in windows and on vehicles and emblazoned on T-shirts, lunchboxes, and other artifacts. In the popular cultural arena, the television program *The Dukes of Hazzard* was wildly popular with the general public, as well as with many of my elementary school classmates; its underlying theme of youthful defiance animated many breathless playground synopses of the previous Friday night's episode. Likewise, the southern rock band Lynyrd Skynyrd was also a favorite among both my peers and the wider community, with its album covers worn proudly on clothing and exhibited on posters. Both the show and the group prominently featured the Confederate flag, equating its symbolism with an innocuous spirit of rebelliousness that was part and parcel of their popular appeal. Meanwhile, many of my history textbooks spun narratives of southern courage and resilience in the midst of defeat in what was occasionally referred to as the "War Between the States," while painting the Reconstruction era as a period of tyranny that the southern people had heroically endured and overcome. In my mind, all of these phenomena were testaments to the ability of the region to reinvent and reassert itself in multiple arenas.

What also appeared obvious to me was that I was not included in the version of the South that would ostensibly rise from the symbolic ashes of Appomattox to claim its rightful place as the cultural, social, and political center of the United States. My Virginia birth and upbringing notwithstanding, as an African American, I had effectively been written out of the identity of "southerner" symbolized by the flag, the official history, entertainment representations, and other various texts implicated in the dominant narratives constitutive of belonging within the region. The conception of southern "heritage" encouraged by my history textbooks' nostalgic focus on the grandeur and innocence of the antebellum South—and invariably invoked by bearers of the Confederate flag—served to advance a very selective, predominately white version of that heritage. This perception was reinforced every time my family drove past the Confederate monument on the grounds of the old courthouse in the middle of our town's main square. The memorial, "guarded" by two restored Civil War-era cannons and engraved with the names of the local area's Confederate war dead, advanced a material, though markedly one-sided, assertion of the entire town's recognized historical identity.

My perception of the dominant meaning of southern heritage was further reinforced on a family trip to Thomas Jefferson's home at Monticello in the early 1980s. The guided tour of the stately neoclassical mansion celebrated Jefferson's achievements and painted a very pleasant portrait of his family life there, emphasizing the ornate contents of the house and its storied architecture. It was a visual history designed to advance a romanticized, tourist-friendly narrative emphasizing the legendary gentility of the Old South. Keenly aware of the history of slavery even as a preteen, I could sense that there were significant aspects of daily life on Jefferson's plantation that were missing from the narrative. This tour—and, I would find out later, similar tours at other plantation museums represented a narrow reproduction of the past characterized as much by its exclusions as its inclusions. All of these experiences collectively painted a clear picture: whether the content and implications of dominant ideas of southernness took the form of the celebrated elegance and splendor of the Old South aristocracy or of the proudly defiant, so-called redneck culture epitomized by *The Dukes of Hazzard*, they invoked cultural memories and, by extension, a sense of belonging, to which I could never lay claim.

Many years later, while living in Atlanta, I followed with great interest the very public battle that erupted when Georgia's then-governor Roy Barnes persuaded the state legislature to remove the Confederate symbol from the state flag. As I watched the battle unfold, I was particularly intrigued by the ways in which the public debate over the flag hinged on the question of heritage and did so in a way that evoked my earlier experiences with the racially exclusionary version of history I had encountered. While white proponents situated the flag as a proud symbol of their heritage as southerners, African Americans and their allies perceived the flag to be a negative icon of that same heritage: the symbol of slavery, Jim Crow, and other institutions of white supremacy. Both sides viewed Georgia's display of the flag as implying state legitimation of one interpretation of "southern heritage" over others. What this and similar battles in other southern states made clear was that competing Civil War memories were central to the divergent readings of the flag's symbolism. One set of memories invoked the version of the past presented in textbooks, at Monticello, and other venues of traditional historical representation; the other demanded a more critical interpretation of that same history.

The most striking aspect of Georgia's flag war was that the state's African Americans—who had had no public voice when the flag was raised in 1956—were able to use the battle to question not only the dominant meaning of the flag and the official memory for which it stood but also to interrogate the very meaning of southern heritage itself. Their vocal opposition to the status quo symbolized by the flag and the act of its display was a means of asserting their own sense of belonging to the South and its historically significant places and institutions. Thus my observations began to crystallize into broader research questions about the intersections between Civil War memory, collective identity, and relations of power. I was most concerned with an African American southern identity, which, as an identity centered on resistant readings of dominant, culturally powerful historical narratives, necessitated a focus on the practices involved in its construction and articulation. I was particularly interested in the ways in which marginalized groups historically denied access to the more traditional structures of historical knowledge production and representation mobilize the forms available to them as means of producing and expressing identity. This led to the following questions: What is African American southern identity? Where does it fit into normalized conceptions of *southern heritage*? What is the role of Civil War memory in its constitution? What is the nature and form of its practices of representation? What cultural work do these practices perform?

This book takes up these questions. My analysis reveals that there is a form of African American identification with the South centered on Civil War memory, and that this sense of belonging to the region is most productively constructed and articulated through a variety of vernacular cultural practices.[1] It does so amid a rapidly changing South that is experiencing demographic shifts that have not only contributed to the modernization of the region but have also afforded it increasing influence over national politics and culture. According to the United States Census Bureau, the South has experienced the greatest population growth in the country, with urban centers such as Houston, Charlotte, Atlanta, San Antonio, and Raleigh among the areas showing the most dramatic increases.[2] A substantial portion of this demographic trend involves African American return migration to the region, which began in the post-civil rights movement 1970s and includes northern-born blacks as well as those originally from the South. As the Bureau's report notes for 2010, that year the region's share of the African American population was the highest it had been since 1960.[3] Most interestingly, this return has been motivated not only by the aspiration to exploit greater economic opportunities but also by the desire to (re)connect with deeply held notions of the South as a historically significant homeplace.[4] Historian C. Vann Woodward has noted that "the attractions for those returning were mainly old cultural constants . . . the values of place and past, the symbols of traditions of region rather than race," while literary scholar Thadious M. Davis has suggested that African American return migration represents "laying claim to a culture and a region that, though fraught with pain and difficulty, provides a major grounding for identity."[5]

So perhaps the South *will* indeed rise again, though not in the manner that (in)famous declaration was meant to convey. The demographic trends that have transformed Dixie have also included a substantial migration of Latinos and northern whites and have contributed to an ongoing shift in political and economic power away from the industrial North to the region. These shifts have helped precipitate a more critical orientation

toward dominant southern memory, broadening the contours of southernness to encompass multiple identities. It is within this context that African Americans have engaged in a variety of communicative practices
designed to construct an identification with the South via the recovery of
memories commonly perceived as a source of trauma and shame. These
practices are constitutive of what Toni Morrison has referred to as "rip-
ping the veil," a concept describing the discursive acts implicated in the
recovery of "proceedings too terrible to relate"—memories of slavery.[6]
The transformations they reflect have served to construct what I refer to
as the "new New South." In contrast to the old New South, which entailed a post-Reconstruction region focused on modernization and industrialization yet remaining steeped in the Old South values of black
subjugation and white supremacy, the new New South describes a twenty-
first-century region in which inclusion is the default value for all things
southern, particularly its defining memories. This transition, along with
the changes it has wrought, has served to complicate references to the region's anticipated resurgence by enabling the following question: if and
when the South does rise again, what form will this new New South take?

Civil War Memory and African American Southern Identity

Group identity is constructed from the stories a group tells about itself,
prioritizing the inherited values, symbols and discourses garnered from
collective memory. The role of memory in the construction of group
identity has been the subject of much scholarship, beginning with the
Durkheimian notion of "collective consciousness" and most famously articulated by Maurice Halbwachs, who advanced a theory of collective
memory as group-centered and interactive. According to these formula-
tions, memory is constructed and reconstructed through various discursive practices, while group solidarity is solidified through commemorative
rituals.[7] The increasing attention contemporary scholarship has accorded
to the study of memory has foregrounded its various forms, including *collective, social, popular, cultural*, and *public*. Of particular concern here is the
assumed distinction between collective memory as theorized by Halbwachs and *cultural* and *public* memory. My goal is to advance an analysis of black collective consciousness that mobilizes the key features of all
three. This book offers a focus on African American group solidarity produced through collective memory while emphasizing the commemorative rituals at the center of Marita Sturken's distinction between cultural
and collective memory. Sturken defines cultural memory as that which is

"shared outside the avenues of formal historical discourse yet is entangled with cultural products and imbued with cultural meaning."[8] Meanwhile, the importance assigned to the processes of recovering silenced historical narratives from the dustbin of history and destabilizing dominant memory prioritizes their reliance on the very public nature of the memories they produce.

Hegemonic memories of slavery and the Civil War have been advanced for more than a century via centralized master narratives constructed through a variety of dominant systems of representation. These systems fall into two major categories: those advanced by and through the state, its agents, and institutions, and those propagated through the private cultural arena. Primary among the first category are American archival institutions, which are far from neutral repositories of objects and data. The documents, photographs, and other records that archives hold are important sources of historical scholarship, collective memory, and national identity and are therefore "active sites where social power is negotiated, contested, and confirmed."[9] The values and actions that determine which artifacts these institutions choose to include in their collections and therefore valorize (as well as the ones they discard and therefore marginalize) are organized around the dictates of—and reproduce—the same structures of power that have privileged white-centered memories. Additionally, archives draw much of their authority from the fact that the social relations embedded in their creation and maintenance are largely invisible and rarely questioned.[10]

Other meaningful ways in which state institutions construct dominant memory occur in the political arena. Political rituals generally have among their uses the construction of collective identity. Those that have served as conduits for southern identity have historically used the Lost Cause as a powerful binding agent for a white collective consciousness heavily invested in Civil War memory.[11] In addition to state-sanctioned displays of the Confederate battle flag, the Lost Cause paradigm that characterized the oratory of many southern politicians in the early- to mid-twentieth century has found its legacy in contemporary celebrations of Confederate History Month, Confederate Flag Day, and other festivities.[12] Moreover, the states' rights rhetoric that provided the paradigm's foundation has retained its salience in conservative political discourse in the twenty-first century. While most—though not all—Civil War historians have long ago abandoned the tendency to give the era romantic treatment, periodic political controversies erupt over campaigns to separate the war from slavery in school textbooks. These conflicts are infused with important meaning and therefore have contributed to the construction of southern identity in both the past and the present.

At the same time, the cultural arena remains the primary means through which dominant memories of the Civil War have been advanced, as individuals and groups invested in the Lost Cause version of Civil War memory and its legacy have enjoyed preponderant access to the means of production of historical narratives. The early-twentieth century memorialization campaigns of the United Daughters of the Confederacy, which resulted in hundreds of monuments dedicated to the Confederate dead, rendered the region's memorial landscape both a symbolic and material paean to southern whiteness. The tourist discourses constructed at these and other sites—such as plantation museums and battlefields—advance official versions of history packaged neatly and unproblematically for mass consumption. Filmic depictions of slavery and Civil War history have privileged the experiences of the antebellum aristocracy while relegating black people to at best supporting roles and at worst dehumanized caricatures in the very time period that defines their identity as African Americans. Contemporary cultural productions of the era have been marked generally not by hostile or paternalistic and stereotypical depictions of Civil-War-era blackness—though these do indeed exist—but by symbolic annihilation, or the lack of representation, of African American experiences.[13] In contrast to the overt distortion of stereotypes, symbolic annihilation is manifested in more subtle practices, ensuring that the hegemony advanced through the resulting narratives is masked and therefore more powerful. For example, the steadfast devotion to authenticity and battle minutiae enables traditional Civil War reenactors to shift the discursive focus away from the causes and consequences of the war, while an emphasis on the grandeur and ornateness of the main house allows plantation museum tour guides to avoid discussing the slaves who performed the labor there and elsewhere on the grounds, and whose bondage provided the backbone of the social and economic systems that gave rise to such opulence. These cultural practices have had the cumulative effect of constructing and representing a southern identity characterized by very narrow and exclusionary parameters.

While the critical memories constructed in response to this trend invoke the collective and cultural aspects of memory practices, they rely heavily on the discursive resources available in the very public nature of their expression. Public memories, according to Blair, Dickinson, and Ott, build collective consciousness through the cultivation of shared memory "in constituted audiences, positioned in some kind of relationship of mutuality that implicates their common interests, investments, or destinies, with profound political implications."[14] This connection between a group's shared memories and the representation of those memories in the public sphere prompts the observation that stories about the past are really focused on the needs and power relations of the present. It informs, for example, the civic processes involved in the production of history museums, as well as the rhetorical strategies deployed in the cultivation of these institutions' various publics. Similarly, it engages the variety of ways in which different practices of memory—from participating in a battle reenactment to sharing a museum experience with others—create meaning. It also underlines the very public nature of battles over Confederate artifacts and sites, where competing discourses pointing to the presumption of a communal "heritage" are often at the core of the conflict. In essence, practices of representing memory in the public sphere acknowledge and respond to the pluralistic character of the publics from which they issue. It is at this intersection of group consciousness that collective, cultural, and public memories intervene in the formation of southern identity, as museums, monuments, battle reenactments, films and other cultural institutions and practices work to strengthen sectional consciousness.

The Civil War has always been more than a definite, singular event in American history. It has traditionally served as a collective script upon which multiple discourses of race and gender have played out. These discourses were and are represented in the romanticized images of the Old South that emerged during the post-Reconstruction period and remain resonant in the contemporary era: gallant and heroic white gentlemen, passive and ultra-feminine white belles, and loyal and contented black slaves. In this vision, the Civil War was a white man's war: a conflict between northern and southern "brothers" that was fought not over slavery but rather for the preservation of hearth and home. Propagated and assiduously maintained by white political and economic elites, this interpretation prevailed throughout the twentieth century as a means of ordering society by containing any fissures among southern whites while ensuring the subservience of African Americans and women. Southern society thus drew its identity from a history that privileged the domination of white men.[15]

Though the idea of a distinct sectional identity was rooted in the plantation economy and attendant conflicts over slavery, it was memories of defeat in the war that gave rise to the modern conception of southernness from the post-Reconstruction period onward, as Lost Cause mythologies served as powerful and sustaining binding agents cutting across geographical and class lines. As the war ended and became part of the past, cultural memories began to form the basis for southern solidarity. These memories, along with their foundational racialized and gendered discourses, have underwritten the contemporary construction of southern identity with respect to both its conventional (white) form and its emergent (African American-centered) form. However, as the unmarked norm, whiteness has historically served as the default identification associated with the term "southerner."

As is the case with most racialized identities, hegemonic white southern identity has produced resistances, and black southern identity is, in its essence, an oppositional identity. My goal here is not to rehash the descriptions of traditional southern identity that have been examined in other scholarly volumes.[16] However, because African American southern identity cannot be understood in isolation from its white counterpart, my objective is to use the conventional understanding of southern identity as a springboard, a means of articulating its relationship to the emergent black identity foregrounded in this book. The constitutive practices of black southern identity are intended to disrupt the hegemony of those aligned with traditional southern identity. The following two accounts of the war are illustrative of this relationship.

In describing the importance of history to southerners, novelist and poet Robert Penn Warren made a case for a regional distinctiveness based on the primacy of Civil War memory, including the sense of identity solidified through the collective experience of defeat. Speaking to a group of faculty and students at Union College in Schenectady, New York in 1966, he stated, "the South is a special case. It lost the war and suffered hardship. That kind of defeat gives the past great importance. There is a need somehow to keep it alive, to justify it, and this works to transform the record of fact into legend. In the process, pain, dreariness, the particulars of the individual experience become absorbed in the romantic fable."[17] Less than thirty years earlier, in 1937, former slave Robert Glenn had offered an alternative memory of what the war had wrought—and a vastly different interpretation of southern belonging—when speaking to Pat Matthews in Raleigh, North Carolina: "I broke down and began to cry. Mother and Father did not know me, but Mother suspicioned I was her child. Father had a few days previously remarked that he did not want to die without seeing his son once more. I could not find language to express my feelings. I did not know before I came home whether my parents were dead or alive. This Christmas I spent in the county and state of my birth and childhood with Mother, Father, and freedom was the happiest period of my entire life, because those who were torn apart in bondage and sorrow several years previous were now united in freedom and happiness."[18]

There are a number of striking differences between these two interpretations of Civil War memory. Warren was speaking before an elite audience during the final years of the civil rights movement; Glenn was speaking before an oral historian with the depression-era Federal Writers' Project. The former describes a group identification based on an admittedly-selective longing for a mythical era, while the latter employs an individual narrative to acknowledge and describe what was, for many, the collective trauma of forced familial separation. Most importantly, Warren's interpretation represents a culturally authoritative, dominant voice that adheres to the convention of deploying a white racial frame to construct a narrative framework based on assumptions equating sectional identity with dominant white memory. In this historical knowledge regime, an emancipatory war and its aftermath are positioned as "defeat" and "hardship." In contrast, Glenn's perspective represents a vernacular voice, previously silenced and much less socially influential, yet centered on the freedom from enslavement and despair that was the most significant consequence of that same war. Though proffered decades earlier, mediated through a professional writer, and articulated in a much different context, Glenn's memory offers an oppositional narrative, an interrogation of the white-centered ideological frame underlying the conception of southern identity advanced by Warren and other powerful cultural producers.

It is the profundity of the differences between these two accounts that has provided the grounding for African American southern identity in the contemporary era. Black sectional consciousness is constructed through both the revision of dominant white memory and the recovery of black-centered memories of slavery and agency in the war and during Reconstruction. In effect, black southern identity is a rejection of the Lost Cause version of the war in favor of what historian David Blight refers to as the conflict's emancipationist vision.[19] The alternative memories created through this revision and recovery constitute what Nietzsche referred to as critical history, or that which brings the past to the fore for the purpose of interrogation.[20] The memories that spring from critical history are those that represent an acknowledgment of past injustices, while the practices with which they are constructed are motivated by a desire for redemption.

However, the resistant nature of this identity extends beyond the revision of dominant historical memory. It represents a broader critical interrogation of the racial and gender discourses that have privileged the historical agency of white men while symbolically annihilating the experiences of black men and women, as well as a subversion of the power structures that have facilitated the perpetuation of racially exclusionary historical narratives.[21] The very concept of a southern subjectivity that foregrounds blackness challenges the romantically sanitized versions of slavery presented in films such as *Gone With the Wind*, at plantation museums, in monuments, and at other memory sites. It offers an alternative vision to the neo-Confederate rhetoric that prevails at battle reenactments and other venues and which depicts the causes of the war as being deliberately divorced from slavery. It resists the imposition of narrow meanings upon the Confederate battle flag and other icons and opposes their sanction by the state and its agents while arguing for the existence of other perspectives on their symbolism. It also offers a post-civil rights voice to those who would oppose the valorization of the Confederacy and its central figures, which continues to operate powerfully within southern culture and politics.[22]

In engaging these objectives, black southern identity broadens the discursive contours of southern heritage. Additionally, because collective memory deploys narratives of the past in the service of the goals of the present, African American southern identity enables a disruption of the continuity of racial and gender stereotypes rooted in southern mythology: the Uncle Toms, mammies, Jezebels, bucks, and other popular images of the era whose modern incarnations still inhabit the pop cultural realm. In this sense, it refutes the narrow range of identities assigned to contemporary blackness by the dominant culture.

At the same time that African American assertions of Southern belonging mobilize the idea of difference from Lost Cause mythology and dominant memory, the shared focus on Civil War memory offers a more complicated form of resistance. In its grounding in narratives from this epoch, the emergence of a black subjectivity opposes dominant notions African Americans hold about themselves. Collective memories of slavery have always been a source of ambivalence among black intellectuals, elites, and common folk, being commonly characterized not by stories of resilience and self-determination but by a sense of trauma and shame. The stigma associated with a heritage that includes bondage has led to a type of "forgetting as humiliated silence."[23]

Moreover, the popular image of the Civil War as a story for white people, by white people, and about white people—with African Americans playing supporting roles as passive victims whose emancipation came at the hands of white saviors—remains pervasive within the black community.

Dominant memories of Reconstruction pose another barrier. Narratives foregrounding African American empowerment during the post-war period have been erased in favor of a popular positioning of the era as a tragic mistake in which the "southern people" were unduly victimized. Indeed, the history of Reconstruction had become so distorted by white historians that W. E. B. Du Bois lamented in 1935 that "we have got to a place where we cannot use our experiences during and after the Civil War for the uplift and enlightenment of mankind."[24]

This ambivalence about the past has contributed historically to resistance to the idea of an African American southern identity. During the early years of the twentieth century, the combination of white sectional reconciliation and an emergent black uplift ideology that superseded previous perceptions of black rural southerners as the quintessence of blackness and racial historicity in the United States initiated the process of disavowal of black southern identity. Additionally, the economic, political, and social oppression that precipitated African American migration out of the South during the middle years of the century enabled race to supplant region as the center of identity. Decades later, when regional identification reemerged as a component of black identity, the South was excluded from the process as the Black Power movement shifted its discursive focus to the urban ghettoes in the North as sites of black redemption. Finally, the persistence of the broad perception of the South as an abject region—a sectional "other" whose culture and politics are widely viewed as reactionary and backwards by both black and white people—further problematizes black identification.

Yet southern identity is fundamentally an articulation of difference, and slavery, along with its legacy, is an intrinsic part of African American culture. A key feature of identities is that they are defined by what they are *not*, and the South has always defined itself as a region in opposition to the North, constructing a sense of collective consciousness from its perceived distinctiveness.[25] Race, slavery, and—later—memories of war and its legacy in Jim Crow formed the basis for this difference. The very liminality of Dixie, with its intransigent social conservatism, reactionary politics, and reverence for the past, has branded it perpetually as a "foreign" country within the United States and therefore positioned it as a prime site for the construction of an identity based on its (both self-proclaimed and assigned) distinctiveness. It was the experience of slavery that collectivized people with diverse languages and cultures into the population we refer to as African Americans; the legacy of that experience has further cemented group consciousness. As the primal scene of the black experience in America slavery has been central to attempts to forge a collective black identity, as has the remembrance of this traumatic history.[26]

While attempts to redefine and expand southern identity had begun earlier during the Harlem Renaissance, the dissolution of the Jim Crow system marked the beginning of transformative efforts to construct and assert a new vision of southern belonging. The recovery of the region as the center of African American identity took root in this novel cultural milieu. Even the 1960s' Black Arts Movement, the aesthetic branch of the Black Power movement, began to create works that identified slavery as the formative black experience in America.[27] The historical knowledge producers whose cultural work is described in this book articulate a subjectivity that has taken root during the last few decades, preceding by a few years the return migration that has enhanced its material, economic, and political dimensions.

The collective consciousness born of memories of slavery is rooted in critical history's intersection with trauma. Trauma is an important aspect of the critical history of the South, just as it is of the nation as a whole; together they form the basis upon which black southern identity is constructed. Recent scholarship on collective memory has positioned trauma not as a destructive force but rather as a productive one that allows individuals to see themselves as a collectivity for whom a shared ordeal is the solidifying experience. Trauma theory situates suffering as a cultural process, one that is experienced not directly but as collective memory.[28] The experience of slavery—which defines individuals as members of a race—constitutes a set of culturally traumatic memories crucial to the cohesion of the group we know as "African Americans."

The emergent identity I describe here involves a usage of traumatic memory that deviates from the connotations ordinarily associated with the definition of trauma. In this formulation, the memory narratives that are constructed through trauma situate it as an experience of endurance rather than of victimization. Though the pain associated with memories of slavery is acknowledged, it is not used to construct a historically victimized subjectivity. The discursive focus is rather on the experiencing and overcoming of suffering through narratives of survival. Cultural memories of the war that ended slavery are an indelible part of its story and are therefore an essential aspect of black southern identity. In the new narratives created through the production of this critical history, it is southern blackness, rather than whiteness, that occupies the central position.

Thus, the discourses surrounding the emergent black southern identity highlight the question of historical agency. In its most basic sense, agency refers to the power earned and effected through action. As Sidonie Smith and Julia Watson remind us, memory produces agency through its "power to intervene in imposed systems of meaning."[29] Historical agency is the power attained through discourses that position individuals or groups as actors in, rather than passive witnesses to, significant events of the past. It is also located in the ability to act in the present to bring the past back to life. In the case of black southern identity, historical agency is produced both in the sense of representing African Americans as actors in one of the defining eras in US history and in the sense of constructing memory through the processes of representation itself. In the first case, African Americans evolve from historical objects to historical subjects; in the second, they advance from historical consumers to historical producers.

The processes of producing historical agency—that engage both the content and process of producing memory—constitute the key features of black southern identity. The first of these features is that black southern identity, like most non-dominant identities, requires its members to engage in identity work as a means of sustaining collective consciousness. According to sociologist Barbara Ponse, identity work includes "the processes and procedures engaged in by groups designed to effect changes in the meaning of identities."[30] Those participating in this work perceive it as a necessary part of the project of asserting a notion of blackness that veers away from its dominant, essentialized form toward more complicated conceptions; the practices of recovering black-centered narratives of the past perform the work of articulating connections between the antebellum, Civil War, and Reconstruction eras and current sociopolitical realities. This includes positioning public policies—such as those resulting in persistent residential segregation, mass incarceration, and inequitable tax structures—as part of the heritage of slavery. It also includes the historical contextualization of social problems commonly attributed to presumed deficiencies in black culture, such as inner city violence, high unemployment, teenage pregnancy, and wealth and educational disparities. In essence, African American southern identity acknowledges the transhistorical nature of contemporary inequalities through an encapsulation of slavery's present-day legacy. This helps construct it as just as much a political identity as it is a cultural identification. These practices perform the identity work of interrogating popular images of antebellum and Civil War-era blackness, marshaling discourses of gender and citizenship to offer an alternative vision of both the past and the present. Thus, the social actions constitutive of black southern identity are intrinsically connected to broader structures of representation, and are further entwined with the goals of community liberation and empowerment, or *cultural work*. Thus, these practices are reflective of what I refer to throughout this book as "identity/cultural" work.

Another key role agency plays here is expanding the contours of southern identity to encompass twentieth century freedom movements. Those engaged in constructing and expressing this identity do so in part by positioning the Civil War as the first struggle in the ongoing battle for African American freedom. As part of the identity/cultural work of demonstrating the continuing legacy of slavery, they build crucial connections between memories of the Civil War and those of the civil rights movement, thereby constructing a much broader memory base than the one offered by a traditional southern identity insistent upon a focus on Lost Cause assumptions that separate the two eras. Furthermore, black identity offers a vision of southern subjectivity that positions African American Civil War memory as an integral part of the American story. This represents an important contrast with traditional southern identity: while white southern identity is constructed from the notion of southern distinctiveness, African American southern identity simultaneously acknowledges a sectional identification while remaining grounded in an ideal of belonging to the national community. In other words, it deploys Civil War memory as an assertion of Americanness.

Similarly, black southern identity is expansive in the sense that, compared to traditional southern identity, it relies less on the lingering cultural divide between North and South and more on the ways in which the southern past may be mobilized to address contemporary goals.[31] For those engaged in the work of constructing this identity, regional differences are less important than the objective of attaining empowerment through an understanding of history. It is this feature of identity that enables, for example, a black man who was born and raised in Chicago to build southern identity by participating in a Civil War battle reenactment in Virginia as a Union soldier and positioning his activities as a contestation of the dominant memories etched on the battlefield landscape. Black southern identity expands southern identity, in other words, by de-territorializing it.

The most important way in which agency intervenes lies in the fact that cultural memories and the identities they produce are constructed rather than reproduced. As Stuart Hall has cautioned us, we must think about identity not as an already accomplished fact but rather as a "production" always in process and constituted within systems of representation.[32] This is particularly the case with identities constituted through cultural trauma, as mediation and representation are critical to the establishment of events as sources of suffering and endurance. Traumatic cultural memories are not experienced directly. As a cultural process, trauma is mediated through various forms of representation.[33]

The contemporary moment has afforded a ripe sociocultural milieu for the emergence and representation of black-centered Civil War memory and identity. In concert with the South's demographic restructuring, a number of cultural shifts have also facilitated this evolution. The hegemonic authority of the Lost Cause is gradually dissipating, as post-civil rights society has ushered in an era where material images of the Old South are contested and erased from a southern landscape in which the population is attempting to take its place in a national and increasingly global community. The emergence of the new New South has worked to enable resistant readings of southern history and culture and to destabilize conventional understandings of southern identity.

These more critical interpretations of the past have extended to the lucrative heritage tourism industry.[34] The resultant memories have served to reorder many of the narratives advanced through tourist sites that had traditionally privileged the experiences of white elites and have stimulated increasing interest in those sites foregrounding black history. As black heritage tours—which include sites associated with the history of slavery—have become more popular, the result has been an expansion of the concept of southern heritage. Not coincidentally, the African American return migration to the region has been accompanied by increasing claims of regional belonging: of all of the region's ethnic groups, African Americans are most likely to identify as southerners.[35] These developments, in turn, have created a conception of modern southernness that is fluid and dynamic, foreclosed the further imposition of a narrow and exclusionary southern identity, and opened up possibilities for multiple southern *identities*.

Vernacular Voices, Sites of Opportunity: African American Cultural Memory and Identity Practices

One final question remains: what is the nature and form of the practices analyzed in this book? A significant aspect of the resistant nature of black southern identity and the memory in which it is grounded lies in the practices associated with its construction and articulation. The history of the mass mediated symbolic annihilation of the African American experience, combined with a distrust of official history, has necessitated the development of an identity grounded in a set of vernacular memory practices constituting a sense of belonging to the South. Memory is not something that exists. It is, rather, something we *do*, something we produce through social practices. We construct, maintain, represent, articulate, and contest memories. "Vernacular" refers to the cultural expressions of "ordinary" people, as opposed to organized elite or official sources. Vernacular voices spring from communities that have been historically ignored and typically function as a response to dominant discourses. The articulation of vernacular memories remains a powerful form of cultural expression. Whether the articulations in question are ethnic, individual, or local, they are situated as both a critical response to the normative authority of official history and as an interrogation of the assumption that the production of history is the exclusive domain of the powerful. It is through vernacular practices that the processes of memory negotiation and renegotiation are implemented. The official memories to which vernacular expressions respond do not occur in a vacuum. They are agenda-driven enterprises designed to create a narrative infrastructure for the promotion of various interests. They are in general promulgated as a means of producing and maintaining social cohesion and loyalty to established institutions and structures. In the South, the Lost Cause and its vestigial myths and assumptions have traditionally served these purposes.

At the same time, dominant southern memory and identity reflect the problematics inherent in any attempt to simplify the "vernacular" as one half of a dichotomy easily collapsible into the categories of dominance on the one hand and resistance on the other. Official histories are generally national in scope, as cultural and political elites and other state actors attempt to deploy memory as a binding agent amid the continuous "threat" of fissures rooted in class, race, religion, geography, and other social formations. While traditional southern memory has served this purpose with respect to the maintenance of sectional identity, it has also functioned in tension with national memories. Nevertheless, the similarities between the functions of southern memory and identity and those of the nation are significant to the construction and vernacular expression of black southern identity, as southern memory shares another key feature with national memory: the marginalization of the historical experiences and contributions of non-whites, with the corresponding valorization of whiteness as essential to American identity.

Thus, any project that takes up an analysis of African American southern memory and identity, as this book does, is by definition an analysis of vernacular modes of expression. The main reason for the utilization of grassroots practices is pragmatic: top-down, traditional memory structures and practices are typically characterized by significant entry barriers and by commercial imperatives. These factors shape the content and uniformity of historical representation and disallow the mainstream circulation of alternative, critical narratives. The appeal of bottom-up practices as modes of memory-making is as ideological and agenda-driven as that of the practices associated with dominant memory, but in a significantly different way: alternative, vernacular practices enable practitioners to exercise a significant degree of agency over their own representation. The ability to assert this agency requires an engagement with dominant memory while necessitating an end-run around the imperatives that define many conventional systems of historical representation. This requires a response to power at its constitutive sites. The practices I analyze thus emerge from the intersection of official and vernacular cultural expressions.

The overarching goal of mobilizing these practices to assert southern identity is not merely to acquire the ability to speak but—more importantly—to be *heard*. The nature of the practices that define and articulate black southern identity advances this goal, as it proffers a dialogic relationship between the oppositional, vernacular discourses and traditional southern identity. As Bodnar has argued, vernacular producers are "less interested than cultural leaders in exerting influence or control over others, and are preoccupied, instead, with defending the interests and rights of their social segments.[36] This goal ensures that these practices must construct and maintain dialogue with dominant memory in order to perform effectively the identity/cultural work of building an oppositional subjectivity. Moreover, as a feature of historically conscious expression, dialogism ensures that the resistant and vernacular nature of these practices does not necessarily render them utopian sites characterized by a lack of conflict. On the contrary, they are strategically intended to produce black-centered memory through intervention in the functioning of the very sites implicated in the construction of white southern identity.[37] This ensures that agency is constructed through both the form and content of these practices, as the form itself has its own content. Additionally, the dialogic nature of resistant memory expressions allows those engaged in them to appropriate hegemonic themes and reorder them for their own purposes. For example, African American men's participation in Civil War battle reenactments as Union soldiers works to reinscribe normative, traditional discourses of masculinity and citizenship while challenging the symbolic annihilation of memories centered on black men's agency in the war. Similarly, when constructing and digitally uploading oral history narratives meant to counter paternalistic, Lost Cause-friendly mythologies of black subservience during slavery, many online museum community members incorporate and emphasize conservative themes of individuality, redemption, and self-reliance. In the case of black memory practices, co-optation of dominant discourse advances oppositional strategies. To borrow an idea from literary theorist Mikhail Bakhtin, interaction with hegemonic memory provides the most productive foundation for interrogating it.[38]

The dialogic relationship with dominant memory that characterizes these practices emphasizes the rhetorical nature of the sites through which black southern memory and identity are constructed. The rhetorical strategies that emerge from this construction mobilize the key features of vernacular discourse, pastiche and cultural syncretism. Pastiche involves the incorporation of elements from the dominant culture, while cultural syncretism refers to those expressions involved in the production of a self-affirming community.[39] The resistant potential of these strategies is further enhanced through the incorporation of important elements identified with African American rhetorical traditions. These traditions emphasize the construction of a critical public voice, including the ways in which it is empowered to communicate values both similar to and unique from those of the dominant culture.[40] Dialogism intervenes in the functioning of dominant memory through the cultivation of a vibrant black public voice, and highlights what this voice offers epistemologically to contemporary deliberation on social and political issues concerned with race. As literary theorist Houston Baker has suggested, "black Americans have always situated their unique forms of expressive publicity in a complex set of relationships to other forms of American publicity."[41] Baker also contends that the practices characteristic of the dialogue engaged within these spheres constitute a critical language inseparable from the historical and cultural conditions from which they emerge and to which they continue to respond.[42] Each site may be thus positioned as a public through which a number of historically conscious individuals interact to construct memory.[43] The interjection of a critical black public voice into dominant Civil War memory spheres undermines the notion that these arenas—battlefields, museums, online communities—are sites of objective historiographies and instead resituates them as places where, through dialogue, negotiations over memory and meaning may take place. These sites are thus transformed into black public spheres. This transformation is significant, given the rootedness of contemporary issues within which race is an overt or underlying element in the Civil War era, as well as the one-sidedness of the collective memories that have emerged from the conflict.

As rhetorical scholar Mark Lawrence McPhail has suggested, it is through the cultivation of a sense of genuine reckoning with and responsibility for history (and its erasures) that American society can shed its preoccupation with racial hierarchies and begin living up to its stated ideals. The belief in the possibility of this reconciliation, he adds, provides the necessary sustenance for African American rhetorical practices.[44]

The engagement of a vernacular African American rhetoric is an essential aspect of the power of those working within battle reenactment culture, traditional museums, and cybermuseums to interrogate hegemonic Civil War memory and construct alternative historical narratives. In these spheres, historical producers, consumers, even the natural and built environments are rhetorical. From verbal discourses proffered through visitor conversations in traditional and online museum communities to the visual discourses advanced via the presence of uniformed black bodies on Civil War battlefields, all of these memory producers interact within a context that deploys a multitude of referents—historical, cultural, regional, and racial—as forms of persuasion.

Laying Claim sets forth a detailed analysis of the vernacular communication practices constructed through these sites. These memory and identity practices encompass a broad range, from a very old form of communication—performance—to the very recent form of digital media. Each practice marshals the rhetorical influences of its respective site to construct vernacular memories through a dialogic engagement with hegemonic history, reworking it into a set of alternative narratives that offer an enriched picture of the past. In the chapters that follow, I analyze the enactment of this agenda. Chapter one foregrounds battle reenactment as a means of asserting southern identity. Though typically perceived as a peculiar hobby, battle reenactment is one of the most powerful means through which hegemonic images of the Civil War are conveyed. The tendency of traditional reenactment to focus on "authenticity" and battle minutiae serves to privilege southern whiteness by obscuring the causes and consequences of the war. The very presence of African Americans as soldiers, civilians, and spectators advances resistant memory, while the acts of performing and viewing historical narratives constitute assertions of belonging. These are all means of articulating claims upon the past. Black battle enactment, a vernacular practice *within* a vernacular practice, mobilizes both pastiche and cultural syncretism to produce identity through the recovery of narratives of idealized gender, citizenship, and agency, as well as through the renegotiation of the meanings assigned to the "hallowed ground" of the Civil War battlefield. Black reenactors perform mostly as United States

Colored Troops (USCT) and utilize a variety of verbal and visual discourses to effectively redeploy Civil War battle narratives to redefine both historical and contemporary southern blackness. These performances also highlight the complexities of black southern identity by bringing to the forefront the tensions that emerge with the minority presence of black Confederate reenactors, along with the alternative discourses conveyed through their performances.

In chapter two, I analyze the discursive strategies of history museums in the South centered on the African American experience of slavery, Civil War, and Reconstruction. Museums are more than mere repositories of objects; they are indicative of the ways societies see themselves. In the South, the dominant visual narratives advanced through museums, monuments, and other historic sites have conveyed tourist-friendly narratives that have symbolically annihilated slavery while advancing hegemonic white-centered ideals of southern belonging. Whether the dominant image has been constructed through plantation museums privileging the elite experience of the era, or through obelisks, statues, and other monuments honoring the Confederate dead, the memorial landscape in the South has historically been a prime site though which the Lost Cause interpretation of the past has been advanced. Thus, black history museums focusing on the era are compelled to employ unique strategies extending beyond those of the exhibits themselves interrogate these narratives and to overcome the difficulties in visually representing the history of slavery. African American history museums advance a multi-pronged representational strategy that engages discourses of space and place along with corporeality, interactive performance, and dialogue to present memories of the era that focus on its emancipationist vision. This innovative strategy advances a cultural syncretism that subverts the hegemony of more traditional historic sites.

Chapter three discusses the ways in which cultural syncretism is constructed through digital media to provide a space for local knowledge to intervene in the construction of dominant memory. Traditional media forms, such as film, have historically been among the most influential, far-reaching agents in the production of idyllic images of the Old South, while new media in the form of neo-Confederate websites, blogs, and video games have helped advance the hegemony of the Lost Cause to audiences on a global scale. Additionally, archival institutions have conventionally privileged the perspectives of white southerners in constructing culturally authoritative interpretations of history. Interactive digital museums have provided a space for resistance to these institutions. The

Memory Book cybermuseum uses social networking technologies to allow vernacular "curators" to upload images of private artifacts from the past and share their oral history narratives with other community members and visitors to the site. Visual images make distant memories accessible and render complex historical events more comprehensible. Storytelling, traditionally an important aspect of both southern and African American culture, engenders agency and power, as those who engage in the work of creating and sharing narratives construct memories of the past that reflect realities that often diverge from official histories in profoundly meaningful ways. Social networking technologies shatter the distinction between producers and consumers, an important capacity for those attempting to revise dominant historical narratives. I analyze the ways in which the *Memory Book* community mobilizes these features to construct affirmative memories of black resilience bravery and entrepreneurial success during slavery, Civil War, and Reconstruction, disrupting the hegemonic power of both traditional media and archival institutions.

Finally, in the conclusion, I offer an assessment of the changing cultural landscape in both the South and the nation that has given rise to the expression of southern black identity, as well as a discussion of events suggestive of the reassertion of traditional identity. I revisit some of the sites with which I began this book, describing their transformations within the context of the new New South, and offer a brief glimpse of the future for which these changes provide an opening. I situate my argument about black southern identity and its constitutive practices and sites within broader discussions of cultural memory, offering some additional insights as to how the region's ongoing transformation might affect these conversations.

The fieldwork for this book included interviews with reenactors, organizers, and visitors at reenactments both inside and outside of the South, as well as observations of battles, skirmishes, historical presentations, and guest interactions. This research took place at the following reenactments: the Battle of Olustee, in Olustee, Florida, in February 2008; the Battle of Forks Road, in Wilmington, North Carolina, in February 2008 and 2010; the Battle of Fort Pocahontas in Charles City County, Virginia, in May 2008 and 2010; the Battle of Camp Nelson in Nicholasville, Kentucky, in September 2009; and the Battle of New Bern in New Bern, North Carolina, in May 2010. Additional research was conducted at Kearney Park in Fresno, California, in October 2008, the Tierra Rejada Ranch in Moorpark, California in November 2008, and the Antique Gas and Steam Museum in Vista, California in March 2009.

I also conducted interviews with staff, board members, volunteers and visitors, as well as engaging in participant/observation research at the following museums: the American Civil War Center (now called the American Civil War Museum) in Richmond, Virginia, during the summer and fall of 2007, the African American Civil War Museum in Washington, DC, during the summer and fall of 2007, the summer and fall of 2009, and the fall of 2013, and the Ancient Africa, Slavery and Civil War Museum in Selma, Alabama, during the summer and fall of 2013. All quotations in this book, excepting those attributed to secondary sources, are derived from these research interviews.

Reenactments, traditional museums, and cybermuseums all marshal different rhetorics that operate most powerfully with their respective publics. However, their major unifying thread is that they all constitute new knowledge regimes that harness the power of grassroots interventions to subvert the hegemony of centralized, top-down historical narratives. They are simultaneously sites of resistance and opportunity. Their immediate goal is to displace a system of public memory that enables African Americans to critique, but not control or own, the representations of their roles in history. Ultimately, the identity/cultural work they perform enables practitioners and visitors to see history not as a series of past events but as a continuum, and to see the places of their ancestors and themselves in it.

I

Ghosts of Nat Turner

African American Civil War Reenactment and the Performance of Historical Agency, Citizenship, and Masculinity

The American Negroes are the only people in the history of the
world . . . that ever became free without any effort of their own. . . .
[The Civil War] was not their business. . . . They twanged banjos
around railroad stations, sang melodious spirituals, and believed that
some Yankee would soon come along and give each of them forty
acres and a mule.

W. E. Woodward, *Meet General Grant*, 1928

[Performance] ruptures and rattles and revises history; it challenges
the easy composure of history under the sign of objectivity.
It discomposes history as myth, making of it a scene awaiting
intervention by the performing subject.

Della Pollock, "Making History Go," in
*Exceptional Spaces: Essays in Performance
and History*, 27

"This whole thing is mind-blowing, I knew nothing of this. . . . If I'd
have known this, it would've taken away the inevitability that I was
gonna be nothing."

Comedian Chris Rock, upon learning
of an ancestor who fought for the Union
during the Civil War, as seen on the PBS
series *Finding Your Roots*.

The eleventh annual reenactment of the battle of Fort Pocahontas—held
in Charles City County, Virginia—displayed most of the elements of a
traditional Civil War reenactment: a large, well-maintained battlefield, a
sealed-off area under a tent for spectators to gather, engage each other in
conversation, and watch the battle, and a small number of vendors selling
food, books, T-shirts, and other memorabilia. The scene conveyed a strik-

ing mix of the old and the new, as men, women, and children dressed in antebellum period attire talked on cell phones and sported digital cameras and camcorders. A short path led visitors away from the battlefield toward a small plantation cum museum, where a docent casually announced the guided tours taking place every thirty minutes. There was also a long trail leading into the woods beyond the battlefield to the encampment area—the living space where the reenactors congregated before and after the battle, eating hardtack, singing songs, cleaning muskets, and engaging in other acts deemed authentic simulacra of the daily existence of a Civil War soldier.

This reenactment, however, also contained some decidedly *nontraditional* elements. Down the hill from the encampment area, on the north bank of the James River, was a prayer circle made up of approximately thirty African American men and women, all descendants of many of the men who had fought in the original battle. Some of them wore T-shirts bearing the names and regiments of their ancestors. To the melodic beat of an African drummer, evangelist Sallie Mae Collier—an elderly black woman—led the prayer: "We need to get this history into our souls so we can tell our children that these people died for them. That's why they have it so easy. There is blood in this ground. We as a people, we [are] a rock. We need to tell our children. How can we tell our children if we don't know? This is the truth, this is history. . . . We need to know we are a *somebody* because our forefathers fought for us to be somebody. We have lost our heritage, but praise God it's coming back. . . . We can commend our forefathers for what they did for us. They had to take the banner and honor the flag. How come we can't take this heritage and pass it to our children? What happened here . . . was the beginning of freedom."

Prayer circles and African drumming may seem out of place at an event commonly perceived to be the exclusive domain of conservative white men. The invocation of ancestral spirits is an African-centered expressive practice which, when performed at a battle reenactment, is evocative of the union of spirituality and militant rhetoric characteristic of African American discourse.[1] As such, it exemplifies the resistant interventions put forward through African American Civil War battle reenactment. Black participation in the hobby is a relatively new phenomenon involving increasing numbers of men and women motivated by a desire to reconstruct the experiences of the nearly two hundred thousand black men who fought for the Union in the war as United States Colored Troops (USCT). The participants come from a diversity of backgrounds—from a high school student in Kentucky who participates in local living history

Figure 1. Prayer circle at the Fort Pocahontas reenactment, Charles City County, Virginia. Photo by Patricia G. Davis.

events with his father to a municipal court judge in Chicago who travels south on selected weekends to engage in combat enactments. Some of them took up the hobby after genealogical research yielded the discovery of a USCT ancestor. Many of them participate as part of civic groups that have incorporated living history performance into their community engagement objectives. Regardless of the various factors that motivate their interest in reenactment, they share a common goal: finishing the work initiated with the 1989 film *Glory*, which for the first time presented the story of African Americans' roles in securing their own freedom. In fact, many black reenactors were first inspired to pursue the hobby after viewing the film. However, the cultural work they engage in through their performances extends well beyond that offered through a Hollywood-produced historical drama. As Collier's prayer indicates, they see it as their duty to represent these forgotten memories in a much more meaningful, productive arena: the discursive space of the Civil War battlefield.

Since its revival as a cultural practice during the centennial celebrations of the 1960s, battle reenactment has provided a means by which historically conscious individuals and groups may construct memories of the war by traveling to various sites to recreate its battles and skirmishes. Most of these events take place on or near the actual battlefields, but their reach extends well beyond the region: California plays host to many very well-attended reenactments each year, as do a few overseas locations. Contrary to mass-mediated images of reenactments consisting of a bunch of scattered individuals engaging in loosely organized gunplay on the weekends, it is a hobby that is highly structured, hierarchical, and ritualized, with formal chains of command, rules of engagement, and safety regulations. Though there are some exceptions, most reenactors belong to organized units with designated roles, such as those of officers and chaplains. Reenactment demands substantial commitments from its adherents, both in terms of time and money. Participants' motivations vary, from the enjoyment of the experience of camping out to the thrill of engaging in gunplay without the physical, psychological, or moral consequences ordinarily attached to such activities. Estimations of the numbers of reenactors range from a peak of fifty thousand in the 1980s to between thirty and forty thousand in 2011. The overwhelming majority are white men.[2] As its more traditional practitioners, it is their interpretations of the war, its causes, and consequences that constitute the dominant memories advanced through reenactment, which draw crowds ranging in number from a few hundred to tens of thousands.

While the practice attracts participants enacting the experiences of combatants on both sides of the conflict, it is the Confederate performances that are tied most closely to regional identity.[3] Reenactment reflects an understanding of history that is inherently masculine and constructs a regional subjectivity largely predicated along the codes of idealized masculinity. In the Civil War era-South, hegemonic assumptions of white southern manhood were rooted in ideals of honor, civic identity, and—especially—masterly authority over blacks and women, all concretized and given expression on the battlefields of the Civil War. Part of the attraction for white men to reenactment lies in the desire to recover this diminished ideal.[4]

The production and expression of heritage through enactment ensures that underneath the thrills of camping out and engaging in gunplay lie concerns that are more ideological in nature. Central to these concerns is the belief that one's ancestors—in both the literal and spiritual senses—fought with valor for an honorable cause. This agenda is advanced through the production of narratives in which the Confederacy instigated and engaged in the war as an act of heroic resistance to federal tyranny. In broader terms, the reordering of Civil War memory enables traditional southern identity to sustain its social and cultural power by maintaining the core assumption of whiteness as historically benevolent. One will find instances where the Lost Cause narrative underlying this belief is advanced overtly, such as through the staging of antebellum cotillions and period wedding ceremonies during the reenactment weekend or the selling of neo-Confederate screeds in the sutlers' area.[5]

However, these values are advanced more subtly—and powerfully—through traditional reenactment's shift away from the causes and consequences of the war in favor of a central discursive focus on the ostensibly neutral values of masculine camaraderie, authenticity, and battle minutiae. This is manifested in many ways, most notably through the distinction between "hard core" reenactors—those whose sense of authenticity is absolute—and "farbs," whose commitment to the same is perceived as questionable. Moreover, Leigh Clemons has suggested that the tendency of most reenactors to portray common soldiers, as opposed to specific historical figures, enables them to circumvent the ideological dimensions of war.[6] The result is a set of historical performances in which slavery and emancipation are symbolically annihilated from the represented narratives. Nevertheless, despite many white Confederate reenactors' insistence that race plays no part in their activities and, indeed, played no (or an insignificant) part in the war itself, racial politics are located squarely within the performances, if expressed only through their attempted marginalization or erasure.

It is this discursive terrain that African American reenactors must negotiate when mobilizing the same history to construct their own identity. Some of these living historians (as many prefer to be called) eschew battle recreations, instead preferring to reenact the USCT experience in schools, museums, churches, juvenile detention centers, and other educational venues, as well as in parades, roundtables, and festivals. They are popular speakers at Black History Month events and Juneteenth celebrations.[7] By centering their reenactment activities on these events, they are able to shift the focus away from battle onto the broader history and its historiography, and to direct their cultural work to those who, in their estimation, will derive the most benefit from it. For these men, performance allows them to tell their story on their own terms. Members of one of these "non-battle" units described their activities as consisting solely of giving lectures at educational institutions because they are less interested in ceding any part of the story to white reenactors on the battlefield than they are in getting it out to audiences who, they believe, most need to hear it. As one member from a USCT unit in Kentucky put it, "most reenactors exist for battle. Our concern is telling the story of the USCT. We resist 'reenactor' and prefer 'living historians.' This is about being a black male and our image. This story is something to be proud of and needs to be told correctly. Getting out on weekends and rolling around in the dirt . . . is more for whites. Our mission goes beyond that. Some folks out there don't know. That's what we're here for."[8] Nevertheless, most do engage in battle reenactment, enabling a direct challenge to the normative assumptions dominant in the discourse of "heritage" underlying these events.

Through my own participation as a spectator, I met many white Confederate reenactors who were quite happy to tell me their version of the events that precipitated the war. Though I was encouraged to find that the reconciliationist code phrase "defense of home" and its inherent suggestion of white southern victimhood did not figure among their answers, I also noticed a steadfast reluctance to place slavery at the center of the conflict. Slavery was *a cause*, but not *the cause*, was the typical response given before the launch into the stock explanations of "states' rights" and "taxation." Others suggested slavery played no role at all. The greater the African American presence at reenactments, the scarcer these elisions became.

While black reenactors and spectators represent a very small portion of the general population of reenactment participants, they have a significant impact on the narratives that are constructed at the events in which they partake. The very presence of African Americans represents their claims upon the memories and subjectivities that form the basis for reenactment and works to reorder these battle narratives in a way that re-centers its focus on the war's causes and consequences. This recovery of the emancipationist vision of Civil War memory destabilizes the dominant images of black contentment and passivity subsumed under the discourses of authenticity and battle minutiae and reconstitutes them for African American (and white) consumption. In other words, it initiates a dismissal of the myth of Uncle Tom and advances a subjectivity more aligned with the image of the insurrectionist Nat Turner. In crafting this new representation of southern blackness, African American reenactors mobilize the rhetorical power of live performance and do so while engaging in combat, both literally and figuratively, with white men.

In this chapter, I analyze the construction of African American southern identity through the performance of Civil War battle reenactment. I begin with a discussion of battle reenactment as a mode of black vernacular performance that features a rhetorical and contextual history particularly suited to the production of pastiche and mimesis, cultural syncretism, and corporeality in the construction of narratives of masculinity and citizenship. I then continue this discussion with a detailed analysis of the ways in which African American participation in reenactment has initiated a reconstruction of the battlefield as a dialogic space in which its public nature and rhetorical positioning as sacred ground facilitate the production of alternative narratives. In the third section, I use as case studies three reenacted battles, paying particular contextual attention to their rhetorical histories in order to highlight the alternative frameworks through which we might view reenactment as a resistant practice productive of black southern identity.

African American Reenactment as Vernacular Performance

Shortly before going into "battle" in Florida at a reenactment of the Battle of Olustee, Andre, a reenactor with the Tallahassee-based Second Infantry Regiment of the USCT, explained the utility of reenactment as a vehicle for advancing Civil War memories centered on the African American experience. "[This is a] story that needs to be told," he said. "To me, it's not a hobby; it's a mission to get the story told to as many faces as possible." This view, which was expressed by a majority of the USCT reenactors at this and other events, exemplifies their project of transforming the practice from an instrument of hegemony into a vehicle for the production of alternative historical narratives. The selection of enactment as a representational practice is far from arbitrary. It mobilizes the key features that emerge from the intersection of performance, African American rhetoric, and vernacular discourse to construct a set of black vernacular performances offering resistant readings of history and transformations in the meaning of southern identity.

One of these features is opportunity. For African American performers and spectators, reenactment provides access to spaces of cultural production unobtainable through other venues. Though it requires considerable time and financial commitments from the participants, it does not impose the significant barriers to entry that characterize other memory-making structures, such as film and archives. For the spectators, it affords opportunities to join reenactors as active agents in the construction of history, a capacity inimical to the hierarchical arrangements characteristic of more conventional modes of representation. Moreover, the nation's post-civil rights cultural milieu, which has facilitated the production of a more critical attitude toward dominant national and regional narratives, has afforded African Americans and other disenfranchised groups expanded ideological access to historical production. James Beatty, a National Park Service ranger and reenactor in Philadelphia, described the significance many black reenactors attach to using this platform to emphasize the importance of exploiting this access and using it to adopt a more critical stance toward accepted history. In describing the content of the presentations he and his fellow reenactors from the Third USCT give to school, museum, and prison audiences, Beatty quoted a line from the John Ford western *The Man Who Shot Liberty Valance*. "The first thing I tell them," he said, "is don't get your history from Hollywood. [The Hollywood mantra is] when faced with a choice between truth and legend, print the legend."

The increased visibility of African Americans in these reenactments has also produced a prioritization of historical accuracy with respect to the participation of both black people and women in the Civil War and has transformed a white male-centered reenactment culture into one more accepting of groups whose historical experiences represent potential ruptures in the functioning of the dominant discourses of authenticity and battle minutiae. One of the more interesting ironies of contemporary reenactment is that the same masculine camaraderie that serves to obfuscate the causes and consequences of the war enables a sense of *communitas* on the battlefield, collapsing racial and class distinctions in favor of the immediate interest of engaging in male-centered gunplay.[9] As one reenactor explained after detailing the importance of getting children involved in reenactment as a means of preserving the built environment, "let's face it, I love this shit. I love playing with guns. I love shootin' at rebels. It's a guy thing. . . . It's male bonding."

This sense of *communitas* characteristic of contemporary reenactment extends to the spectators, though in a slightly different way. Many black reenactors report that it is common for members of the crowd to approach them in the encampment areas to tell them that they are happy to see them there. This inclusiveness creates an opening for black men to participate and enact their agenda of transforming the performed narratives. Nevertheless, black reenactors' ideological access is somewhat complicated, as various dynamics, including historical accuracy and battlefield control, mediate the degree of opportunity ceded to the production of alternative memories. The men consider negotiating this challenge to be a significant aspect of the identity/cultural work they perform.

In addition to accessibility, reenactment enables a grassroots intervention in the production of memory that marshals the powers of live performance to construct a sense of southern identity. Vernacular performance offers one of the few cultural forms through which black men and women may exercise control over their own representation. This control is essential to the construction of identity. Identities are in a constant state of negotiation and renegotiation, and self-representation and self-definition are essential aspects of a group's ability to resist oppression in the social, economic, and political arenas. Performance theorist E. Patrick Johnson has suggested that the performative sphere represents opportunities for African Americans to activate a politics of agency and subjectivity.[10] He argues that the performance of self represents not merely the construction of identity but a means of achieving empowerment through self-definition. The agency of self-identification is a crucial aspect of the project of enacting subjugated memories. Embodied performances have always played a central role in consolidating identities centered on memory, reaffirming a sense of collective identity based on a shared history.[11] Thus, black Civil War reenactment presents a particularly provocative mode for the performance of identity because of still-rigid notions regarding "ownership" of Civil War memory: the war itself, the identities and expressive practices it inspires, and the sacred spaces upon which it was waged have all been constructed to valorize a heroic southern white male subjectivity while implicitly designating blackness as existing outside of history.

Moreover, because traditional reenactment itself represents the production of history from the bottom-up, the identity/cultural work black reenactors perform is not limited to challenging the popular narratives produced through the practice. Their performative agenda encompasses a critical orientation toward official historical narratives more broadly, as well as a destabilization of the uneven power relations through which they are produced. Vernacular expressive practices generally are often performed as a means of interrogating, and, ultimately, subverting the status quo. Rituals have the potential to temporarily upend hierarchies of power and reclassify the individual's relationship to society, transforming the social structures that confine participants to the margins of society and inciting the marginalized to action.[12] Political philosopher Antonio Gramsci once suggested that folk rituals possess the capacity to "bring about the birth of a new culture," and therefore "must not be considered an eccentricity, an oddity or a picturesque element, but as something which is very serious and is to be taken seriously."[13] It is this dichotomous characteristic—in which superficial peculiarities serve to obscure much deeper transformative agendas—that makes vernacular performance a powerful means of constructing memory. The "eccentricity" of reenactment draws curious spectators from all over the world to battle re-creations and affords reenactors myriad opportunities to articulate their interpretations of history during visitor interactions that take place before, during, and after the gathering's more spectacular events. Additionally, during large reenactment weekends, the Friday before the battle is often set aside for living history demonstrations for schoolchildren brought to the site on fieldtrips. Amid all of the pageantry, reenactment provides a forum for its participants to exercise a significant influence on our beliefs about the past.

While white reenactors have traditionally wielded this power in a manner that reifies mainstream history and the hegemonic memories constructed through it, African Americans are seizing it as an opportunity to construct alternative narratives critical of the authority of official memories. Black reenactment exemplifies the function of vernacular historical performance as an embrace of different ways of knowing, a radical critique of the ways in which knowledge is organized within dominant institutions such as the academy. This goal is a particularly urgent one for black reenactors, as African American contributions have traditionally been marginalized in American history, with the black experience in the Civil War era boiled down to superficial treatments focusing mostly, if not exclusively, on slavery. As one reenactor explained, "a lot of noted historians fail to talk about blacks. Shelby Foote and Edwin Bearss [are] very detailed, but won't talk about blacks." The co-optation of reenactment rejects the confinement of the black experience of the era to slavery, expanding its focus to include the war and Reconstruction, while re-situating it as a crucial aspect of the American story more broadly. Black reenactments thus have the potential to resist the narrow box into which "official" history has placed Civil War-era blackness and, in so doing, construct a southern identity that, much like its traditional white-centered incarnation, foregrounds heroism, valor, and honor.

In using battle enactment as a vehicle for this identity/cultural work, the men interviewed for this study emphasized their desire to tell forgotten stories that would accord all African Americans a sense of historical agency. One reenactor described his interest in the hobby as having developed in high school, where he noticed that his teachers expressed shock at the notion that blacks had fought in the war. As the only African American in his school, he felt it his duty to fill in the missing pieces. "Somebody else wrote our history; we were left out," he said. "That's why we get the questions we get at reenactments. . . . The ancestors of slaves get to tell their own story. All history is revisionist. We must pay attention to oral history. . . . They've discounted the black soldiers who were there. We need to put our own spin on it." This and similar motivations expressed by other reenactors underscore the centrality of historical agency as a crucial aspect of their effort to mobilize Civil War memory as a means of constructing southern identity. In order for African Americans to build a sense of belonging to the South, they must position themselves as actors rather than as passive victims within the history that is at the core of both southern and black identities. This entails participating not only as USCT soldiers but also as scouts, nurses, and spies, as well as noted historical figures such as Frederick Douglass, Harriet Tubman, and Charlotte Forten-Grimke.

Although black reenactors see it as their duty to convey these narratives to the general population, they are most heavily invested in teaching other African Americans about their history. After relaying a story about a conversation with an African American academic historian who had expressed surprise at the revelation that black men had fought in the Civil War, one reenactor said that the experience "made me realize I needed to keep doing this. You'd be surprised how many of us don't [even] know about *Glory*." Many of the men I spoke to stressed the importance of a sense of historical agency to present attitudes and behaviors, linking black service and citizenship in the war to contemporary feelings of belonging. As one man at a reenactment in Virginia put it, "young men need to know history. [They] will behave in different ways once they know history. Once you know your ancestors did something, you'll walk a little straighter. You know Lincoln didn't just free us—we were more than just slaves."

The enactment of these recovered memories renders representation itself a form of action. Living history performance is a mode of expression that presents cultural memories in embodied form, entertaining spectators while subverting traditional historical narratives. By shifting the focus to representation, it articulates narratives of social and power relations that actually seem to eclipse the history itself. This focus constructs the Civil War battlefield as a vernacular discursive space in which both physical and ideological battles are waged. Black engagement in reenactment constructs historical agency in four ways. First, black participation reconnects the war to slavery, which recovers memories of black people working to emancipate themselves from bondage and contributing to American ideals of freedom and equality. Second, it subverts dominant stereotypes of black contentedness during slavery, passivity during the war, and hyperviolence and hyper-sexuality during Reconstruction. Third, the representation of uniformed black bodies on the battlefield provides grounding for affirmative contemporary notions of black masculinity through the production of an idealized historic subjectivity: the heroic citizen-soldier. Finally, it shifts the meanings assigned to the "sacred" ground of the Civil War battlefield away from notions of blood sacrifice for "hearth and home" toward blood sacrifice for the cause of emancipation.

In order to maximize the agency and power of performance as a means of advancing these objectives, black reenactors incorporate a rhetorical strategy that combines two discourses aligned with African American rhetorical practices—mimesis and corporeality—with the foundational elements of vernacular discourse: pastiche and cultural syncretism. Mimesis has historically served as a performative discourse through which African Americans engage in both critiques of power and struggles over identity. Kirt Wilson has located the roots of the racial politics of imitative practices in the antebellum era, when both enslaved and free blacks used tools appropriated from the dominant culture to attain literacy and to articulate claims of citizenship via the adoption of the norms of white middle class respectability. The expansion of these practices after emancipation to include behaviors consistent with assertions of citizenship increased their potential to further disrupt the prevailing southern social order. Imitation, it was assumed, implied racial similarity and equality and, most dangerously, the possibilities of integration. At the same time, Wilson writes, African Americans such as Frederick Douglass saw mimesis as both providing a "space from which blacks could resist oppression" and as a means of "projecting an identity that was similar to the dominant society."[14]

As a category of mimetic performance, pastiche enhances its subversive potential by appropriating elements from the dominant culture not merely to mimic convention or even to mock it, but to actually celebrate it.[15] In the case of battle reenactment, African Americans strategically redeploy pastiche, mobilizing its traditions in order to assert claims upon the enacted history and to produce alternative, critical readings and meanings that ultimately disrupt dominant assumptions. It is thus a celebration of previously silenced historical narratives, one that reverses the typical flows of cultural appropriation to effect a very bold co-optation of a culturally influential mode of Civil War memory production.[16] As is the case with mimesis more generally, these practices underscore the subjective and ideological nature of memory, the constructed nature of southern identity, and the power relations inherent in the normative suppositions assigned to both. Through imitative, grassroots acts, black reenactors are able to offer historical interpretations that flip the racial script.

Though pastiche shifts the primary mimetic focus away from mockery to celebration, African American reenactment retains the capacity to mock professional history for its erasures of black agency. An approach marked by distrust of official history is characteristic of reenactment culture generally and takes on an even more ideological agenda with African American participants. Part of the strategic importance of utilizing reenactment as a means of interrogating dominant narratives stems from its history as a cultural practice that occupies a liminal space on the margins of both traditional academic historical production and public history, one that is often infused with more explicit ideological agendas. Shortly after the end of Reconstruction, members of the Grand Army of the Republic—an influential Union veterans' lobbying group—staged small reunions and reenactments using National Guard units as Confederates. These rituals, from which African American veterans were largely excluded, were part of a wave of reconciliationist sentiment and heightened ambivalence about race relations. After the turn of the century, amid the changing socioeconomic milieu created by increasing immigration and industrialization, reenactment became an expression of nativist sentiment, as well as an even more significant part of a sectional reconciliation based upon the erasure of race and slavery from memories of the war. Interest in reenactment later declined, as concerns about world wars and depression superseded interest in the pageantry with which these events had come to be associated.[17]

In presenting dominant historical narratives in a melodramatic package designed for mass consumption, Civil War reenactors have always operated on the margins of a multitude of communities, particularly those associated with the more elite structures of official history. Shortly after the first contemporary reenactments were staged during the war's Centennial celebration, Alan Nevins, the second chairman of the Civil War Centennial Commission, dismissed them as "trashily theatrical" and declared that they would proceed further "over his dead body." Shortly thereafter, National Park Service director Conrad Wirth sought a reduced role for reenactments in the celebrations, preferring instead to leave history in the hands of trained interpreters who would construct "a dignified and impressive commemoration beyond reproach."[18] These concerns reflect the tensions between professional and amateur history, a tension many reenactors are more than happy to exploit in positioning their activities as an accessible grassroots intervention.

Additionally, the festivities often accompanying reenactments—such as parades, balls, and other pageantry—seem to mock the more conservative representations associated with academic history. Bakhtin has suggested that the carnivalesque—a concept used to describe satirical challenges to authority and established hierarchies—holds significant potential to upend social relations and strengthen forces for change in the non-carnival world.[19] African American reenactors recognize this mimetic power, and marshal the aspects of it most useful to them. While they share traditional reenactors' disdain for professional history, they often place academic lectures critical of that history with a focus on black history and agency at the center of their events. They also tend to eschew the more theatrical characteristics of the events in favor of a more pedagogical focus, but are able to use the attractions of reenactment's pageantry to draw in visitors to the more educational presentations.

Black reenactors' mobilization of pastiche as part of their identity work extends beyond the co-optation of these useful elements. It also entails the strategic appropriation of hegemonic values from dominant culture. Much like their nineteenth-century forebears, black reenactors are using the war—more specifically, its memory—as a means of asserting their own claims to the ideals of masculinity and citizenship historically denied them. Their identity/cultural work incorporates performances of manhood and belonging. Black men's appropriation of dominant gender and citizenship ideals serves to wed pastiche with cultural syncretism, as the reclamation of these values reorganizes Civil War memory in a way that affirms, rather than devalues, a subjectivity centered on the intersection of southernness and blackness.

Black men's uniformed presence in the encampment and sutlers' areas, in the speakers' tents, and especially on the battlefield, mobilizes a set of corporeal discourses to articulate their claims to the masculine values of honor, heroism, and valor associated with the performances of traditional southern identity proffered through Confederate reenactment. Corporeality, which at its most basic level refers to the various ways in which the body conveys meaning, is an essential component of African American discourse, as it is through the body that race and racial meanings are socially constructed. Corporeal rhetorics position the body as a discursive text that may be read in ways similar to other texts. Ronald L. Jackson II has described the processes of assigning meaning to the body as scripting, which with respect to African Americans involves ascribing certain negative qualities onto black bodies. Dominant Civil War memory is deeply implicated in this scripting, positioning black masculinity as alternately passive and violent, angry, and sexually deviant. Additionally, the body politics that emerge from inscription and are played out in the cultural arena have served the function of providing the marginalized "Other" against which the centralized utopic "Self" is produced.[20] As a cultural practice constitutive of traditional southern identity, battle reenactment adheres closely to this schema, using discourses of authenticity and battle minutiae to construct the utopic southern male—heroic, powerful, and most importantly, white—in opposition to the marginalized black slave. These corporeal rhetorics continue to characterize the overwhelming majority of reenactments where African American participation is negligible or non-existent.

Nevertheless, just as dominant Civil War memory has produced corporeal discourses scripting black bodies as the "Other," African American-centered memory and identity relies on a redeployment of these discourses as part of the rhetorics of resistance. By using the body as a visual tool to centralize blackness and decentralize whiteness, African American memory producers mobilize their corporeality to rescript their assigned otherness. Through enactment, black reenactors assume the idealized masculine values advanced through the practice, redirect them away from the discourses of authenticity and battle minutiae, and refocus them on the struggle for emancipation. As such, they provide a powerful set of discourses for the recovery of blackness as essential to public dialogues about Civil War history. The new memories created from this shift are dismissive of dominant narratives relegating Civil War-era black men to the status of passive victims awaiting freedom through the heroic efforts of white Union soldiers and President Lincoln. In shifting the focus of these masculine narratives, black reenactors evolve from historical objects to historical subjects who worked bravely to free themselves from bondage. This forms the basis for the identity/cultural work conducted through these performances.

Black reenactors' performances of masculinity represent a continuation of the work begun by the men whose experiences they are emulating. The ability to lay claim to then-prevailing notions of manhood was a significant motivation for black men to join the Union Army, an effort that was met with resistance from a variety of quarters. Though black men had served in combat in previous battles, including the Revolutionary War, the last state-chartered group of black soldiers—the New Orleans Free Men of Color—had been abolished in 1834.[21] A number of private black militias were active when the Civil War began, but their offers of service to the Confederacy were rebuffed.[22] With its vastly superior industrial and human resources, the North initially saw no need for black soldiers and also declined their offers of service: this was to be a white man's war. The prevailing belief was that black men were simply incapable of courageous war combat, as *inferior* beings made *inferior* soldiers.[23] However, once the North incurred heavy casualties in the initial campaigns, resistance to the enlistment of black men became more difficult to sustain. Union leaders began to view them as potentially valuable resources, initially recruiting USCT troops from among free men in the North. They soon realized the utility of tapping an even more significant supply of men from the

South; ironically, this recognition came about from the boasts of Southerners that their slaves, who constituted more than half of the region's labor force and were impressed into service to the Confederacy as laborers, enabled the rebels to "place in the field a force so much larger in proportion to her population than the North."[24] The realization that undermining this labor force would weaken the efforts of the Confederacy prompted Union leaders—beginning with General Benjamin Butler—to hold and declare slaves who had escaped to northern lines as "contraband of war," or "contrabands." This population would eventually produce many USCT soldiers. The Confiscation Acts of 1861 and 1862 and the Militia Act of 1862 initiated the processes involved in enlisting black men into the Union Army.[25]

These early organizational efforts were officially authorized with the issuance of the Emancipation Proclamation on January 1, 1863, which initiated a wave of enlistment. Black soldiers, whose numbers had exceeded 180,000 by the war's end, would ultimately be organized into 166 regiments. While three-quarters of black men in the North had enlisted, a majority of the men hailed from the Confederate slave states.[26] Many observers realized that the soldiers of the USCT had the strongest motivation for fighting to secure victory for the Union and framed this incentive within assumptions centered on the attainment of manhood. When asked if slaves would fight, Frederick Douglass responded, "no, the slaves will not fight. But if you ask me will the black man fight, the answer is yes." White contemporaries also recognized the war's stakes in these terms. As one white soldier observed, "put a United States uniform on his back and the chattel is a man."[27]

By 1864 USCT battlefield performances had convinced even some Confederate officials of their own neglect of a valuable resource. They had begun to recognize slavery as a weakness; it had, among other things, provided a potent recruitment tool for the North. The emancipation and enlistment of black men into the Confederate Army, they believed, would remove the only motive black men had to fight against the South.[28] Confederate President Jefferson Davis initially dismissed such appeals and forbade further discussion of the subject. However, by the fall of that year, the South's losses were significant enough to again prompt discussion of arming the slaves. While Davis would eventually sign a "Negro Soldier Law" authorizing the enlistment of slaves in March of 1865, there remained strong resistance to the idea as late as the preceding January.[29] The prospect of black men performing heroically on the battlefield represented potential threats to the ideology of white supremacy that was the foundation of the slave society the South was fighting to preserve. As Georgia Senator Howell Cobb stated, "if the black can make a good soldier, our whole system of government is wrong."[30]

Black men were aware of these sentiments and of the ideological stakes central to their armed service. Thus, for them, proving their mettle as men was conjoined with emancipation and preservation of the Union as central concerns for helping the Northern army secure victory. They asserted these stakes both visually and verbally. For example, the 127th USCT unit's regimental flag contained the inscription "We Will Prove Ourselves Men." J. O. Malone of the Fifth Massachusetts Cavalry, Colored boasted that "the colored soldiers in this four years' struggle have proven themselves in every respect to be men," while Thomas Long of the First South Carolina regiment declared in a sermon that "if we hadn't become sojers, all might have gone back as it was before. . . . But now things can never go back, because we have showed our energy and our courage and our naturally manhood."[31]

Black men's meritorious service was also recognized outside of the black community. Sixteen black men earned the Congressional Medal of Honor for bravery in battle.[32] In May 1864 a government commission investigating the condition of freedmen reported that "the whites have changed, and are still rapidly changing, their opinion of the negro. And the negro, in his new condition as a freedman, is himself, to some extent, a changed being. No one circumstance has tended so much to these results as the display of manhood in negro soldiers. Though there are higher qualities than strength and physical courage, yet, in our present state of civilization, there are no qualities which command from the masses more respect."[33]

Black men's claim to the masculine ideals of the era were rhetorically linked with citizenship. In this configuration, certain patriarchal duties, particularly the support and protection of women and children, were contingent upon the attainment of civic equality.[34] African Americans' position within the national community had always been tenuous. The enslaved were private property with no rights, while the liberties of free blacks in both the North and the South were under perpetual threat. A few years before the war, the limits of African American belonging had been clearly defined and cemented by the Supreme Court's *Dred Scott* decision of 1857, in which Chief Justice Roger Taney infamously declared that blacks were noncitizens and had no rights that a white man was bound to respect.[35] The war would offer an opportunity for black men to prove their worth both as men and as citizens, and USCT recruitment rhetoric was often framed in these terms. During the war, Douglass, whose two sons later served with the Fifty-Fourth Massachusetts, understood the importance of service to the republic. In a March 3, 1863, editorial titled "Men of Color, to Arms," he urged black men to enlist, conflating service with emancipation and full citizenship rights: "Once let the black man get upon his person the brass letters, US, let him get an eagle on his button, and a musket on his shoulder, and bullets in his pockets, and there is no power on Earth which can deny that he has earned the right to citizenship in the US."[36]

The pushback against these assertions, in both the North and the South, further reveals the limits imposed upon African American claims of citizenship. In opposing a bill repealing restrictions on the bearing of arms by black men, Senator Robert M. Hunter of North Carolina argued that the bill was an admission that slavery had been wrong from the beginning and could thus lead to an unimaginable slippery slope: "If we could make them soldiers, the condition of the soldier being socially equal to any other in society, we could make them officers, perhaps, to command white men."[37] The situation evolved only marginally once black soldiers joined in combat. Members of the USCT initially received lower pay than their white counterparts, were denied opportunities for appointment as commissioned officers, and were typically assigned duties more akin to those of laborers than soldiers. Black soldiers captured and held as prisoners of war risked being summarily executed or re-enslaved.[38] Moreover, the rewards for meritorious service extended to black men were fraught with conditions, if not denied outright. For example, in 1864 Union General Benjamin F. Butler was so impressed with the service of the three hundred black troops under his command at the battles of Fort Harrison and Fort Gilmer that he awarded them the US Civil War Colored Troops Medal, a medal commissioned specially for them. However, the medal had no official status, and the recipients were not allowed to wear it on their uniforms.[39] Nevertheless, after the war many USCT veterans continued to engage in the civic activities expressive of their sense of belonging, as well as that of their newly emancipated community. Many returned to the South, working with the Freedman's Bureau and other agencies to implement the rights their service had helped to secure.

As the war faded into memory and the post-Reconstruction years gave rise to the Jim Crow era, the ideology of white supremacy that provided its foundation necessitated a dismissal of black accomplishments. Black men's heroic service would be handily forgotten, neatly expunged from dominant memories of the war. Narratives related to it were kept alive

only by the recollections of individual USCT veterans in personal cor-
respondences and a few mainstream yet non-influential publications from
the perspectives of white participants in battles with USCT.[40] Moreover,
the reconciliationist sentiment that hinged on reunion between North
and South hardened into a Lost Cause mythology that produced popular
memories of both the war and the Reconstruction era in which the conflict's causes had morphed into the "protection of hearth and home," i.e.,
the protection of Southern combatants' particular state of residence or the
"protection of (white) women." These retroactively putative causes for
which the war was fought, which strategically emphasized a set of traditional masculine values privileging the defense of revered institutions, allowed southern white men to not only retain the masculine ideals forged
during the war in the face of defeat but also to strengthen their sense of
belonging to the region. These revisionist memories of the war, combined
with assumptions of whiteness as central to national identity, also enabled
them to simultaneously retain their membership in the national community while maintaining assertions of sectional identity.

These new southern memories situated black men as objects rather than
as subjects with agency over their own lives. Their primary roles in the war
were limited to serving as Confederate laborers or spies or, more often, as
contented slaves taking care of the plantation household while the "real
men" were away fighting the war. Moreover, the discursive construction
of the postwar occupation as a period during which the white South was
victimized by uncivilized freedmen and unscrupulous Yankees gave rise
to another popular image: the bestial black buck. This mythological figure became a prominent symbol in the film *The Birth of a Nation* (1915)
that—in addition to creating the most infamous incarnation of the vi-
cious would-be rapist in the figure of the character Gus—features a scene
in which marauding black soldiers from the First South Carolina wreak
havoc on the fictional town of Piedmont and its white citizens. Black men,
according to these mythologies, could be neatly categorized as dehumanizing archetypes, not as heroes who had fought honorably and bravely for
the preservation of the Union and for their own freedom, as well as for that
of their wives and children. These revisions produced hegemonic memories in which idealized Civil War-era white manhood was established, defined, and concretized through the discursive construction of black masculinity as pathological.

Additionally, while the continuing endurance of the Lost Cause vision
has enabled southern white men to claim a masculinity rooted in the ideals of the past in spite of (or, perhaps, because of) the framing of the South

as the nation's "abjected regional other," it has had a markedly different bearing on the formation of contemporary black masculinity. As Riché Richardson has argued, gender and racial discourses constructed through popular culture have produced dominant notions of authentic blackness and masculinity that marginalize the South as a productive location for black subjectivity.[41] These conceptions, advanced by both black and white cultural producers, have yielded images of southern blackness associated with indolence, backwardness, and submission to white male authority, as well as with behaviors consistent with what is colloquially referred to as "coonery." Thus the intersectional effects of race, gender, and region, combined with the marginalization and erasure of black men's heroism from dominant memory, have situated southern identity as a source of embarrassment rather than as grounding for affirmative notions of manhood. According to Richardson, in this configuration southern history has placed an emasculating burden on black men.[42]

One of the foundational assumptions of memory studies is that acts of remembrance are less focused on the narratives and mythologies of the past than on the ways in which these discourses may be put to use in the service of present agendas. Black reenactors' identity work incorporates performances designed to reorder southern history, reconstituting it into a useable past that provides a foundation for affirmative notions of race, gender, and region in the contemporary era. By engaging in this identity work, they are simultaneously performing the cultural work of enacting new memories in which black men are the chief occupiers of the masculine and citizenship ideals foregrounded through the dominant history of the war. Luther, a self-described entrepreneur and member of a Fifty-Fourth Massachusetts regiment in Chicago, explained the importance of this goal while relaxing at his campsite in Florida: "To me, the Civil War symbolizes the evolving endurance of African American people. When it was all over, they fought and fought valiantly. They were able to take a bullet and die like the white guys. What the Civil War symbolizes to me is paying homage to those who did what they didn't have to do. The Civil War would not have been won without the black men. The Fifty-Fourth stood their ground in this battle. Some said, 'I'd rather die fighting and free than live a slave'. . . . The bonding part is not the issue. For two days, you get to leave all the problems of the world behind and give homage to someone else . . . not letting what they did be in vain."

Black reenactments are simultaneously performances of history, race, and gender, rendering the black male body an archive for the recovery of previously silenced memories. These performances mobilize the mutability of memory to enact an agenda centered on what Bryant Keith Alexander refers to as passing.[43] The racial and gender passing that underwrites these performances does not resemble passing in the classic sense, in that the participants are not performing an identity outside of the prescribed borders of the one to which they may "authentically" lay claim. After all, the central point of these enactments is that black men's agency during the war, while traditionally symbolically annihilated from dominant representations, remains historically accurate. Rather, black participants are "passing" in the sense that they are mobilizing these performances to construct an alternative identity from the one centered on traits rooted in southern mythology and hegemonically ascribed to contemporary black male alterity: the hyper-violence, hyper-sexuality, hyper-athleticism and general hyper-deviance typical of dominant images of African American masculine enactment. Their passing performance reflects not the multitude of southern masculinities that characterize the present but the gender values of the Old South, a controversial proposition for, among other reasons, the patriarchal values and problematic respectability politics it invokes. They are also passing in the sense that their performances engage a conservative martial frame. Military service has historically provided a means by which African American men could assert and reassert claims to normative masculine citizenship, with early- and mid-twentieth-century black intellectuals, journalists, and other public figures constructing advancement ideologies discursively positioning racial uplift and the expansion of democracy as interdependent goals.[44] Nevertheless, these claims, which have been met with mixed results, have existed in tension with black men's perpetual status as outsiders and societal problems potentially and perpetually in need of containment. This position has been advanced through the arena of popular culture and underwrites many of their contemporary racial and gender performances.

However, the centrality of Civil War memory in the production of both southern and African American identity transcends these concerns. Black people were fighting to secure their own liberation at home rather than fighting imperial wars overseas. This notion is so fraught with meaning anathema to dominant discourses that the World War II-era recruitment film *The Negro Soldier* detailed black service in every war up to that time *except* the Civil War. Additionally, performances of history foregrounding the heroism of black men who fought not only for their own freedom but also for that of their women and children articulate a vision of manhood that, though patriarchal in nature, subverts the hegemonic images of misogyny, absentee fatherhood, and general familial pathology essential to the perpetuation of African American "Otherness." It is for this reason that black women's gender performances at reenactments are crucial to the production of black memory and identity. Dressed in antebellum attire as enslaved or free women and often providing lectures about their historical characters' activities as abolitionists, nurses, Union spies, and Reconstruction-era reformers, they represent stories of black female agency before, during, and after the war. Just as importantly, their presence around the perimeter of the male-dominated space of the battlefield serves as a visual reminder that the ultimate goal of the sacrifices the men were making included the emancipation of women and children. Their enactments, which are also evocative of performative passing, help facilitate the masculine passing essential to the USCT's identity/cultural work. These revisions enable black men to claim the Old South values of honor and gallantry for themselves, all the while reordering them for contemporary consumption.[45]

These performances of racial and gender passing highlight the fluidity of identities. Black men's bodily occupation of the image of the citizen-soldier exposes the socially constructed nature of traditional southern identity, as well as that of the narrow repertoire of African American masculine identities. In so doing, it breaks the boundaries imposed by the dominant memories that provide the foundation for both. Many of the men I interviewed emphasized the ways in which various aspects of their performances contribute to their identity/cultural work. One of these is the authority assigned to the soldier's uniform. The cultural veneration of the warrior-hero transfers all of the myths, symbols, and ideals of society onto the bodies of men (and a small number of women), both living and dead. Military uniforms connote an image of protection and salvation, which in the national imaginary is rarely occupied by black men. The visual rhetoric of the uniform is especially powerful when performed in strikingly anomalous contexts, particularly as it offers a rebuttal to the ways in which many white southerners perceive their own identity—some of which have the support of state and commercial institutions. As one reenactor put it, "to go to South Carolina, where there are still a lot of Confederate flags and a lot of 'Lee surrendered but I didn't' [T-shirts and bumper stickers], to see blacks go down there in Union blue is interesting to me. They're gettin' it." Just before going into "battle" in Wilmington, North Carolina, George Reid of the 127th Ohio Volunteers (Fifth USCT) described to me his habit of venturing into Civil War souvenir shops near the sites of many of the reenactments in full uniform. In discussing the ways in which his appearance presents a stark and interesting contrast to the reams of Confederate memorabilia inside the shops, he said, "we like dispelling [myths] by our own presence. We put on our uniforms and that is the statement—we don't have to *say* anything. I like doing that. I even do it at work." Additionally, the cultural power implicit in the visuality of black bodies in uniform is, according to many of the men, an important aspect of fostering an identification with Civil War memory among African Americans. After explaining the historical fears of Confederates and their allies at the sight of former slaves armed and in uniform and fighting for their own freedom, Reid suggested that a significant aspect of his work involves mobilizing this combination of visuality and corporeality to facilitate African American desire to lay claim to the history. "This is a tough sell in the black community," he said. "It's our mere presence [in uniform, with guns, that makes it sellable]. I do it proudly and I do it a lot."

Moreover, the mimetic nature of reenactment fosters a deeper appreciation for what the USCT accomplished, while appropriating antebellum notions of honor and mastery. Black reenactors are using their bodies to exhibit what Kirk Fuoss refers to as demonstrative performances, which operate in the fashion of the "how-to" and the exemplary.[46] Through the occupation and performance of the idealized citizen-soldier, reenactors undermine discourses positioning black masculinity as outside of and in opposition to the elements associated with ideal citizenship. At an event in Nicholasville, Kentucky, Malcolm—a reenactor with the Camp Nelson Foundation—suggested that the enthusiastic acceptance black participants receive at battle simulations is due in part to their mastery of the artillery process. "We are held up often as the example of how it should be done," he explained. "People are willing to be educated." In explaining his attraction to the hobby, a reenactor in Florida put it this way: "It's about doing something others can't do. I can load and fire an 1861 Springfield [rifle]." That black reenactors are able to function as exemplars in this way is remarkable in a culture in which the image of black men with guns inspires fear in many.

The sense of cultural syncretism that underlies this work is most evident in the participants' goal of using reconstituted memories to provide a more productive model for black youth. Situating their work within broader efforts to counteract what they perceive as destructive attitudes among young men, many reenactors expressed the importance of passing the hobby on to the next generation in order to improve its future prospects. These sentiments are based upon the perception that a sense of historical agency and an awareness of the principles associated with heroic masculinity lead to greater self-esteem and a higher sense of purpose among youth. One

Figure 2. Ritual performances of exemplary masculinity and citizenship at the Forks Road reenactment, Wilmington, North Carolina. Photo by Patricia G. Davis.

reenactor expressed this in blunt terms: "Not having a history and not knowing your place in things creates a psychological vacuum and self-hatred. This leads to gangsterism." Demonstrating exactly what African Americans have accomplished subverts discourses that imply that "you're nothing, you're not a man. . . . [It] rids us of the 'I'm worthless and you're worthless' black-on-black killing. It is our job to set up the next generation. If you listen to Clear Channel, Fox, you're not getting it."

Several outreach efforts targeting young men of color have resulted from this aspiration. The Philadelphia/Trenton-based Third USCT reenactment unit travels to schools and community organizations, sponsoring young men in their late-teens and early-twenties by providing funds to purchase uniforms. Some of the men involved have taken this outreach a bit further, institutionalizing their reenactment activities in the form of after-school youth programs. Participating in battle re-creations is among these activities. Rob Goldman of the Fourteenth Rhode Island Heavy Artillery (Colored) runs a youth internship program in Providence. He and his cadets participate in the reenactments at Olustee and Fort Pocahontas. The young people attend school three days of the week and spend the other

Figure 3. Enjoying downtime in the encampment area before the battle at Camp Nelson, Nicholasville, Kentucky. Photo by Patricia G. Davis.

Figure 4. Engaging in battle at the Forks Road reenactment, Wilmington, North Carolina. Photo by Patricia G. Davis.

two in their internships. The program's focus is on history and historical preservation. Goldman suggested the importance of getting younger men and women involved in preserving history, noting that the average reenactor is forty-eight to fifty-five years old. He also admitted that his motivation in this vein is far- reaching: "If you don't know your history, you're doomed to repeat it. . . . If we don't get kids involved in preservation, we're gonna lose it. Otherwise, they move into the suburbs, get a car, etc. [This is] my way to get back at America—change society." Art Liggens, whose great-great grandfather fought with the Twenty-Second USCT and whose teenage son is the drummer in his unit, said that immersion in the hobby helps alleviate the peer pressure that typifies the experiences of those in his son's age group. He surmised that although his son might at some point yield to other youthful temptations, he would eventually get back into reenacting, "like other wholesome things." Liggens, a former Marine, leads a unit of teenage boys who travel to various reenactments and battlefields during the year. At the close of the battle that I witnessed at Fort Pocahontas in Virginia, they were planning to tour Petersburg Battlefield a short distance away before heading back to New Jersey.

Dexter Akinsheye of the Fifty-Fourth Massachusetts, Company B unit in Washington, DC, co-founded the Marie Reed Cadet Academy in the city. Akinsheye, who declared that he perceives USCT soldiers to be "a much better set of heroes to admire than rap stars," uses as his chief selling point the fact that children between twelve and fourteen years of age served as unit drummers on the battlefields during the Civil War. He and his young cadets make the annual trek to the Forks Road reenactment in Wilmington, North Carolina, and perform at events at the African American Civil War Museum in Washington. At each event, the highly disciplined boys participate in drills and inspections. In addition to their other scholastic duties (which emphasize history), the primarily black and Latino youths learn leadership, responsibility, and character building skills. When asked to elaborate on what he saw as the connection between these qualities and battle reenactment, Akinsheye replied, "I've given them internal ranks. . . . They say to their peers who are doing something wrong, 'a cadet's not supposed to do this.'"

While most reenactors are middle-aged, there are a few young men engaged in the hobby, often as the result of the influence of an older, influential male figure. There were several father-son dyads among the groups I studied. While I was interacting with visitors at the Forks Road reenactment in Wilmington, a young man named Adrian said that he had entered the hobby at the suggestion of his mother's boyfriend as a means of staying out of trouble. When asked what his friends had to say about his activities, the nineteen-year-old replied that they had initially found it strange, telling him that he should be doing something more fun, like breaking into houses. He also stated that eventually some of them came around and expressed interest in reenacting, but refused to wear the clothes.

The discourses of masculinity and citizenship constructed through African American reenactment perform work rather differently when enacted through the very small number of black Confederate reenactors. The notion that blacks fought for the Confederacy became part of a modern, organized memorialization campaign in the 1970s and has since gained increased currency as the Sons of Confederate Veterans and other heritage groups have exploited a multitude of commemorative venues to push the claim.[47] White Confederate reenactors cling steadfastly to this narrative thread and use their interactions with visitors to advance it, even making the assertion that black Confederate "soldiers" were treated more equitably than their USCT counterparts. Imagining blacks as having taken up arms for the Confederate cause would seem to lend credence to the notion that the war could not possibly have hinged on slavery. It also reifies the images of white benevolence and black contentedness underlying the Lost Cause-infused narratives that pervade traditional reenactment. Both of these myths are central to the ability of white Confederate reenactors to vindicate the Confederacy and to maintain the honorable, heroic masculinity that underwrites their own performances. The narrative is a significant point of contention with USCT reenactors, most of whom are quite hostile to the idea and consider engaging in friendly verbal skirmishes with Confederate reenactors and spectators over this point to be a significant aspect of their work. Claims of the historical existence of black Confederate combatants have served as an ongoing source of tension at some of the larger reenactments. Before the day's official skirmish began at the reenactment I witnessed at Olustee, one of the men explained that part of his motivation in participating was to challenge the Confederates over the claim of black support for the Southern side. After the battle, many white visitors approached the African American reenactors to ask them about black service to the Confederacy. A common phrase among the USCT reenactors in response to any question regarding possible black service to the South is "show me the records," meaning that as long as there are no pension records proving black men were paid for their services to the Confederacy, they were laborers rather than soldiers. The men typically combine this response with a discussion about the facts of forced black labor during the war.

Only the rare black Confederate reenactors—who are generally treated as pariahs by those who perform as USCT soldiers—are willing to give beliefs about armed black rebel soldiers any credibility and to enact the associated agendas into their own performances of southern identity. In contrast to USCT reenactors' construction and expression of a resistant identity centered on the recovery of marginalized memory, black Confederate reenactors construct their subjectivity through the hegemonic history circulated at the events, particularly those where the black presence as reenactors and spectators is negligible. When describing to me their motivations for participating, they articulated a sense of purpose that represented a mixture of neo-Confederate discourse with assertions of the South as an African American homeplace and the primal scene of black subjectivity. John, a member of a Thirty-Seventh Texas unit in southern California, suggested that although he has three ancestors who fought as USCT he views his expressed identity as more aligned with the values of the Confederates. He also put forward that these values were more productive of black southern subjectivity: "The Union army was seen as an invading force; [the South] was the black man's home," he said. "If you're gonna reenact history, you gotta be true to it. There were free black men who fought for the Confederacy and were paid more than the USCT." Darrin—a Vietnam veteran, former schoolteacher, and member of the same unit—reiterated these claims and detailed the ways in which he invokes his southern heritage in responding to spectators who question his choice to reenact as a Confederate soldier. "I've gotten looks like, 'you're on the wrong side,'" he said. "I'm on the right side. [My] mom's from Tennessee; dad's from Louisiana. These are my southern roots." Don, a member of another Thirty-Seventh Texas unit based in Virginia, told me that he learned about "black Confederates" in a college course on military history and ascribed his motivation for engaging the hobby to the desire to represent their "neglected narratives," arguing that the production of an "authentic" black subjectivity necessitates the recovery of these memories. "Ever since *Glory*, every brother I know wants to reenact the Union blue," he said. "But I want to tell this side of the story. No one else will tell it. You gotta honor your whole history; you're not part of a person."

Black Confederate reenactors represent a minority enactment that relies more heavily on sectionalism and questions of historical agency than the masculinity and citizenship discourses at the core of the identity constructed through the majority of these performances. It is tempting to view their engagement as potentially disruptive of the identity/cultural work performed through the articulation of new battlefield narratives.

However, these performances invoke tropes of *passing* similar to those implicated in the USCT enactments, only with a different set of negotiators. In this case, black southern identity is negotiated primarily through interactions with white Confederate reenactors which, in addition to the geographical attachments associated with traditional southern subjectivity, entails an acceptance of some of the assumptions underlying Lost Cause mythologies. For example, in articulating his motivations for reenacting as a Confederate soldier at the invitation of a white friend, Neil, another member of the Thirty-Seventh Texas unit based in southern California, suggested history as the primary factor. The version of history to which he subscribes, however, is filtered through a neo-Confederate interpretive lens. "[I do this] because [the history] is accurate. I didn't agree with some of the things Mr. Lincoln did," he said, in reference to the unilateral presidential suspension of habeas corpus in 1861. "I wanted to be different, [to] be historically accurate. How could [USCT soldiers] be fighting against slavery if the units were segregated?"

In the event, black battle enactment, whether centered on an adherence to hegemonic memory or on resistant readings of it, merely underscores the complexities of black southern identity. By situating performed discourses of masculinity, citizenship, and agency within the historical context that produced them, we can more clearly comprehend these complexities, and begin to develop new analytical frameworks for evaluating reenactment as a practice productive of African American subjectivity. In the next section, I discuss the ways in which the discourses implicit in another important element in these performances, the battlefield, intervene in the identity/cultural work advanced through them.

The Civil War Battlefield as a Dialogic Space

As the mobilization of mimesis, pastiche, cultural syncretism, and corporeality underlying these performances makes clear, black men's participation represents not a radical restructuring but rather an intervention in the functioning of reenactment—a disruption of the power of its dominant narratives claiming southern belonging as synonymous with whiteness. Thus, the new memories constructed through reenactment are characterized by a dialogic relationship with the dominant memory. The most important aspect of this relationship involves the ability to cultivate a number of publics and counterpublics within a meaningful discursive space.[48] The rhetorical effectiveness of the reenactments relies on their very public nature, which confers fluidity upon the forgotten narratives of black service in the war and enables them to circulate within and outside black communities.

The dialogic aspect of the performances helps advance this fluidity in two ways. First, it offers unique opportunities for reenactors to engage spectators about all aspects of the enacted history, including its historiography. Second, the co-optation and restructuring of the dominant meanings assigned to the sacralized spaces on which the battles occur enables both reenactors and spectators to become active participants in shaping their own identities through a continuing dialogue with the dominant memory. Both of these dialogic aspects of reenactment are crucial to its transformation into a counterhegemonic cultural practice constitutive of black southern identity.

The spectatorial agency produced through live performance also allows visitors to reenactments to construct their own subjectivity. One of the primary differences between live performance and other forms of representation lies in the relationship between performers and audiences. Reenactments are structured in such a way that there are no hierarchies between the two sides, as spectators are invited and encouraged to engage in one-on-one conversations with reenactors both before and after battle simulations. The performer works with an audience that has the same repertory of images that he or she has, which provides the necessary common experience.[49] Jill Dolan asserts that performances represent more than just an intersubjective encounter between performers and spectators; instead, the very act of viewing a performance can stimulate a sense of civic participation and belonging among audience members. Theater, according to Dolan, is a vital part of the public sphere in that it offers a public forum for debate. Performative reenactment is thus a component of critical civic engagement, a "public practice through which radical democracy might rehearse."[50] It provides an especially productive means for African Americans to intervene critically in the functioning of hegemonic history, as it eschews the hierarchical arrangements typical of dominant public discourse in favor of more African-centered norms prioritizing communal understanding among diverse peoples. This is a significant aspect not only of social justice but also of the transformation of African Americans from "objects" to "subjects."[51] In actively participating in the production of memory, spectators join the reenactors in constructing the agency essential to identity.

In explaining the reasons reenactment offers such a productive venue for the representation of previously silenced African American memories, many reenactors expressed opinions that pointed to the advantages of live performances, particularly those allowing for substantial performer-visitor interaction, in constructing this agency. Ricky Davis of the Third USCT unit said, "History for most folks is a hard sell. Reenactments are flesh and blood—smacks them in the head. . . . It's fun to see people charged up, saying 'I didn't know that.'" James Carney summed up the objective of his reenactment regiment by quoting Confucius: "'What you hear, you will forget. What you see, you will remember. What you experience, you will understand.' This quote personifies us. We invite audience participation."

Nevertheless, the importance of the audience at reenactments presents a unique challenge for black men, as the spectatorship remains overwhelmingly (98 percent, in the estimation of some reenactors) white. Despite the fact that attendance at reenactments is generally seen as an educational experience for the men, women, and children who attend them, most spectators have no idea blacks participated in the Civil War and therefore don't expect to see them there as performers. The men described the reactions of white spectators as generally positive, with a little bit of surprise and skepticism mixed in. "Glad to see you," "let's talk," "we didn't know," and "you guys didn't do this" were typical reactions, according to my respondents. The reenactors see these responses as starting points in their mission to cultivate a conscientious counterpublic focused on the black role in the war. The reactions of the white reenactors are similar. At a battle recreation in Florida, a woman describing herself as a "third-generation reenactor" approached the USCT reenactors and told them that because of their presence at these events she made a trip to the principal's office at her teenage son's school in order to "correct" a history teacher who had told his class that no black men fought in any Civil War battles in Florida. At the same event, a white male Union reenactor simply told the men, "I didn't see any black guys here last year . . . happy to see you here. You guys saved our bacon." When asked about the reactions of Confederate reenactors, the men replied that they are the most likely group to be unaware of black men's agency in the war: "The 'beer and pretzels group' [of southern whites] most likely to make claims of 'heritage' are the least likely to know about blacks in the Civil War," a Philadelphia reenactor declared.

For black reenactors, the greatest obstacle is engaging potential African American audiences in the performance of memories perceived as traumatic and white-centered, a perception that makes it less likely other blacks will see Civil War battle as a common experience. My interviewees offered explanations as to why they felt this to be the case, pointing to the continuing wariness with which African Americans hold these memories. Kendall Reynolds and Fred Moore, both members of the Fifth USCT (originally the 127th Ohio Volunteers) lamented the lack of African American interest in their battles. "We ask, 'why are our middle-aged brothers not rallying to this history?' Blacks have issues with Civil War history. We haven't come to terms with slavery," said Reynolds. "Civil War history brings a bad taste to us," added Moore. "When you ask for heroes, they can name jump shots, iPods, etc. But not this."

The importance of representation for claims upon the enacted memories and identity lies not only with the performers but extends to spectators as well: in discussing their responses to the challenges inherent in African American engagement with Civil war history, the men suggested that a significant aspect of the effectiveness of their performances lies in the presence of blacks at the events as visitors. According to the men, most African Americans who do attend reenactments are historians and *Glory* fans, with a few curiosity-seekers mixed in. Aside from these groups, the numbers of interested black Americans is very small. While two of the reenactments I attended were centered on black history and therefore drew significant numbers of black visitors, this is not typically the case. Among thousands of attendees at the other reenactments, only a handful of spectators were identifiably African American. Ronnie, a middle-aged black man with dreadlocks visiting the Olustee reenactment in Florida, said that he attended the event simply out of curiosity and afterwards was glad he came. "Most people don't know," he said. He added that he had some questions about African Americans' place in Civil War memories: "Where are we? Where do we fit in? I come because I don't know these aspects of history . . . not much pertaining to us. This is black history month." A reenactor in Kentucky explained that members of his unit view increasing black interest in battle simulations as their primary duty, tying increased knowledge of this history to a better contemporary reality. Describing their mission as a "cultural shift," he said that "blacks have seen reenactments as a negative thing, rather than an educational opportunity. . . . It should be seen as an opportunity for blacks. There are negatives, but blacks should see how these negatives affect the present and keep us at a disadvantage. We should arm ourselves against current policies." Away from the battlefield, lack of interest is much less of an issue. As the featured speakers at living history events at schools, juvenile detention centers, museums, and other venues, the men retain complete control over the narrative. Though they did note in their conversations with me that they typically encounter wariness about viewing and touching artifacts they bring to their presentations—such as slave shackles and chains—the opportunity exists for them to use these events to stimulate interest among their audiences in attending the battle reenactments.

The dialogic nature of battle reenactment also involves the battlefield itself in the production of meaning central to southern identity. The notion that the landscapes on which the war's battles were waged constitute hallowed ground is an essential aspect of this identity and is generally an unquestioned assumption within the traditional community of reenactors. The veneration of the land, with its focus on the blood spilled in battle, is an essential component of the discourses of authenticity and battle minutiae shifting the focus of reenactment away from the war's causes and consequences. More importantly, it assists in the construction of a subjectivity in which heroic masculinity and honor are exalted, and combat is interpreted through a frame emphasizing tragic death.[52] African American reenactors retain this assumption when performing their identity/cultural work. However, their performances, along with those of the spectators they draw to reenactment, restructure the rhetoric of battlefield sanctity to foreground blood sacrifice in the service of freedom. The appropriation of the language of sacred space as part and parcel of a reinterpretation of the battlefield functions to demonstrate that they, like most landscapes, are contestable. The capacity to assign more critical meanings to the landscapes highlights the fracturing of the contemporary narratives built around them and is central to the production of an alternative, black-centered vision of southern identity.

America's battlefields are simultaneously sacred spaces and places. They are sacred spaces in the sense that they are the scenes of great violence, sacrifice, death, and destruction; a patient and determined search can still yield shell casings, bullets, and bone fragments from wars waged more than a century ago.[53] After battles were fought, makeshift funerals were often conducted right on the spot where the dead had fallen—many Civil War battlefields contain small or large cemeteries with stone records of those who gave their lives. They are also sacred places in the sense that they signify the history that constitutes a significant part of group identities, and—to an even greater extent—national identity and heritage. In suggesting that consecration is "part of the cultural work of sacralizing space, time, persons, and social relations," David Chidester and Edward T. Linenthal cite Claude Lévi-Strauss's contention that the value of the sacred is itself empty of meaning and therefore susceptible to the reception of any meaning whatsoever.[54] Geographer David Harvey has referred to sacralizing practices as the "aestheticization of politics . . . in which appeal to the mythology of place and person has a strong role to play."[55] This highly subjective process of imparting meaning to geography renders the nation's battlefields as spaces upon which social relations are played out.

The construction of discursive relationships among place, time, and persons on Civil War battlefields began even before the war's end, with Lincoln's address at Gettysburg on November 19, 1863. Declaring that the sanctification of the field had been completed by the heroic actions of the soldiers, Lincoln declared that the living could not further "consecrate" nor "hallow" the ground, as "the brave men, living and dead, who struggled here have consecrated it far above our poor power to add or detract."[56] This declaration of the ground as hallowed and the subsequent valorization of the heroic Civil War soldier that was a part of the culture of reconciliation laid the foundation for the designation of battlefields as sacred spaces.

At the same time that the discursive construction of these historic landscapes as hallowed ground was taking place, another critical development was initiated, namely, battlefield preservation. The project of constructing Civil War memory through battlefield preservation began during the war, with monuments erected on the fields at Manassas, Stones River, and Vicksburg. Later, in 1864, the Department of the Interior—of which the National Park Service (NPS) is now a part—designated the battlefield at Gettysburg as federal land. Today, a slight majority of battlefields (53 percent) are either maintained by the NPS, supplemented by state agencies, private interests, or a combination of all three, with the rest controlled exclusively by private interests.[57] Both of these factors—the perception of battlefields as sacred spaces and the control of historic sites either by state and federal agencies or by private entities—are important to the construction of the new battlefield narratives performed by African American reenactors.

There are very few sacred spaces so closed as to disallow the potential for what Chidester and Linenthal refer to as "counter-maneuvers of resistance and recovery."[58] What one sees and hears on the battlefield during a reenactment or learns during on-site tours of the grounds and the visitors' centers is the result of a process of negotiation, as individuals and groups seek to present complex events visually.[59] For the nation's Civil War battlefields, such a process was set in motion with an act of Congress in 1989. In legislation prescribing park boundaries at the Fredericksburg and Spotsylvania County battlefields, Congress inserted language specifically instructing the Secretary of the Interior to interpret the parks "in the larger context of the Civil War and American history, including the causes and the consequences of the Civil War and including the effects of the war on all the American people, especially on the American South."[60] This was followed by similar legislation regarding the interpretations at Gettysburg and Vicksburg. As a result, the NPS began developing interpretations positioning slavery at the war's epicenter on the grounds of the battlefields under its control.[61] The new legislation—which was opposed by Confederate heritage organizations that had spent decades working on the inscription of Lost Cause-friendly monuments to the Old South on public lands across the southern landscape—facilitated the circulation of African American memories within these sacred spaces. This increased access helped constitute the battlefield as a contemporary public sphere in which a multitude of narratives may be constructed, represented, and contested.

Places are sacralized through the cultural labor of ritual. Memory constitutes an important aspect of this ritual.[62] Decades of reenactments have worked through their ritualistic nature and reverential verbal discourse to reinscribe the sanctity of the battlefield landscape, with the sacrifices made by those who died in battle constituting its central theme. According to Blight, this prioritization of masculine sacrifice has transformed battlefields into places of sectional healing while foreclosing their prospects as places of racial healing.[63] Indeed, the status of reconciliation as the default discourse underlying traditional reenactment is exemplified in the ritualistic mutual salute between opposing sides after the conclusion of battle. However, as Chidester and Linenthal have suggested, *reinterpretation* also constitutes a practice by which battlefields are reproduced as sacred sites.[64] In enacting new memories upon these spaces, black participants combine the traditional rituals of re-consecration that occur before, during, and after battles with the imposition of alternative meanings on the notion of blood sacrifice that forms the essence of the lands' sanctity. The modified nature of the sacralizing themes black reenactors and spectators construct centers on the addition of another perspective on the virtue of blood sacrifice, that of *freedom*. Freedom, in this sense, represents concepts both material—as in emancipation—and abstract, as in adherence to the nation's professed democratic ideals. Both serve to recover memories of slavery and emancipation and to insert them into battlefield narratives.

The men articulated to me the importance of blood sacrifice to both of these conceptions of freedom, describing their duty both to honor their ancestors and to respect the ground as sacred by telling the story of the USCT. It was because of the blood spilled on the ground, they told me, that African Americans earned the freedom that enabled their very presence at reenactments, and that America was forced to live up to its promise as a democracy. Of primary importance is the fact that the sacrifices made were those of African Americans freeing *themselves*. "It is on their shoulders that we stand," said one of the men in underlining the importance of preserving the sanctity of the ground upon which they were about to engage in battle. Another reenactor expressed his interest in the hobby in similar terms, stating, "I love being on the hallowed ground where your ancestors were." Yet another described his attraction to reenacting partially as a response to his interest in the paranormal. The spirits of the dead on the battlefield, he explained, draw him to the hobby. Moreover, veneration of the sites of ancestral struggles for freedom is not limited to the reenactors. As the prayer circle at Fort Pocahontas illustrates, spectators are sometimes drawn to reenactment for the same reason. A visitor to the reenactment there who has written a book on blacks in the Civil War said that he sees these sites as the "hallowed ground upon which freedom was won." This represents a significant intervention in the discourses advanced through traditional reenactment, and not only in terms of differences in the meanings embedded in the invocation of ancestors. It also represents a fusion of conventional southern articulations of battlefields as sacred ground with a set of expressions associated with an important African-centered cultural tradition: recognition of and reverence for the ancestral presence among the living as a source of guidance and inspiration.

The veneration of battlefields is also reflected in the preservation activities of both black and white reenactors. As centuries-old sacred spaces in the midst of an increasingly modernizing and globalizing South, battlefields also represent cultural clashes between the old and the new. The 1960s ushered in increasing pressures for the conversion of these lands to "higher density uses" such as parking lots and housing complexes. Like their white counterparts, African American men have answered calls to campaign for keeping these places free from encroaching modernization, which, in the parlance of reenactment culture's veneration of these sites as sacred, represents defilement of the land on which their ancestors died. Shortly before embarking on a trip to Morris Island, South Carolina, with other members of his Fifty-Fourth Massachusetts unit based in Washington, DC, to attend the annual memorial to the fallen USCT and to protest the proposed residential development of the site at Battery Wagner, Mario Baker described the protest's purpose in terms of the importance of fending off any threats to the site's sanctity.[65] "This is something we have to do," he said. "Our ancestors shed their blood there. It is hallowed ground. To stand on the hallowed ground where black heroes were is momentous. It is our job to honor their sacrifice by protecting the land."

The discourse of sacred ground emphasizes the dialogic relationship between traditional and African American-centered reenactments. As is the case with the performative construction of masculinity, citizenship, and historical agency, dialogism advances the power of cultural syncretism and pastiche through a restructuring of the meanings assigned to the battlefield. In the next section, I use the reenactments at Olustee, Forks Road, and Fort Pocahontas to examine the ways in which this collaboration repositions reenactment as a resistant practice.

New Memories at Olustee, Forks Road, and Fort Pocahontas

The new memories constructed through African American engagement in reenactment highlight the ways in which multiple aspects of the practice intervene in the production of the narratives produced in its course and offer new frameworks through which we may analyze the identity/cultural work being performed. This includes all aspects of the built environment surrounding the battlefield. The expanded history presented allows us to more clearly see the ways in which the entire tourist experience—from the guided tours to the gift shops on the larger battlefield sites—constructs the way we remember the Civil War. For example, the items for sale in the visitor shop inform us as to what aspects of history are considered important by the particular event's organizers, as well as which aspects they consider marginal. The short films describing the battle in question typically shown at small theaters located inside the visitors' centers serve the same function.

The discursive environment for this identity/cultural work also includes aspects of the battles and sites that are not visible. Factors such as location, racial geography, ownership, and local history influence the narratives presented during reenactments. The Petersburg National Battlefield may be thought of as a representative example of this point. The site, located in Petersburg, Virginia—a town that is part of the Richmond Metropolitan area—is home to the historically-black Virginia State University and has a local population that is just under 78 percent African American.[66] The siege of Petersburg resulted in a decisive and pivotal Union victory, with significant USCT involvement. The battlefield is maintained by the NPS and thus falls within the purview of the legislation mandating the presentation of an expanded history. The gift shop features books, toys, and other souvenirs detailing the Confederate, Union, and African American perspectives on the war. Notable examples include *Battle Cry of Freedom* by James McPherson, *Uncommon Valor* by Melvin

Claxton and Mark Puls, and a children's book about slavery titled *Life on a Plantation*. The film shown inside the media room prominently features the contributions of the USCT in the battle. What is particularly striking here is the representation of USCT men as "typical" Union soldiers.

When I interviewed Nathaniel Walker, a ranger at the Petersburg Battlefield, he noted that there has been a greater push since the early 1990s within localities, states, and the NPS to preserve battlefields that showcase a wider history. Most of the people who visit the Petersburg park are middle-aged whites; the few African Americans who tour the site tend to be soldiers from nearby Fort Lee. Because the black presence at the Battle of the Crater—as the conflict is often called—was so significant in terms of strategy and numbers, Walker informed me that the then-operational management plan provided for the eventual inclusion of narratives detailing the work of African American civilian and supply efforts.[67] Walker, who is a USCT reenactor at Petersburg as well as a civilian reenactor at other battles (often playing a "contraband" and/or "slave"), said that he often hears blacks complain that "that's not my history, that's *their* history." Yet, he argued, "blacks considered themselves American—this is American history. . . . To be more inclusive, we present the history to everyone. . . . There's no way this can just be one segment of the population and history."

The national battlefield park at Lookout Mountain provides a striking contrast to the Petersburg site. The surrounding area of Chattanooga, Tennessee, is larger than the Virginia town and has a much smaller—though not insubstantial at nearly 35 percent—African American population.[68] The battle there constituted a Union victory without the involvement of USCT troops. While this would seem to justify the lack of narratives about black service in the Civil War at Lookout Mountain, any mention of slavery as a cause of the conflict is also missing. The guided presentation of the battle focuses mostly on the mechanics of the armed clash. While the NPS-operated visitor's center offers a presentation foregrounding the experiences of soldiers from both the North and the South, the privately-run gift shop next door features reams of Confederate memorabilia, from bumper stickers and mugs to hats and T-shirts and a smaller collection of Union-themed items.

These are but two examples of the contrasts between the traditional and expanded presentations at the nation's battlefield parks. Many of the dynamics mentioned here are operative at reenactments, with two significant factors determining the narratives as well as the tenor of the celebrations. The first factor involves the historic significance of the battle.

The NPS has developed an elaborate classification scheme that ranks each battle in terms of its significance.[69] "Class A and B" battles represent the "principal strategic operations of the war," while "Class C and D" battles were of "limited tactical objectives of enforcement and obligation." The USCT saw combat in 449 engagements, of which 39 were major battles.[70] With a few exceptions, most battles involving the USCT were "Class C" or "D." These battlefields are most likely to be owned by private interests, and the battles staged there are geared more toward education than toward pageantry. The combination of these features—battle significance and battlefield control—has resulted in presentations more likely to highlight black military and civilian involvement in the war at these sites. The second factor involves the histories of the battles, specifically those that evoke memories of southern victory. Civil War reenactments are, above all, tourist attractions and, as is the case with organized sports, most spectators want to be on the "winning team."[71] This is particularly the case in rural pockets of the Deep South, where regional identity is heavily invested in Confederate nostalgia.

The battles at Olustee, Forks Road, and Fort Pocahontas are among the small number of reenactments in which significant numbers of USCT reenactors participate. There are striking differences characterizing each of the three remembrances, with divergent factors influencing the rhetorical power of the new memories. A comparison of the reenactments is therefore particularly fruitful.

The Battle of Olustee took place on February 20, 1864. Holding a "Class B" designation, it was relatively small (though part of the largest campaign in Florida) but of great strategic significance. Historically, the invasion by the Northern army entailed an agenda that was primarily political in nature, meant to return Florida to the Union in time to send a pro-Lincoln delegation to the Republican National Convention. Its strategic objectives included capturing vital transportation routes, cutting off the flow of supplies from the peninsula, allowing the export of cotton and timber to the North, and bringing thousands of freed slaves into the Union army.[72] The battle included the engagement of three USCT units, the Fifty-Fourth Massachusetts Infantry, the First North Carolina Colored Infantry, and the Eighth US Colored Infantry. Of the three, only the Fifty-Fourth Massachusetts had seen prior combat. Along with previous battles at Port Hudson and Millikin's Bend, Olustee would serve as a proving ground for black soldiers to demonstrate their valor. Most accounts of the battle suggest that they and their white Union comrades performed as well as they could under difficult circumstances, particularly the relative lack of training and experience of two of the USCT units.[73] Neverthe-less, Olustee would become a decisive and strategically important Confederate victory.

The importance of these factors is reflected in the tenor of the annual reenactment held at Olustee every February. The event is one of the largest battle re-creations held in the Southeast and draws hundreds of reenactors and thousands of visitors from all over the United States, as well as a handful from abroad. The Olustee Battlefield Historic State Park is located in a rural area near Lake City, Florida, approximately fifty miles west of Jacksonville, in an area of the state described as more distinctly *southern* than many of its other parts that have been culturally transformed through decades of migration from the North and from Latin America. The battlefield became the subject of controversy in late 2013, when the Florida chapter of the Sons of Union Veterans sought permission to add an obelisk commemorating fallen Union soldiers to the three Confederate memorials erected on the grounds by the United Daughters of the Confederacy during the early twentieth century. Chief among the intense objections raised to this plan was the fact that many residents in the surrounding area were descendants of Confederate soldiers who had fought at the battle, implying that the proposed monument would stand as a material insult to their memories. Invoking the rhetoric of "hallowed ground," opponents argued that the establishment of a monument to the Union dead, many of whom were black Floridians, would represent a defilement of the sanctity of the battlefield and, consequently, a denigration of the area's southern heritage.[74] Finally, Olustee represents a combination of state and federal control: a federally-controlled 600 acre park surrounds the three-acre state park. The battlefield thus falls within the purview of the federal legislation requiring more even-handed representation of the conflict. All of these factors—the site's history and symbolic significance, its geography, and its ownership—influence the capacities of black reenactment to reshape its memories.

I attended the reenactment of the Battle of Olustee in February of 2008. Of the three events described here, Olustee adheres most closely to the celebratory tenor characteristic of most traditional reenactments. The reenactment encompasses an entire week of festivities in the nearby town of Lake City—including craft shows, dances, parades, and a Miss Olustee pageant—before culminating in weekend combat on the battlefield. The signature event, besides the battles, is an antebellum ball held on Saturday night. The site features large, separate encampment spaces for reenactors from each side to cook, eat, sleep, and interact with visitors, a large sutler's area for vendors to sell food and hawk their war-themed wares, and a large field adjacent to the battleground for practice drills. During the event that I witnessed, numerous large tents housed lectures on details about the battle as well as first-person accounts of historical figures of the era. There was a booth for visitors to take sepia-toned photographs designed to look like they were taken during the era. One of the tented areas even featured a space for couples dressed in period attire to renew their wedding vows.

The battle enactment itself was generally marked by an atmosphere more characteristic of a sporting event, with the audience divided into two groups in stands on their favored sides, cheering as "their" team "scored a victory." Sophisticated pyrotechnics enhanced the more spectacular aspects of this scene, producing the impression of real gunfire and heightening the drama on the battlefield. The standing-room only crowd was herded onto a set of bleachers, which overflowed long before the battle began. Though the Union maintained a heavy presence among the fans, it was clearly outnumbered. The cheers and shouts from the crowd and the ubiquitous presence of the Confederate battle flag signaled a deep investment in the outcome for many of those attending. As the battle was waged, a chorus of whoops and hollers issued from the stands when the rebels, after twenty minutes or so of pummeling by the Union forces, regrouped and started advancing. As the Confederate reenactors drove the Union men across the field, one woman exclaimed, "here come the Johnnies," a comment striking in its affectionate familiarity suggestive of identity. At the close of the battle, both sides saluted each other and the audience in the discourse of reconciliation typically performed at reenactments. There were only a handful of African Americans in attendance.

Nevertheless, even this small African American presence, as both military and civilian reenactors, presents significant ruptures in the dominant functioning of the Lost Cause discourse on display at Olustee. Mary Fears is a retired educator, filmmaker, and civilian reenactor. Every year she, her husband, and their two sons drive their RV from Orlando to Olustee to spend the weekend educating other reenactors and spectators about the African American role in the war. She and her group are allotted an hour's worth of space in the program to discuss the history of black involvement as smugglers, soldiers, servants, and spies. I watched as her group finished its presentation, left the stage, and then mingled with a steady stream of visitors eager to learn more about the subject. Her older son, perhaps the most recognizable figure at the festival as "Frederick Douglass," appeared to be a crowd favorite. Ms. Fears's display tent, which featured her book on black reenacting, a poster describing little-known facts about slavery, and various slave artifacts was one of the more popular attractions. A constant flow of visitors stopped by to peruse the artifacts and ask questions. "Many of the black men have stopped coming to Olustee," she said. "For the last few years, they have gone to Wilson's Wharf (Fort Pocahontas) instead." When asked why, she explained that the environment here had gotten a bit less welcoming over the years. As if to illustrate this point, several yards away, in the sutler's area, items of a different stripe were on display: whips, miniature Confederate battle flags, pro-Confederate books (including those arguing the existence of armed black Confederates), and other artifacts more reminiscent of the idealized Old South.

In addition to the sale of these items, the importance the event held for traditional notions of regional identity was exemplified by a flyer placed on the windshield of every car parked along the rural stretch of road along the battlefield by the white supremacist organization the League of the South.[75] Besides stating the group's primary aim to "advance the cultural, social, economic, and political well-being and independence of the Southern people by all honorable means," the flyer listed the irrelevance of the US Constitution, the need to control both legal and illegal immigration, and the devolution of states' rights as reasons why "Home Rule for Florida and the South is Necessary." K. Michael Prince has described the organization's ethos as resting on the belief that the social changes wrought by the war and its aftermath have emasculated the South, with the league's cultural work as centered on restoring regional manly honor and identity through opposition to the above-mentioned "threats."[76] Both the assumptions underlying the language in the flyer and its distribution emphasize the symbolism of Olustee, along with the constraints its meaning as a historically significant place imposes on the capacity for black participation to influence dominant memories. More importantly, they serve as a reminder of the tensions that arise when narratives of the Old and New South come together on the battlefield. Nevertheless, Olustee provides a useful illustration of black reenactment's potential, as well as of its limits, particularly those imposed by history, geography, and battlefield control.

The importance of these factors is further demonstrated at two other battles, both of which offer useful contrasts to Olustee. The reenactments of the battle of Forks Road—which I attended in February 2008 and 2010 in Wilmington, North Carolina—and the skirmish at Fort Pocahontas (which I visited in May of 2008 and 2010 in Charles City County, Virginia, a rural area situated approximately halfway between Richmond and Williamsburg), are centered on the African American experience. As such, both events are much more focused on pedagogy. Forks Road and

Fort Pocahontas are battles that fall into the NPS "Class D" category, with much smaller total numbers of reenactors and spectators but higher proportions of USCT and black visitors. Moreover, private interests control both battlefields, which locates them outside of the purview of the NPS mandate. However, in an interesting twist in these two cases, private control of the battlefields has worked to advance the representation of new narratives, as organizers have realized the events' potential to develop a new market focused on African American heritage. Both reenactments provide illustrations of reenactment's capacity to serve as a vehicle for the construction of new memories and black southern identity.

The battle of Forks Road—part of the Fort Fisher Campaign and the last fight in the Battle of Wilmington—involved the participation of approximately sixteen hundred men from five USCT units on February 20 and 21, 1865. Many of these soldiers had escaped slavery and joined the army in nearby Union-occupied New Bern, which hosts its own annual reenactment weekend. The battle was a decisive Union victory.[77] In contrast to the Lost Cause-infused, crowd-centered theatricality of Olustee, Forks Road is a much more low-key affair. The battlefield is now part of the grounds of the Cameron Art Museum, which hosts the annual USCT Symposium and Living History Weekend. The event's location at the museum is in keeping with its mission to be more of a cultural heritage conference than a staged tourist event. Though there is an opening ceremony, a period dance, and artillery demonstrations before each battle, there is no sutlers' area. Nor are there tents for guests to indulge in period photography or engage in wedding vow renewals.

The recurring theme of each year's event is "Earning the Right to Citizenship." Although during the event that I attended a slight majority of the reenactors were white, the weekend was focused mostly on the contributions of the USCT. Concerns about authenticity were supplanted by educational objectives, as many of the black reenactors chose to spend the night in a specially-booked local hotel rather than remain with the white men who were camping outside in the cold February rain. Before the actual battles on Saturday and Sunday, spectators were treated to academic symposia titled "The Underground Railroad and Frederick Douglass," "The Black Spy Network" (featuring a reenactor as "Harriet Tubman"), and "Name Changing and USCT Genealogy Research." On Sunday morning, there were church services for reenactors and spectators. Afterward, William B. Gould IV, author of *Diary of a Contraband*, discussed this book about his ancestor who escaped slavery to join the Navy. In another workshop, "Marketing African American History and Culture," a moderator discussed the challenges in promoting this era of African American history. Past reenactments had included a panel discussion on the controversies over the notion of "Black Confederates," with scholars explaining the differences between "man-servants" and "weapon-equipped soldiers."

The symposia and, especially, the battle reenactment drew substantial numbers of African American visitors. Many of the attendees were children from area schools accompanied by their parents. Event organizers worked in conjunction with the local Board of Education to provide the state's teachers with continuing education units for attending the symposia; the teachers, in turn, encouraged their students to attend. Of the three reenactments detailed in this chapter, the Forks Road experience, with its focus on educating the public about the little-known service of the USCT, best illustrates the potential for the construction of new memories at these events, transforming these performances from racialized spectacle to a more pedagogical experience focused on African American history.

The skirmish at Fort Pocahontas, also known as Wilson's Wharf, commenced on May 24, 1864, when twenty-five hundred Confederate cavalry attacked two Union-occupied points on a peninsula of land between the James and Appomattox rivers. The Union had engaged in a series of coordinated assaults in Virginia featuring the involvement of the first brigade of the Army of the James, made up solely of black regiments under the command of General Edward A. Wild. These units, which had seized the site in order to provide both a supply base and a threat to the nearby Confederate capital in Richmond, included the First and Tenth USCT.[78] After a five-hour fight, the attack was successfully repelled. Afterward, the USCT built an earthen fort on the site that they named Fort Pocahontas. The USCT performance in the battle was important in advancing the black soldiers' ongoing mission to prove their bravery; in fact, journalist and chaplain Henry McNeal Turner would later use white soldiers' praise of black heroism at Fort Pocahontas to push for equal pay for African American combatants.[79] It was also an important symbolic victory, as the commanding general of the defeated Confederates was none other than Fitzhugh Lee, nephew of Robert E. Lee.

The annual reenactment at Fort Pocahontas is one of the most significant African American battle re-creations and is regularly hosted by the Thirty-Eighth USCT, a local unit from Richmond. The weekend represents a hybrid of Olustee and Forks Road: when I attended, its tenor was much less pedagogical than that of Forks Road, while the event was more focused on the actual battle simulation, as Olustee had been. Yet, as was the case with Forks Road, Fort Pocohontas's theme was centered on the

USCT troops. Harrison Tyler, the grandson of tenth US President John Tyler, had bought the land that contains the battlefield out of bankruptcy court in 1994, began developing it in 1996 and, after meeting and consulting with some reenactors from the Fifty-Fourth Massachusetts in Washington, DC, began staging annual reenactments there in 1998. The first year featured only three reenactors. The following year, the Fifty-Fourth unit from DC participated. Every year since then, the crowd has grown more substantial. Tyler, who lives nearby in his family home—which also hosts plantation tours—said he eschews the politics implicated in reenactment culture. "I'm a strict believer in interpreting history as it happened," he said. Nevertheless, at the same time that Fort Pocahontas provides an illustration of the transformative potential black participation brings to reenactment, it also exemplifies its limits. One of the complaints that many of the African American reenactors have about this event is that it involves a rupture in the culture's focus on historical accuracy, as well as a significant contradiction of its discursive focus on authenticity. Over the course of the reenactment weekend, the Confederates are allowed to stage one battle in which they secured victory. When I asked Tyler about this, he explained that, in order to get adequate Confederate reenactor participation, he had to allow them one "triumph." "The Confederates wanted to win one day, so we integrated Fort Stephens," he said. "We wanted to make everybody happy. We try to keep the rabid ones away. We have to live in a world where everybody gets along."

In spite of this incongruity, the Fort Pocahontas event demonstrates the ways in which battle reenactments may be used to redefine the contours of southern identity, by focusing on African American heritage tourism. The most distinctive feature of this reenactment is the spectators, a slight majority of whom are black. In addition to the men, women, and children from the nearby cities of Richmond and Williamsburg, the event I witnessed featured a group bused in from Norfolk, approximately ninety miles away; this was the Bells Mill Historical Research and Restoration Society, whose members are USCT descendants. All of them were wearing T-shirts printed with the words "We Are the Proud Descendants and Relatives of Afro-Virginian Union Army Civil War Patriot Heroes Who Fought at the Battles of. . . ." Many of the shirts bore the names of the particular ancestors who had fought at Fort Pocahontas. The head curator of the society, Dr. E. Curtis Alexander, delivered a lecture on the first day of the reenactment weekend in which he highlighted the actions of the black soldiers at Fort Pocahontas and argued that the battle has been erased from dominant memory for "obvious reasons." Afterward, he suggested that

Lee's surrender at Appomattox represented the emergence of a unified nation more consistent with its expressed ideals, and that the bravery of the USCT was instrumental in the formation of this version of "America." "This is marginal history," he said. "We [African Americans] are history."

After the completion of the prayer circle, several visitors explained their motivations for attending the reenactment. One middle-aged man said that he had become interested in the Buffalo Soldiers while serving in the military.[80] This interest led him to find out more about the USCT. One man became interested after he noticed the graves of thirteen USCT soldiers in the cemetery of the church of which he is the pastor and decided to learn more about their lives, as well as the lives and experiences of other colored troops. A married couple said that they were there as part of a larger genealogical project in which they were seeking any USCT ancestors they may have. These responses reveal the potential for reenactments to become stimuli for black citizens to rediscover not only a marginalized African American history but to connect with their own personal histories. At the end of the battle, before the customary salute of reconciliation each side pays to each other and the spectators, an African American woman from the Contraband Society (based in the nearby city of Hampton) sang "Amazing Grace."

Conclusion

The prayer circle held at Fort Pocahontas is illustrative of the multiple ways in which African American reenactment undermines assumptions of normative whiteness within the practice, as well as the broader assumptions embedded in the memories underwriting it. This call to the ancestors, combined with the performative arrangements and place attachments appropriated from traditional battle reenactment, has helped construct the reenactment as a resistant practice and reconstruct the battlefield as an oppositional site. The fusion of these practices, in turn, strengthens the forces of pastiche and cultural syncretism associated with the performances and is representative of the diverse sources fueling the emergence of African American southern identity.

The performances at Fort Pocahontas, Olustee, Forks Road and other sites help construct black southern identity through the production of memories foregrounding historical agency before, during, and after the war. Specifically, the performances enacted by black bodies on the battlefield and in the visitors' areas shift the discursive focus of reenactment away from authenticity and battle minutia to the war's causes and consequences. This shift creates new narratives, in which dominant Civil War memories positioning blacks as either passive victims or malevolent bucks are reordered through the creation of discourses of masculinity and citizenship. In this way, hegemonic images rooted in southern mythology are supplanted by affirmative memories productive of an oppositional identity centered on the intersection of southernness and blackness.

Black reenactments serve as vernacular expressions that facilitate and mediate performative conversations in which the multiple and intersecting lenses of this identity—race, gender, citizenship, and region—coalesce through the mobilization of pastiche and cultural syncretism. African American Civil War battle reenactment represents an alternative practice within an alternative practice, one that leverages the latter's perceived eccentricity, accessibility, and influence among "average" consumers to recover memories of slavery and emancipation as central to the war, to demonstrate the agency black slaves and freedmen exercised in securing their own freedom, and to offer alternative readings of the meanings assigned to the sacred space of the battlefield. Reenactment deploys the vernacular discourses embedded in embodied performance to transform the dominant meanings ascribed to Civil War-era memory and, by definition, those available to the formation of contemporary southern blackness. In the next chapter, I examine the role of grassroots discourses associated with slavery and Civil War museums in the construction of black southern identity.

2

So That the Dead May Finally Speak

Space, Place, and the Transformational Rhetoric of Black History Museums

"We can talk about slavery for a few minutes, if y'all *want* to," said the young African American docent in response to a question about the slaves who had performed the work required to maintain the elegant and stately Shirley Plantation, located on the north bank of the James River in rural Charles City County, Virginia. The guided tour I attended of what is billed as America's oldest plantation included detailed discussions of the wealthy, elite planters who had lived there, their descendants over the last two centuries, the members of the family who still occupied sections of the house—even the ghost that, according to legend, haunted it—but no mention of the "other" residents who had also lived on the grounds in the past. The tour consisted of thirty minutes of cheery tourist discourse peppered with the passive voice to describe how draperies *were sewn*, items *were brought in*, and food *was served*. When the subject turned to the furniture in the room that *was made* by American hands (after all, the docent explained, the Carter family that owned the plantation had been a patriotic clan that did not believe in importing furniture from England), someone in our small group of fifteen tourists, mindful of the lack of discussion about *who* had actually carried out these duties, finally asked if slaves had performed the labor necessary to construct the beautiful chairs and tables in the dining room in which we were standing.[1] In a spiel that seemed as though it were designed to be left out of the narrative if he deemed a particular tourist group to be less receptive to such discussions, the docent provided a brief description of the African Americans who comprised a majority of the inhabitants of the grounds, devoting a significant portion of his talk to their treatment. "The slaves here were treated well," he added, "they had ample food and good medical care."

At this former plantation, guided tours are limited to the planters' living quarters. On the remainder of the estate's grounds, including the kitchen and stables where the specter of slavery looms more insistently, visitors are on their own. In these spaces, the placards, rather than the docents, perform the work of glossing over the realities of slavery and race, often describing the African slaves as "servants" and using the passive voice in descriptions of the tasks they performed. Furthermore, the written descriptions provide detailed information about the white indentured servants who had worked there during the period before Africans were brought to Virginia as slaves, a rhetorical ploy that obscures the racial subjugation essential to North American slavery by suggesting that whites were also victims of exploitation.

These linguistic tactics are all components of a process of social forgetting reliant on a representational strategy Jennifer Eichstedt and Stephen Small refer to as symbolic annihilation.[2] This type of erasure produces tourist narratives foregrounding the lifestyle of wealth, privilege, and gentility of elite southern whites while minimizing or completely omitting the role of slavery as the backbone of the social and economic system that supported this regime.

Though it is important to note that the symbolic annihilation of slavery from plantation house narratives is not a universal practice among such tours, when it does occur it is an aspect of a much broader set of decades-long cultural practices designed to carefully reconstruct cultural memories so that they are unmoored from their racialized, gendered, and classed historical contexts. These practices, as Michael S. Bowman has suggested, "legitimize an ideology that works to reproduce a hegemonic discourse that goes back to the Old South," which serves the interests not of the antebellum planters of the past, but rather those of a "class of professionals whose business is the control of information, meanings, values, and images within and across cultural lines."[3] They are the contemporary proprietors of a heritage industry that, according to geographer Derek Alderman, has "disinherited black travelers from their heritage."[4] The broader effect of these practices is that they, and those who perpetuate them, have been instrumental in privileging elite southern whiteness in the construction of the very narrow, exclusionary parameters of traditional southern identity.

These parameters are even more sharply delineated through another element of the region's geography: its memorial landscape. Once specific sets of memories are fixed upon a landscape, they become part of the official memory of the community, be it local, regional, or national. In this respect, race has had a significant impact on the spatial development of the South (as it has on the American landscape more generally), transforming its monuments, museums, and other aspects of its material culture into sacred artifacts serving the particular needs of white citizens.[5] Steven Hoelscher has suggested that landscapes of race and memory are at the center of the South's struggle for identity with the contemporary representational battles between the Old and the new New South stemming from a complex web of political, economic, and cultural relationships.[6]

The South's memorial landscape is heavily saturated with monuments to the Confederacy. The Civil War, contends Kirk Savage, "provoked the greatest era of monument building ever seen in this country."[7] Spearheaded by white women's civic groups, most notably the United Daughters of the Confederacy, the movement began shortly after the war's end as a widespread project to memorialize the war dead in cemeteries. As this campaign became a critical aspect of sectional reconciliation during the latter years of the nineteenth century, it eventually grew to encompass the broader project of creating monuments to generic "honorable" Confederate soldiers in highly visible public spaces and continued well into the twentieth century.[8] Another important aspect of the work of legitimating the Lost Cause through the regional landscape involved attempts, usually though not always successful, to erect monuments representing one of its other foundational archetypes, namely, the image of the "faithful slave." Attempts to create memorials in this vein often faced stiff opposition from progressive African Americans appalled at the possible memorialization of a stereotypical and regressive figure, as well as paradoxically from white southerners dismayed at the lack of loyalty displayed by "unappreciative" former slaves who abandoned their plantations after the war and later expected monuments suggestive of social equality.[9] Nevertheless, these memorialization efforts would later be taken up by state agencies, with the underlying racial assumptions left largely intact. Historian W. Fitzhugh Brundage has contended that these projects were undertaken as a means of controlling the memories assigned to the war and exerting cultural influence over public history. It was this monopolization of public space, he argues, that helped define the conception of "southern" as one that excluded the region's African American citizens.[10]

The most visible landscape artifact in the South is the Confederate battle flag, which represents a powerful rhetoric combining the specific mythology of the Lost Cause with the equally potent sacred meanings associated with flags in general. Symbols are used to invoke a shared understanding that is already present among the groups for whom they carry meaning; the semiotics implicit in the presence of the flag on homes, monuments, in cemeteries and other places within the South's symbolic landscape suggest that the Lost Cause version of history still carries significant currency in the region. These meanings become even more pointed with government-sanctioned displays of the flag, gaining authority from the legitimating institution of the state. While the dominant class has always controlled commemorative resources, in the twentieth century government officials came to be included among those "disciplining authorities" seeking to promote loyalty to the state and its leaders.[11] This ideological function of commemoration, which has been performed throughout history and in most developed societies, has shown itself to be particularly salient during periods defined by social upheaval. One such moment occurred in the aftermath of the *Brown v. Board of Education* Supreme Court decision in 1954, when the Confederate flag went up on statehouses throughout the region and was incorporated into state flags as a response to the racial "crisis" precipitated by the order to desegregate with "all deliberate speed." Though the turn of the twenty-first century saw many public battles resulting in the removal or reduction of state-sanctioned displays of the rebel flag, the banner remains highly visible in some places and continues to function as a powerful symbol of the normative assumptions underlying dominant Civil War memory and traditional, white-centered southern identity.[12]

The significant role of geography in the production of southern identity points to the importance of the resistant memories constructed through African American history museums, particularly those located in the South. Museums centered on the black experiences of slavery, Civil War, and Reconstruction interrogate the linear narratives constructed through plantation home tours and destabilize the Lost Cause interpretation privileged throughout the memorial landscape. In revising the regional landscape to include artifactual representations of black agency during the era, museums are especially instrumental in altering the dominant memories and parameters of southern identity. Moreover, the material and visual cultural fields are especially fruitful sites for the vernacular production and contestation of the meanings etched into the landscape. As institutions of memory that draw their narratives from a number of constituencies—visitors, source communities, background and frontline personnel, and others—they enable "average" people to become agents in the production of history through "re-visioning" the landscape.

In this chapter, I detail the identity/cultural work of three museums: the

African American Civil War Museum and Freedom Foundation (AACWM) in Washington, DC, the American Civil War Museum (ACWM) in Richmond, Virginia, and the Ancient Africa, Slavery, and Civil War Museum (AASCWM) in Selma, Alabama. These institutions demonstrate the power of visual, material, and corporeal representations of African American-centered Civil War memories to disrupt the white hegemony of the southern landscape and expand the parameters of southern identity. Each museum establishes and asserts African American belonging to the region through the deployment of what I refer to as a *transformational rhetoric*. This set of discourses responds to the demands associated with the representation of what Geoffrey Cubitt, Laurajane Smith, and Ross Wilson refer to as "dissonant history," which is comprised of narratives of the past that contradict the essential narratives of established history.[13] The history of slavery disrupts the assumptions of white benevolence undergirding regional (and national) memory and identity, while those offering a narrative focus on black agency in the war and the Reconstruction era undermine the presumptions of normative whiteness central to the dominant narratives of those eras. These oppositional memory institutions utilize a variety of rhetorical strategies in carrying out the additional work required of museums engaged in consciousness-raising.

A transformational rhetoric also responds to the complexities involved in the display of a painful heritage to African American publics whose interest in visiting museums generally and whose receptivity to exhibitions of slavery specifically have traditionally been described as ambivalent. This discomfort springs from a "humiliated silence" about slavery that calls for considered representational approaches.[14] These offer a set of unique display strategies that acknowledge and respond to the particular challenges involved in the transformation of the landscape and the memories and identity that define it. The cultural syncretism advanced through these discourses does not rely on the rhetorical power of the exhibits alone, but draws its meaning from the complex relations among a multitude of intersecting elements. Specifically, each institution's capacity to alter dominant memory extends beyond the basics of visual and/or material museum displays to encompass unique revisionist strategies incorporating place, space, interactive and affective performance, and corporeal agency. Each museum constructs memory and identity through the interplay of two or more of these discursive elements, enabling vernacular historical producers to resist the dominant memory and identity constructed through white monopolization of southern public space over the last one hundred years.

In the following sections, I describe the power of history museums in constructing memory and identity, examine the productive capacities of a transformational rhetoric, and delineate the ways in which its constituent discourses operate at the AASCWM in Selma, the AACWM in Washington, DC, and the ACWM in Richmond. First, I look specifically at the role of history museums in the construction of African American identity. Second, I articulate the contours of transformational rhetoric by describing its features. I then devote three separate sections to analyzing the ways in which its particular discourses interact to construct black southern identity at the AACWM, ACWM, and AASCWM, respectively.

Slavery/Civil War Museums, Resistant Memories, and Black Southern Identity

Sturdivant Hall is located in the Old Town Historical District in downtown Selma, Alabama, and is the most majestic of a number of impressive properties on the beautiful, tree-lined residential street. For just a few dollars and ninety minutes of their time, visitors can participate in a very detailed guided tour of the ten-room mansion and get a peek into the intimate antebellum lives of the Watts family. At the end of the tour, they will learn that the kitchen, along with the quarters that once housed the very small number of "servants" who lived and worked there, is now a gift shop. Overall, the excursion—which is concentrated mostly on the inside of the main house—offers tourists a perspective on the prewar era that is nostalgic, glorious, and relatively untroubled.

A little over a mile away, in an area of downtown Selma no less historic yet considerably less elegant, another museum offers a much different perspective. The Ancient Africa, Slavery, and Civil War Museum (AASCWM) is devoted to the experiences of the enslaved people whose exploitation underwrote the grandeur on display at Sturdivant Hall. Unlike the plantation museum, which is maintained by a combination of public and private interests, the AASCWM is self-sustaining and relies completely on volunteers.

Attorney Faya Rose Toure founded the museum in 2002. Together with her husband, also an attorney and state senator, Toure moved to Selma forty years ago to continue the legal services work and activism the couple had begun earlier in New York City and later Huntsville, Alabama, shortly after graduating from Harvard Law School. She sees the museum as a crucial aspect of her grassroots civic activities, which—in addition to her legal work—have included organizing campaigns on behalf of low-income women and public school students and founding a cultural arts center, a youth organization, and the AASCWM's sister institution, the National Voting Rights Museum. Many of the museum's volunteer staff also work with these other bodies. "[We] wanted to bring northern activism here, [so] we decided to build institutions and political organizations. All of this work begins to interrelate," she explained. "History is a continuum. We are an activist museum. A museum that just exists without making connections is nothing. [The] museum reminds us [of] who we are, where we've been, where we must go and do to achieve a democracy of inclusion. True liberation embraces this concept."

Far outside of Selma's Black Belt, in Washington, DC, is the African American Civil War Museum (AACWM). Its founder and chairman, Dr. Frank Smith, is a former DC city councilman and veteran of the civil rights movement with a professional background in urban planning. These experiences, he explained, helped plant the seed in his mind for the museum. After being arrested during a civil rights demonstration in 1960, he became a member of the Student Nonviolent Coordinating Committee (SNCC) and chairman of the Atlanta Student Movement while attending Morehouse College. In 1962, during a voter registration drive in Holly Springs, Mississippi, he met a descendent of a soldier with the USCT. "I didn't know [about the USCT] and was shocked," he said. "Even with three years of college." The encounter spurred Smith to read John Hope Franklin's *From Slavery to Freedom*, which included a section on the USCT. In 1968 he moved to Washington, DC, in the midst of the uprisings that followed Martin Luther King Jr.'s assassination and, two years later, was elected to the city council. It was at this time that his long-term interest in the stories of the USCT began to take the form of concrete plans. "The city, especially U Street, went up in flames," he explained. "We wanted to build something [there] to attract tourists from the Mall. What would be notorious enough to do that? Why not build a monument to the soldiers? They saved the Union and have not gotten their recognition. When we build it, it will be a phenomenon."

Thus, Smith's motivation for constructing the museum was twofold: first, to create an institution to counter the traditional elision of slavery from Civil War memory while honoring those who fought for its abolition, and secondly to revitalize the neighborhood. Under his leadership as a member of the DC city council representing the area, the African American Civil War Memorial Freedom Foundation was incorporated in 1992. In January 1999, after many years of planning and funding drives which attracted donations from individuals, black churches, local organizations, government agencies, and corporations, a bronze monument bearing the names of the more than two hundred thousand black men who served in the war—including in the Navy—was erected at the corner of Vermont and U streets. In 2000 the museum opened two blocks west of the memorial, with the objective of placing the Civil War in the foreground of African American history. "People were skeptical about a Civil War monument, [believing] Confederates would be coming up here," Smith said. "But some saw *Glory* and knew better. Confederates, sometimes via the UDC [United Daughters of the Confederacy], had stolen the show, and the Civil War was identified with whites. We had to create something equivalent to that for black people." Smith estimates that the museum draws some seventy thousand visitors annually, most of whom are under the age of thirty. In April 2011 it moved from its former location in a seven-hundred-square-foot building to a five-thousand-square-foot newly renovated space across the street from the monument.[15] As of 2015 the museum was the only institution dedicated solely to the display of African American combat in the Civil War.

Approximately one hundred miles south of DC off of Interstate 95 lies Richmond, Virginia—a former capital of the Confederacy, the current capital of the Commonwealth of Virginia, and home of the American Civil War Museum (ACWM). Of the three museums discussed in this chapter, the ACWM is the sole institution not founded by an African American, and its exhibits do not focus exclusively on the African American experience of slavery and the Civil War. It is, however, notable as the only Civil War museum in the South dedicated to representing the northern, southern, and African American perspectives on the war. In keeping with this mission, its discursive focus relies heavily on black memories—including those of slavery—in representing the war. The museum is located in downtown Richmond in the historic Tredegar Ironworks building and is therefore alternately referred to as the Tredegar Museum. It was founded by Alex Wise, the great-great grandson of Henry A. Wise, the governor of Virginia during the years immediately preceding the Civil War and later a combatant in the Confederate army. According to Wise, this ancestry played a major part in inspiring him to found the museum. Having grown up during the civil rights movement and been profoundly affected by it, Wise, a lawyer by training, spent a significant amount of his post-law career involved in educational initiatives geared toward African Americans.

The ACWM was founded as a sister institution to the nearby Museum of the Confederacy (MOC). While serving as Chairman of the Board of the MOC in 1993, Wise was moved by the unanticipated success of

"Before Freedom Came," a temporary and controversial exhibit that explored the significance of slavery to the Confederacy. He was particularly intrigued by the exhibit's ability to draw black visitors to the museum. A year later, while serving as the state's Historic Preservation Officer, Wise decided that a new museum would be the most appropriate forum within which to tell the complete story of slavery. "My job was to derive the greatest benefit possible from state historical sites," he said. "I realized there was no place in the country that has presented the Civil War from three sides—Union, Confederate, and, if you really wanted to understand it, [the] black side—a key part of the story that gets lost. You can't understand the story unless you include that."

The Tredegar National Civil War Foundation was charged with the development of the new museum, which was incorporated in July 2000 through a public-private partnership between Congress and the Richmond Historic Riverfront Foundation. The idea of the museum encountered pushback from both black and white constituencies. African Americans on the city council were concerned about yet another museum comprised of Confederate artifacts, while neo-Confederate groups were intensely opposed to the possibility of museum narratives in which the memory of their "heroes" might be sullied. The attitude, suggested Wise, was "let's get back to the days where the only discussion was whether [Robert E.] Lee was in the New or Old Testament. The only way you could have a modern museum about the Confederacy was to share the stage with other constituencies." The planners thus developed a strategy to construct the site with the Confederacy on one side and the Union on the other. However, given Richmond's politics and the existence of a substantial black public for a Civil War museum, Wise found this arrangement insufficient. "You had to have the African American legacy, too," he stressed. The museum opened in October of 2006 and hosts approximately twenty thousand visitors a year.

A common thread among the vernacular historians I interviewed for this chapter is the desire to utilize the visual cultural arena to revise dominant historical narratives through the display of a neglected aspect of African American history. In so doing, they have used a very old media form to give shape and presence to this history by constructing the space for a ritual encounter with the past. Though there are many other representational forms through which Faya Rose Toure, Smith, and Wise could have presented these narratives, the choice of the museum arena was not arbitrary. As anthropologist Ivan Karp contends, museums are repositories of knowledge that "educate, refine, or produce social commitments beyond those that can be produced in ordinary educational and civic institutions."[16] Thus, the fact that each of these cultural producers has an illustrious civic background is no coincidence. For them, opening museums to showcase a forgotten or erased history is part and parcel of their civic duty, which involves enabling more inclusive conceptions of belonging to the South and its cultural memories.

Historian Spencer R. Crew has suggested that African Americans have unique concerns with preserving, controlling, and recounting their history. He argues that the erasure of the depth and breadth of black accomplishment in America and in Africa—which rationalized and facilitated enslavement and second-class citizenship—has played an important role in defining the status of black Americans. The preservation of black history becomes thereby an even more critical project.[17] Indeed, civic-minded African Americans recognized the importance of their historical representation even before emancipation. As early as 1828 African Americans formed organizations devoted to demonstrate their historical and literary achievements. These early efforts were mostly in the forms of publications, such as James W. C. Pennington's *Text Book of the Origin and History of the Colored People* (1841), William C. Nell's *The Colored Patriots of the American Revolution* (1854), and George Washington William's *History of the Negro Race from 1619 to 1880* (1882). These works were designed to counter the then-rampant denigration of black historical achievements and to preserve black history for future generations.[18]

During the nineteenth and early twentieth centuries, books and journals remained the primary sources of information about black accomplishment. The civil rights movement, which spurred a newfound interest in black history along with an acknowledgement of its neglect, ushered in a new era in which museums devoted to black history were constructed. Many of these museums, such as the Museum of Afro-American History in Detroit (1965), the Museum of Afro-American History in Boston (1969), and the Anacostia Museum in Washington, DC (1967, now part of the Smithsonian), were all community-based and community-oriented museums.[19] In addition to opening up a discursive space in which African American communities could preserve and represent their histories, the movement also led to ideological and structural changes that facilitated the construction of larger cultural institutions. These changes were designed to present visual narratives that included, rather than glossed over, the historical origins of the uneven social relations that continue to characterize American society. Two factors led to the presentation of African American history in these new institutions. First, a new focus on the historical origins of inequality prompted inquiries into black history. Second, the achievement of political power through the civil rights movement enabled blacks to secure funding from elected officials for museums foregrounding black history. These changes led to the creation, among others, of the National Civil Rights Museum in Memphis (1991), the Birmingham Civil Rights Institute (1992), the National Voting Rights Museum in Selma (1992), the Ralph Mark Gilbert Civil Rights Museum in Savannah (1996), and the Albany (Georgia) Civil Rights Museum (1998).[20]

However, the fact that these museums all display *civil rights* history underscores a significant obstacle for the three museums detailed here: the display of the history of slavery is problematic for both black and white citizens. According to historian James Oliver Horton, confronting the contradiction between the American ideal and the reality of American history can be "disturbing."[21] As is the case with any nation, the narratives that make up American identity are the product of a great deal of selective remembering and forgetting. The historical fact of slavery runs counter to the romantic notion of America as the land of the free. As such, it is often excluded from public presentations of history. Ira Berlin has suggested that it is the mixture of history with the politics of slavery that is at the root of this discomfort. The question of race in the twenty-first century, he argues, cannot be addressed without recognition of its roots in the slavery of the past.[22] Thus, the representation of this history has implications not only for the past but for the contemporary moment as well, resituating slavery and its legacy as context for many concerns in which race is implicated. The visual display of African American history helps transform current discourses on affirmative action, poverty, educational disparities, and crime and punishment. All too often, comprehensive public discussions of such controversial policy issues are difficult.

The display of slavery has been as much or more problematic for African Americans as it has been for the population at large. The historical societies established by blacks immediately after the Civil War eschewed the gathering of materials about slavery in favor of presenting materials about the black influence in Europe.[23] The ambivalence with which African Americans have held these memories since then has been reflected in public debates about their utility among political figures such as Frederick Douglass, Alexander Crummell, Booker T. Washington, and W. E. B. Du Bois. In spite of the resurgent interest in black history borne of the civil rights movement, the cultural trauma associated with memories of slavery has continued to infuse the collective black psyche even into the modern era. Anthropologist John Michael Vlach has detailed the frustration he and other organizers confronted when they attempted to stage an exhibit on slavery at the Library of Congress in 1995. The exhibit, titled "Back of the Big House: The Cultural Landscape of the Plantation," was cancelled after a series of complaints about its staging. The pressure to cancel the exhibit, it turned out, came not from a general public uncomfortable with such a display, but rather from the Library's African American employees. The thought of daily confronting the visual images of slavery apparently took too much of a psychological toll.[24] For museums looking to confront this history by focusing their mission on the representation of slavery, this can be daunting. Writing about the most recent North American literature on slavery in 2000, George Fredrickson observed that "one hundred and thirty-five years after its abolition, slavery is still the skeleton in the American closet. Among the African-American descendants of its victims there is a difference of opinion about whether the memory of it should be suppressed as unpleasant and dispiriting or commemorated in the ways that Jews remember the Holocaust. There is no national museum of slavery and any attempt to establish one would be controversial."[25]

The experiences of the proposed US National Slavery Museum are illustrative of these difficulties. On the initiative of L. Douglas Wilder, the first African American Governor of Virginia (1990–1994), the museum was set to become the first museum to focus exclusively on slavery. Organizers set up a non-profit corporation in 2001 to raise funds for its completion and in 2002 a local developer donated a large tract of land for its construction in the historically significant city of Fredericksburg, Virginia.[26] Moreover, the museum's organizers had drawn their planned exhibits from artifactual donations representing a very large and diverse source community, including from as far away as Liberia in western Africa. However, the construction of the museum was controversial in the local community, with opponents objecting to what they saw as its potential to instigate racial tensions. Specifically, they were concerned that the proposed institution would serve as a reflection of an "ugly" brand of slavery that, they claimed, was practiced elsewhere and was unlike the "benign" type of slavery practiced in Fredericksburg—of which the city was (and supposedly should be) proud. Its supporters, on the other hand, invoked the economic and cultural benefits of representing a long-neglected aspect of the area's African American heritage. The museum, they suggested could play an important role in subverting untroubled declarations of southern heritage contingent upon the erasure of memories of slavery and its central role in building the South.[27] Ultimately, the museum's organizers were unable to raise the necessary funds to begin construction and filed for bankruptcy in 2011.[28]

An additional obstacle with which these museums have had to contend concerns the issue of African American interest in and attendance at museums. During my 2007 interview with John Motley, the African American chairman of the Board of Directors of the ACWM, he lamented the fact that the vast majority of those interested in visiting museums, and Civil War museums in particular, are white. "We go more towards entertainment than museums," he explained. "One of the challenges of museums is—how do you bring in more [visitors]?" In order to stimulate black interest in the museum, he gave lectures at black churches and at the historically-black Virginia State University. He suggested that other societal institutions could be useful in bringing in black visitors, proposing that African American history museums would benefit if, for example, "black history [were to be] taught in a more interesting way in high school. [There is] no quick fix. *Glory* was helpful, [as was] the Ken Burns series for more intellectual types. When more things happen in the pop cultural arena, [it] would be helpful. . . . The black family reunion crowd, more re-enactments would further interest."

In response to these concerns, museums showcasing slavery and/or the Civil War have had to develop new strategies to attract visitors, devoting energy to refuting misconceptions about the era. According to Berlin, discomfort over displays depicting this traumatic slice of American history could be ameliorated by the cultivation of a greater understanding about exactly what slavery was, including an exploration about who the slaves were and what they experienced.[29] The enslaved gain a voice through institutions presenting the history from their perspective, and not merely in the narrow terms of the labor they performed but in the more comprehensive terms of the lives they led. This would also help dispel the perception that Civil War museums are one-sided and perhaps racist.

This is the mission of the museums in Selma, Washington, DC, and Richmond. One strategy employed in attaining these ends involves changing the discourse about slavery in such a way as to emphasize black agency. In this regard, museums that focus on lesser-known aspects of African American life during the period are particularly instrumental. In describing the role his museum plays in facilitating discussions about slavery, AACWM founder Frank Smith explained the approach his staff has adopted. "It's hard to get black people to talk about slavery," he said. "You have to get them to talk about freedom. When they see the USCT exhibit, it is easier for them to talk about slavery. It parallels the civil rights movement—black people led the civil rights movement."

Motley contends that the most positive aspect of the Civil War was the ending of slavery but sees a disconnect between this fact and the beliefs most blacks hold about the war. "Blacks, by and large, are ashamed of slavery. It's unfortunate, but true," he said. But a cultural shift is possible, in his view: "You don't find many who collect any of these things, or art. Affordability is an issue. The vast majority I compete with [for these artifacts] are whites. When people come to my house or exhibits I curated, they are blown away. [They] had no idea about black agency. [They then have a] positive reaction, more pride and surprise. . . . The Civil War is crucial to black identity. The reluctance of blacks to study the Civil War and visit sites is unfortunate. It should be more central to black history and what we contributed to America. Without the Civil War, there would have been no civil rights movement. Blacks think we did nothing. There is a connection between the Civil War and the Revolutionary War. The Civil War is often referred to as the second revolution."

Motley's viewpoint is shared by ACWM President Christy Coleman. In discussing the unique challenges she and other African Americans in the museum field confront, she traced their roots to black discomfort with memories about the experience of slavery: "We in the museum field have challenges—African American museums face challenges confronting the more difficult parts of our past. The challenge is, one would conclude, the subject matter and audience are seen as the same. [There is] historic amnesia. Our heroes and heroines have been selected for us. We tend not to support even our own institutions because we're marginalized by the field. History museums in the South are even more challenging."

The AASCWM in Selma takes a broad approach to overcoming these difficulties, situating slavery as one part of a much longer continuum of African American advancement that stretches back to ancient African civilization and encompasses the civil rights movement, as well as the post-civil rights era. This strategy, according to museum staff, emphasizes to visitors that their heritage includes significant contributions to the world and does not begin or end with slavery. "We were an enslaved people, but we were not slaves," Toure says of the narrative the museum advances through its exhibits, its use of space, and its performances.

The strategies mentioned here underline the role the institutions under discussion assume in building cultural syncretism. Through a discursive focus on memories of slavery as part of national memory and of a long march toward *freedom*—with all of the rhetorical power implicit in that construction—they perform the identity/cultural work of constructing a new conception of southern heritage centered on the production of an affirmative black southern subjectivity. This entails restructuring narratives of slavery in a way that aligns with, rather than departs from, broader societal discourses. Such a dialogic relationship, in which narratives of slavery are shifted away from discourses of victimhood toward dominant memes of resilience and self-reliance, situates the era as instrumental in constructing a sense of black historical agency while providing a fuller accounting of American history in general. The culturally prevalent erasure of the black perspective from common narratives propagated through the educational system, the entertainment industry, the tourist industry, and other cultural arenas obscures the complexity of the political, social, and economic realities of colonial and antebellum America. As Berlin has suggested, "simply put, American history cannot be understood without slavery. Slavery shaped America's economy, politics, culture, and fundamental principles. For most of the nation's history, American society was one of slaveholders and slaves."[30] This point—that black history is *American* history, emphasizes the importance of the cultural syncretism advanced through the museums and highlights the identity/cultural work of recovering memories of slavery from the margins. My fieldwork indicates that many of the visitors to the museums share these sentiments. Written comments about the exhibits at the American Civil War Museum in Richmond revealed responses such as "we enjoyed your more balanced telling of the causes and effects of the war" and "finally—black history fits into American history."

Additionally, the restructuring of these narratives performs the work of undermining essentialist assumptions of "authentic" blackness as being narrowly defined by accounts of degradation and suffering and provides a foundation for the recovery of southern memories centered on more fluid, affirmative notions of identity. These include the recovery of stories of blacks resisting slavery, fighting in the war to secure their own freedom, and working as Reconstruction-era social reformers. Moreover, in the case of the AASCWM museum in Selma, it also involves building an affirmative identification with blackness through the display of ancient African achievements.

In building this cultural syncretism, the institutions described here draw their identity-producing capacities from those associated with museums more generally. Museums are more than mere repositories of objects, they are material reflections of the ways social groups, regions, and nations define and represent their identities. They are spaces of public culture in which various collective identities are formed, maintained, and contested through a multitude of practices, processes, and interactions. First, the engagement between museums and their geographical and source communities advances identity within those communities, enabling constituents to become agents in the production of memory through a variety of practices. These may range from contributing artifacts and family oral histories to the museum's collection to comprising its frontline staff and incorporating local histories into its exhibits and narratives. Thus agency is cultivated through the development of a dialogic relationship between the museum and the communities it serves. Second, at the audience level, visitors' interactions among themselves and with other visitor groups help form a sense of shared history at the same time that viewing and assigning meaning to exhibits further advances a sense of communal identity.[31] All of these practices, processes, and interactions are instrumental in the production of the new memories advanced through African American history museums foregrounding the Civil War era.

Another aspect of museums' role in producing memory and identity provides much of the foundation for the resistant nature of work these institutions perform: the involvement of culture in the viewing and interpreting process ensures that museums are bound, or at least subject to, a politics of display. As is the case with the construction of identities through other representational systems, issues of power are also to be found here. Still, museums have a unique influence in the production of meaning because of the cultural authority generally assigned to them. Richard Sandell has contended that, unlike more traditional media forms, museums are positioned to effect social change precisely *because* of the experience of visiting and the perception of them as objective, trustworthy sources.[32] In fact, Roy Rosenzweig and David Thelen conducted a study on the popular uses of history in which they found that 80 percent of those surveyed trusted museums and other historic sites to provide "real" or "true" history. This percentage of respondents was greater than those who trusted high school teachers and college professors to present an accurate accounting of the past.[33]

In addition to their assigned credibility, museums wield cultural power in another important way. Karp has suggested museums, archives, and other similar institutions possess the cultural capacity to define peoples and societies by "reproduc[ing] structures of belief and experience through which cultural differences are understood." These institutions, he contends, are crucial aspects of civil society, and, as such, "become places for defining who people are and how they should act and as places for challenging those definitions."[34] These capacities become an even more critical and explicit discourse within history museums. "Community," in the context of a history museum, may involve the shared responses of visitors to the collections and the exhibitions contained within it; it may also serve as a referent to the people whose histories have inspired the collections.[35] It is this aspect of the intersection of museums and culture that is more explicitly ideological, as it entails the assertion of broader claims about a group's heritage, which may either be constructed through multiple perspectives or be the result of one uncontested narrative. Museum displays privileging one set of memories over alternative, competing versions define the heritage of very broad and heterogeneous communities in a way that marginalizes local or alternative memories that are in tension with those institutionally legitimated. Ultimately, museum displays make culturally authoritative statements about a community's (be it local, regional, or national) ways of seeing the world, particularly about whose histories and memories matter, and whose do not.

For this reason, museums and other cultural institutions are often ground zero for battles over historical interpretation—which are really struggles over heritage, with its attendant constructs of race, region, and nation. As is the case with other representational forms, museums are arenas in which wider social relations are played out. Visitors to museums, or audiences, enter into the site with certain expectations molded by interactions with and within other social and cultural arenas. The institutions' fidelity to these expectations, or lack thereof, may form the basis for public battles. For example, according to the staff of the ACWM and its sister institution, the Museum of the Confederacy, both museums are nearly constantly engaged in struggles over exhibits with the Sons of Confederate Veterans (SCV), the self-described "Guardians of Confederate History and Heritage." During my initial visits to both museums in July of 2007, they were embroiled in local controversies with the SCV over their representation of history. The board of the ACWM was deciding whether or not to display a statue of Confederate President Jefferson Davis that had been donated in response to the prominence, in the museum, of a statue of Abraham Lincoln. For their part, the MOC staff members described their battles with the SCV as an ongoing "headache." The MOC's troubles with the group had begun with the "Before Freedom Came" exhibit in 1993, and had since taken the form of periodic, minor skirmishes over particular displays. The employees of both institutions suggested their problems with the SCV and other heritage groups involved the more inclusive interpretation of history the museums presented. Although museums mean many things to many different people, part of their mission includes the promotion of critical analyses of the connections between the past and contemporary concerns.

For African Americans, these "contemporary concerns" include the display of an erased past and the forging of a relationship between the recovered history and its legacy. The same cultural forces empowering museums as institutions in which dominant narratives, ideologies, and identities are produced and articulated may also be mobilized to reconstitute them as spaces of resistance and social justice. As Sheila Watson has pointed out, museums are also places where identities can be challenged, explored, and rethought.[36]

Slavery and/or Civil War museums are increasingly assuming this role, becoming spaces for the transformation of southern identity. Two interrelated phenomena have worked to facilitate the identity/cultural work they perform. The first concerns the role of museums and other archival institutions within the estimated $30 billion African American travel market, which situates them as one of the three fastest-growing demographics in the travel and tourism industry and includes the burgeoning interest in African American heritage tourism.[37] The second concerns the changing orientation of history museums in the South. In order to attract new visitors, southern Civil War museums are increasingly broadening their scope and offering more modern interpretations of the war.[38] This includes featuring displays foregrounding the experiences of those who fought for the Union as well as the causes and consequences of the war. In so doing, they expand their scope to construct more comprehensive memories for both black and white visitors.

These changes in the southern heritage tourism infrastructure have assisted in the development of museums as viable public spheres for African American vernacular producers to transform the landscape and thus to effect changes in the meaning of Civil War memory and southern heritage and identity. In order for these institutions to exploit these changes effectively, they must employ unique strategies essential to their counterhegemonic project. In the next section, I present a detailed analysis of these strategies.

Toward a Transformational Rhetoric of Black History Museums in the South

While this new infrastructural environment has assisted in smoothing the pathway for the development of archival institutions displaying multiple perspectives on Civil War memory, the museums in question must confront some very particular challenges. These include displaying memories contradictory to the fundamental narratives of established memory, upending the white hegemony of the regional landscape, and overcoming the difficulties associated with the legacy of African American "humiliated silences" concerning the display of a heritage centered on enslavement.[39] They have developed unique strategies to meet these challenges and advance a set of transformations: of the landscape, of the dominant perception of slavery as an era of victimization rather than of resistance and resilience, of dominant memories of the war and its aftermath, and of the assumptions of normative whiteness underlying the southern identity at the center of these constructions. The identity/cultural work the museums must perform in order to facilitate these transformations requires representational strategies that engage in various degrees of consciousness-raising and extend beyond those of the traditional exhibits characteristic of most museums.

These representational strategies are rhetorical in nature. According to Carole Blair, rhetoric may be construed as "any partisan, meaningful, consequential text," with "text" conceived of as any "discourse, event, object, or practice."[40] At its core, it encompasses a set of practices designed to influence audiences in particular situations. Museums constitute rhetorical institutions in many ways, in which the most apparent mode of influence is through exhibits and their spatial arrangement and where both visual and material stimuli are used to "invoke a collective sense of civic and cultural understanding."[41] They are also rhetorical in less tangible but equally powerful ways. The very public nature of the identity/cultural work they perform makes certain values and experiences—particularly those connected to the salience of particular historical narratives—concrete to wide audiences. Moreover, the very experiences of visiting a museum and assigning meaning to the exhibits build identification among visitors, which constitutes a key aspect of rhetorical work.[42]

In its transformational sense, the rhetorical strategies of museums incorporate and expand this work to marshal the discursive power produced through the interplay of several of its dimensions. In addition to oral discourse, the material, symbolic, geographical, spatial, corporeal, and performative aspects of the displays are involved in constructing critical black-centered memories. A transformational rhetoric accounts for the fluidity of identities and the dynamism of landscapes, implicating multiple features of museums in this regime of representation. For the three museums at the center of this analysis, these dimensions include the exhibits themselves, space, place, interactive and affective performance, and corporeality.

Exhibits

The cultural work performed by museums in the production of memory and identity is most explicitly articulated through their exhibits. These include objects, texts, images, audio-visual installations and other artifacts, along with the spaces in which they are situated. The meaning of museum exhibits constitutes a more complex mode of communication than other apparatuses of historical production—such as books, articles, and films—as the capacities of visitors to view and, perhaps, interact with objects in material form involves multiple processes. Flora Kaplan has suggested that because exhibits encompass processes that are both cognitive and cultural, they may be seen in the Durkheimian sense as social representations of a "collective self."[43] The sizes of the artifacts, their relationships to the other displays, and the written texts created to describe them all contribute to visitor understandings of the past. While the visitors assign their own meanings to the objects they see in museums, the ways in which they are arranged ensure that the motives of the creators influence their interpretations.

The museums examined here construct resistant memories through the production of exhibits featuring artifacts representative of a society in transition from one in which the "collective self" is coded as white and southern to one that is more racially and geographically inclusive. This entails presenting exhibits that not only engage with the war itself but—unlike traditional Civil War museums in the South—also resist presenting the conflict as a discrete event divorced from its most significant cause and most transformative consequence: slavery and emancipation.

While all three museums construct the war as inextricably tied to slavery and emancipation, the ACWM in Richmond is uniquely situated to articulate this through its exhibits, as its mission involves serving constituencies who identify with the Confederate, Union, and African American perspectives. The museum's displays are centered on the theme of "Union, Home, and Freedom," which are positioned as the "three ideals that defined post-Revolutionary America" and signify each of the three sides involved in the war. In keeping with this theme, the exhibits foreground slavery as a cause, include displays of its postwar legacy of Reconstruction, and present events of the twentieth and twenty-first centuries as part of its long-term legacy. Christy Coleman, the museum's president, characterized the display of the war's legacy in the ACWM as central to its mission. "Our museum and exhibits are about causes, which is why we include slavery. But, more importantly, it is about the *legacy* of the war," she said. "Our discussions [are] about social engagement. The Civil War represents the birth of black leadership, Reconstruction." Included in this exhibit are photographs of the Robert Gould Shaw memorial in Boston, Stone Mountain in Georgia, a ship approaching Ellis Island, the Tuskegee Airmen, the civil rights movement, and an ERA march, as well as a film still from *Gone With the Wind*. In keeping with the museum's mission to serve multiple constituencies, the photographs present an image in which the effects of the war represent better opportunities for *everyone*. In so doing, it informs us of its continuing relevance in broad and inclusive terms.

In addition to foregrounding the significance of the display objects, a rhetorical analysis of the transformative meanings created through museum exhibitions should include attention to the films shown and the digital media narratives displayed. Early in the visitor experience, the ACWM rebuts neo-Confederate discourse asserting that the war had nothing to do with slavery with a display inviting visitors to participate in an interactive quiz that poses the question, "what caused the Civil War?" Visitors may choose among "disagreement over federal versus state powers," "competing economies and cultures," "westward expansion," and "slavery." As part of this exhibit, visitors then watch a film explaining the conflict's causes. The film makes clear that the first three options were all essentially arguments over slavery, informing viewers that "each of these causes contributed to the war and each was linked to slavery. Take slavery out of the mix and it's hard to believe there would have been a war."

Museum rhetorics also include the items sold in the gift shop. As is the case with visitors' centers, highway markers, and other tourist-oriented, seemingly neutral artifacts, gift shops are heavily imbued with meaning as to the relative value the museum and the multiple communities it serves place on particular interpretations of history. In addition to the standard fare of books on the major battles and figures of the war, commemorative mugs, caps, T-shirts, dolls, and figurines, the ACWM sells books on slavery and black military combat. These volumes include *Black Soldiers in Blue* by John David Smith, *The Negro's Civil War* by James McPherson, *The Slave's War* by Andrew Ward, and *Where Death and Glory Meet* by Russell Duncan.

Finally, the rhetorical elements implicit in museum exhibits are particularly useful when it comes to the display of traumatic histories such as slavery, which often features artifacts that historian Geoffrey Cubitt has referred to as *atrocity materials*. These include those museum displays "whose common feature is their capacity to depict, represent, evoke, or imaginatively reconstruct the physical brutality of slavery and the physical sufferings of the enslaved."[44] Such artifacts contain the power to evoke emotional responses in visitors and trigger moral outrage and empathy. These reactions become even more powerful when the objects are not just featured underneath glass enclosures but are displayed in an interactive manner that allows visitors to touch and pick them up. This enables them to "touch" the past in a more visceral manner and to acquire a more intimate and concrete experience with the displayed memories.[45]

Both the AACWM in DC and the AASCWM in Selma include tac-

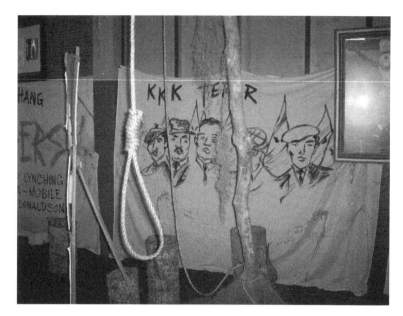

Figure 5. Lynching noose in the Ancient Africa, Slavery, and Civil War Museum in Selma. Photo by Patricia G. Davis.

tile displays of atrocity materials in their exhibits. The AACWM displays slave shackles, while the AASCWM incorporates a small-scale slave ship and a lynching noose into its guided tour, staging an interactive performance wherein visitors sit in the ship and later position their heads in the noose. This aspect of the performance heightens the rhetorical power of these materials, as it allows visitors to not only acquire a tactile perception of the brutalities of slavery but also to attain a corporeal experience that involves, somewhat literally, putting themselves into the shoes of those oppressed through enslavement and its Jim Crow legacy. Though the display of these materials entails navigating the potential risks associated with "compassion fatigue," it helps to disabuse visitors of any notions of complacency about the past and to provide them with a heightened sense of the resilience required to overcome the subjugation enforced by these materials.[46] The sense of trauma at the core of southern memory is thus restructured to produce affirmative notions of African American identity.

Space

The rhetorical power embedded in a museum's exhibits does not operate independently of the spatial arrangements in which they are situated but rather combines artifacts with space in order to construct meaningful historical narratives. Much of this power lies in the ways in which the strategic use of space purposefully directs the gaze of the visitor and in its potential to evoke the emotional reaction necessary to identify with a distant past. Garry Wills has used the case of rural cemeteries to discuss the ways in which displays are made more powerful through arrangements meant to manipulate the attitudes of visitors, and which are useful for understanding the strategies involved in museum displays. He writes: "The material structure of a place's tangible features resonates with symbolic implications generated through selective namings, conventions, styles, narratives, and rituals. Places are thus deposed rhetorically in their physical design so that their arrangement works to dispose the attitudes, feelings, and conduct of those who visit, dwell within, or otherwise encounter them. All constructed and designed places can be considered as material embodiments of preferred attitudes, feelings, and valuings. Thus, an important dimension of the rhetoric manifested in display is the symbolic resonance of material places that inclines those who occupy them to experience social meaning from particular, selectively structured vantage points or perspectives."[47] Accordingly, the impact of material culture on memory and identity formation includes its form and location in addition to its texts. The spacing of museum exhibits is not arbitrary but rather is designed in such a way as to facilitate not only *what* is to be remembered but—more importantly—*how* this remembering should be conducted.[48] In this sense, architectural design becomes a discourse as or more powerful than written or spoken language. Space becomes an evocative discourse through the external design of the museum and through the internal design and layout of the artifacts.

This mobilization of space becomes particularly salient for museums displaying dissonant narratives, including those emphasizing histories of enslavement. Because the cultural trauma of slavery can only be experienced indirectly through various modes of representation, empathic exhibition design defines the ways in which an exhibition becomes meaningful for the individual visitors. Such a strategy, according to Hadwig Krautler, combines "all material elements of an exhibition and the respective framings (building, specific location within a certain type of architecture, style of announcements) and does so by connecting the intended message with each person's specific repertoires of associations and connotations, as well as the pertinent and relevant social facts."[49] It is for this reason that the ACWM's placement of the display emphasizing slavery as the primary cause of the war is so significant. By positioning this interactive display near the entrance of the museum and to the visitors' right as they begin engaging the artifacts, the layout encourages them to read the rest of the exhibits in terms of their impact on African Americans. Given the ACWM's diverse visitor base, this is a very important way in which design elements are utilized to advance particular interpretations of the exhibits.

The history museums discussed here use space in another important way, one that maximizes the abilities of staff and visitors to construct meaning collaboratively and is therefore part of their transformational rhetorical approach. The strategic creation of social spaces for visitors enables them to engage in dialogue with museum staff and with each other about the displayed history, their understandings of it, and the meanings they ascribe to it, including its historiography. Social spaces designed to facilitate dialogic narration are central to the capacities of museums to build collective identities. In his discussion of what he considers to be the various forms of symbolic space embodied by history museums, Sheldon Annis has described the "social space" as that which provides for a museum experience in which visitors bond over the sharing of experiences through the exchange of personal and collective memories.[50] Visitors bring their own perspectives to their museum experiences and may have these reinforced, contested, and refined through dialogue with others. This function of space in museums presenting dissonant histories may be enhanced by the actions of museum staff who engage in what Tamar Katriel refers to as dialogic narration, which exploits the roles museums play as arenas for ideological assertion. These "dialogic threads" are advanced through docents, curators, and other personnel who combine factual representations and communal narratives to construct a museum discourse that ultimately serves as a guide for the visitor conversations that will take place in the institution's designated social space.[51]

The AACWM in DC mobilizes these spatial features to enable visitors to construct connections between slavery, African American Civil War history, and the contemporary legacies of both. The Spirit of Freedom monument itself was designed to create a welcoming space for community gatherings. It is in this space that the museum holds ceremonies and dedications, with the participants interacting in the monument's shadow. Inside the museum, the use of space operates even more powerfully and has served an important function in both the former and current buildings housing the museum. In the older structure, the primary discursive power embedded in the museum's exhibits was associated with the social space referred to as the "Soldier's Room;" in the new building, this function has

Figure 6. Social space outside the African American Civil War Museum and Freedom Foundation in Washington, DC. Photo by Patricia G. Davis.

been assumed by a sizeable auditorium with a stage for the oral presentation that provides the bulk of the visitor experience. In this space, visitors gather before or after perusing the artifacts and listen to lectures on African Americans' historical experiences in the war presented by either founder Smith or Hari Jones, the museum's curator. Visitors are then invited to engage in conversations with each other and with museum employees about the lecture, as well as about their own personal experiences with broader aspects of the history and memory emphasized in the oral presentation.

Moreover, at the same time that this organizational scheme functions to create a shared space for visitors to gather and converse, it simultaneously allows museum personnel greater agency over directing the visitors' gaze toward the artifacts inside and outside of the room. Ultimately, the museum's use of space ensures that visitors are not left to examine and interpret the exhibits on their own but are directed to collaborate with staff and each other to assign meaning to the displays. This process assigns agency to both staff and visitors in a way that constructs vernacular memory.

The AASCWM in Selma also exploits the possibilities of social space and employs performance as a means of doing so, but in a much different way from the DC museum.

Figure 7. Social space inside the African American Civil War Museum and Freedom Foundation in Washington, DC. Photo by Patricia G. Davis.

The museum's visitors are made up almost solely of pre-constituted tourist groups, often from churches, schools, and universities. The museum tour is centered on an interactive performance in which the guide plays the role of plantation overseer, while visitors play the roles of slaves. The tour takes the "slaves" on a trek through history that includes the transatlantic trade—complete with small-scale ship—and a Jim Crow-era lynching. After the tour the group is directed to a large room where the docent facilitates a group conversation in which the participants are encouraged to share their thoughts on the experience. The museum illustrates the ways in which the use of social spaces meant to facilitate dialogue among visitors is particularly productive with respect to the display of atrocity materials, as it provides opportunities for visitors to engage in conversations about their emotional responses to the experience of interacting with the artifacts and about the impact these reactions may have on their historical understandings, worldviews, and behaviors.

Place

As Deborah Atwater and Sandra Herndon have suggested, museums play communicative roles in the construction of public memory through, among other aspects, their physical location.[52] As is the case with space, place is a powerful discourse that helps construct narratives of belonging and identity. The specific building, neighborhood, and city in which each museum is located constitutes a significant aspect of its rhetorical power, as particular sites perform the identity/cultural work of engaging visitors in what it means to be members of a larger community.[53] Much of the work of constructing collective identities through the built environment involves the production of sites as places. Geographic spaces become *places* once meanings are ascribed to them, carrying powerful associations and investments for particular communities.

These ascribed meanings are often historical in nature, as their foundation is largely provided by public histories. Rhetorics of place operate most powerfully when they evoke the history and memory of a site. As historian David Glassberg has noted, "historical consciousness and place consciousness are inextricably intertwined; we attach histories to places, and the environmental value we attach to a place comes largely through the memories and historical association we have with it."[54] Powerful, historically symbolic places may carry more meaning than words, often conveying a sense of home, communal belonging, and, most importantly, identity.

Symbolic places that serve as the embodiments of the cultural myths, narratives, and memories that tie a group together provide an even firmer grounding for collective identification. As white monopolization of public space demonstrates, the combination of history and race helps ensure that identities tied to landscapes are constituted through exclusion as well as inclusion. As sociologist Les Back has suggested, racism is, by nature, a "spatial and territorial form of power which aims to secure and claim native/white territory but it also projects associations on to space that in turn invests racial associations and attributes in places."[55] The racialization of place is even more impressive in a built environment constructed for the preservation of dominant regional memories rooted in white supremacy, as is the case with the impressment of the Lost Cause upon the southern landscape. Architectural scholar Craig Barton has contended that, as a social construct and concept, race "has had a profound influence on the spatial development of the American landscape, creating separate, though sometimes, parallel, overlapping or even superimposed cultural landscapes for black and white Americans."[56] In the South, this phenomenon has manifested itself in a white-centered hegemonic landscape on which denial and rationalization have been etched and on which celebratory narratives of heroism, valor, and triumphalism have been concretized, effectively conflating southern heritage and identity with whiteness.

Museums employing a transformational rhetoric seek to destabilize this hegemony by mobilizing and restructuring the discursive power of the symbolic places used to construct southern memory as white. Stephen Legg has used the term "sites of counter-memory" to describe spaces and practices subaltern groups use to refuse to forget and to force public recognition of their achievements, historical contributions, and struggles.[57] The identity/cultural work these museums perform serves this function but goes even further. These institutions invite alternative readings of history not through the construction of "separate but ostensibly equal" spaces but through the material and symbolic occupation of the very sites implicated in the dominant memories. The reconstitution of these sites as resistant constructs a sense of black belonging by appropriating and claiming them as places for African American memory, a process that forces a renegotiation of their meanings. Thus, the practice of locating museums in historically significant places crucial to traditional southern identity constitutes an assertion upon that identity, a way of relocating silenced narratives from the confines of "local" memory and imposing new perspectives on the dominant history constructed through the landscape. These places may be historically significant cities or towns, as well as symbolic sites within those cities and towns. Because museums are emblematic of cities, deeply connected to their civic projects, and critical to their tourism infrastructures, the relevant discourses function in urban landscapes distinctly from those of more rural areas.[58]

The transformational rhetoric of place operates particularly powerfully with the ACWM. Its location in Richmond enables it to present its racially and geographically inclusive narratives in a way that subverts the symbolic power of the city as the birthplace of the Lost Cause and the most vaunted symbolic place of traditional southern identity. Memories of slavery are an indelible part of the city's history: in the 1800s, Richmond was second only to New Orleans in terms of the number of slaves bought and sold. Nevertheless, its cityscape has served as a geographical reflection of values that have marked African Americans as existing outside of the memory and identity of the city and region. To illustrate this point, ACWM President Christy Coleman recounted a quote from a prominent white business leader: "there are two lies Richmond was built on: blacks are inferior, and tobacco doesn't kill." The ACWM brings this aspect of the city's history out of the confines of silenced memory to the forefront.

The AACWM in Washington, DC, mobilizes place in many ways similar to the ACWM. The metro area's urban landscape is also heavily saturated with monuments to white heroism, albeit privileging those figures whose alliances were with the Union. The AACWM, located in an area of the city off the beaten tourist path, implicitly performs the cultural work of presenting readings of the past that serve as alternatives to those privileged on the National Mall and other sites. However, the AACWM's rhetorical approach departs from that of the ACWM in a significant way: rather than offering resistant memories through a renegotiation of the symbolism of the wider urban landscape, it mobilizes community-specific history in its use of place. As Blair, Dickinson, and Ott have suggested, a significant aspect of the rhetorical power of memory places is that they propose "a specific kind of relationship between past and present that may offer a sense of sustained and sustaining communal identification."[59] The AACWM exploits this relationship by promoting the little-known role of its surrounding community in the struggle for emancipation and positioning it as an exemplar of African American freedom and progress, which staff position as the fruits of black heroism during the war. The counter-narratives the museum constructs thus use location in a way designed to create meaning tailored to a constituency primarily interested in learning about black agency in the war.

The AASCWM in Selma also marshals the discursive power of place, but does so in a way that differs substantially from the other two museums. Unlike DC and Richmond, Selma is a Deep South small town with a contemporary image that remains firmly rooted in the past. The complex and intersecting economic, cultural, and social relationships that characterize larger urban centers and underwrite the development of their built environments do not factor as heavily in the small towns of the region's Black Belt. Nevertheless, Selma, which was a wealthy area of cotton production in the antebellum era and an important munitions center during the Civil War, is historically significant as a symbol of the civil rights struggles of the twentieth century, particularly the push for voting rights and the violence associated with it. The museum draws upon this symbolic power to position the Civil War era as critical in the ongoing African American freedom movements. In making legible the linkages between the two, the museum marshals the discursive power of place to perform the work of transforming common conceptions of Civil War memory and identity held by both black and white citizens. Sister Yomi, a volunteer at the museum, explained to me the way the museum uses its location in Selma to present a broader, little known narrative about how the connection between slavery, the Civil War, and civil rights constructs blackness as resilient. "We are a comeback people," she said. "If you can't get inspiration from our story, where do you get it? People draw inspiration from our story. That's why people are drawn here to the Deep South, to walk in our history-making shoes."

Interactive and Affective Performance

While most museums continue to occupy a more traditional model in which visitors are left to view and interpret the displays on their own, many are increasingly developing exhibitionary repertoires in which performance is an essential aspect. Tamar Katriel has characterized heritage museums as "ideological performative arenas" in which museum encounters are situated as "narrative events," with the tour guides as central figures in performing and enacting these narratives. Scott Magelssen has suggested that staff enactments in museums perform the function of constructing perceptions of "real" history by filling in gaps in common historical knowledge.[60] While these functions enable museum personnel to exercise greater control over the meanings visitors assign to the displays, enactment further works to empower visitors to become active participants—or agents—in the production of narratives. Interactive performance situates visitors as central figures in the narratives; they are then able to use their own personal and shared memories to fill in the gaps in dominant history. The give-and-take between performers and the audience characteristic of live theater thus allows them to become co-creators in the production of historical knowledge.

Performance is a particularly valuable resource for museums showcasing dissonant heritages. For both staff and visitors, the body becomes an archive for silenced memories, transmitting historical knowledge through the collaborative relationship forged between staff and visitors.[61] These participatory aspects of the museum experience stimulate personal memories, offering visitors opportunities to see the ways in which their own experiences fit into larger historical narratives. The agency they attain through their direct engagement then empowers them to adopt a broader, more critical orientation toward accepted history. According to Susan Evans, director of the Smithsonian's American Food History Project, museum performances encourage visitors to coalesce into learning communities charged with confronting history in a familiar and more comfortable form (theater) and to perceive it as a series of acts, rather than as "an inevitable story written in a textbook."[62] It also empowers them to engage in conversations about the history—as well as their places in it—and to create the shared knowledge essential to the formation and maintenance of a sense of community. This, in turn, creates a transformational museum experience, one that subscribes to a view of truth as socially negotiated and constructed from a shared repertoire of inventional resources and reveals the possibilities embedded in the linkages between performance and rhetoric.[63]

This linkage is crucial to the construction of a transformational rhetoric, as the agency and identity constructed through performance make it a particularly useful strategy for the institutions seeking to destabilize dominant memory. It marshals the visual, corporeal, tactile, and aural features of enactment to transfer the cultural authority of hegemonic structures of memory production—including other archival institutions—to museum personnel and visitors. These transformational rhetorical performances may be affective, interactive, or a combination of the two.

The AASCWM in Selma uses performance in a way that combines affect and interaction. The performances assume the form of reenactments in which visitors participate in a re-creation of the transatlantic slave trade, which enables them to build an emotional connection to traumatic memory. The museum houses a replica of a slave ship that is large enough to seat approximately twenty persons at a time. As part of the performance, visitors are seated in the model, while the image and sound of ocean waves is projected onto the room's walls as the ship is rocked in a manner meant to simulate an actual journey. The slave ship is an image that has operated powerfully in the African American symbolic universe, functioning in emotionally specific ways that make the past meaningful to the present. Indeed, the image of the slave ship has become a carrier of group meaning, signifying the genesis of slavery and the black experience in America. The AASCWM uses the exhibit to create a sense of living history, enabling visitors to experience a simulation of the Middle Passage as well as to reflect upon that journey and its contemporary legacy of racism and socioeconomic inequality. Thus, the replica may be understood as embodying what Carel Bertram refers to as the "felt real," in which the discursive power of affect is mobilized to capture the trauma of enslavement in emotional, psychological, and physical terms.[64] The complexities involved in such experiences are underscored by the varying reactions to its use. Museum staff describe the reception to the experience as mixed, often upon racial lines. In particular, some African American visitors express feelings of hurt, embarrassment, denial, and disbelief. Others express a sense of empowerment, hoping to learn more about the history. Many white visitors articulate feelings of shame in the failure of the nation—and whites specifically—to live up to its ideals. These mixed responses point to the risks inherent in the performance of traumatic memory. Nevertheless, museum founder Toure insists that this is a necessary part of depictions of enslavement, as many visitors arrive at the museum confessing to having been told by white residents in and around Selma that slavery was not that bad. Moreover, as a staff member told me, many participants respond to the performance with exclamations pointing to the difference between what the experience offers and what they were previously taught about slavery in school. They are encouraged to use the experience to gain a sympathetic understanding of what the enslaved had to endure and to apply that knowledge in a way that promotes a more comprehensive perspective on slavery's contemporary heritage as well as the attempts to disconnect its legacy from its historical context. In this way, the enactment provides opportunities for visitors to become agents in the production of history, a function Toure emphasized when explaining the reasons staff include the performance among the museum exhibits. "We believe history is made every single day," she said. "What good is a museum that only records history and doesn't participate in making it? It is worth nothing. We don't want history to be bland. . . . [We] use theater to infuse, to teach, to get people excited about history."

Upon completion of the transatlantic "voyage," visitors are ushered into an adjoining room where the abuses of plantation life are enacted. Afterward everyone congregates in a large room called the Hall of Resistance, where the tour guide facilitates a discussion about the experience and solicits visitors' thoughts on the ways in which it might have affected their understandings of the era and its contemporary legacy. This social space prompts the development of learning communities productive of critical history and encourages visitors to use the experiences of others, rather than more official sources, to build their own memories. Indeed, during my fieldwork one visitor remarked that the experience was much more educational than reading about slavery. The ultimate goal is to inspire visitors to use embodiment to engage in social action productive of change in the present.

The AACWM in DC also uses its social space to engage its visitors in an interactive performance. While there is a constant flow of individuals or small groups into the interior of the museum, a significant part of its constituency consists of large groups of twelve or more visitors who attend specially-designed lectures. These are usually black family reunion participants, tourist groups, summer youth program participants, or schoolchildren. The presentations are typically adapted to emphasize the particular histories of the areas from which the visitor groups have traveled and include discussions of the ideologies implicated in the silencing of historical narratives. Curator Hari Jones typically delivers the lecture, though founder Smith or the museum's small network of volunteers does so when he is unavailable. After gathering information about where the visitors are from, Jones delivers the lecture using a commanding tone that solicits verbal feedback and draws powerfully upon the call-and-response pattern often deployed in African American oratory. This serves the purpose of building identification with the visitors and allows them myriad opportunities to engage the performance interactively, often through affirmative verbal responses uttered throughout the lecture.

Corporeality

The incorporation of visitors into a museum's production of resistant memory through interactive or affective performance advances a corporeal logic that utilizes bodies as rhetorical resources. Bodies are crucial components of both narratives and representation, and these two categories coalesce powerfully in the performances at the museums.[65] The shared experience of enacting the slave trade or participating in a lecture—and the conversations that occur around each—serve as powerful binding agents instrumental in the construction of anti-hegemonic identities.

Within a transformational rhetoric of museum display, corporeality operates in an additional important way. Because a significant aspect of a museum's rhetorical power lies in its very public nature, the bodies that represent the museum constitute an important aspect of its ability to construct resistant memories and dissonant heritage. An institution's public face is rarely considered to be a critical aspect of its rhetorical strategy. Nevertheless, when one considers the importance of credibility, or *ethos*, in other rhetorical arenas such as public address, it is useful to interrogate its potential with respect to history museums. For museums attempting to subvert dominant historical narratives, a rhetorical strategy that evokes credibility—primarily through its attendant trope of identification—is an essential resource.

In the case of Civil War museums, bodies representing the public face of the institutions are raced and, to a lesser extent, gendered and classed. However, in the context of transforming hegemonic historical narratives premised on assumed racial distinctions and the cultural power attached to them, the redeployment of these social constructions becomes a crucial element of these museums' rhetorical repertoire. It constitutes a resistance to the narrow social location to which the dominant scripters have assigned black bodies with respect to Civil War memory.[66] For example, situating black administrators, staff, and board members as the public faces of a Civil War museum asserts claims upon the memories constructed therein and articulates these claims in powerful terms to both black and white constituencies. It does so in perhaps stronger terms than might be communicated through the exhibits. It is a way of using the body to say "this history belongs to *us*, as well. It is part of *our* heritage."

It is similarly important for white museum officials, particularly those with assumed credibility tied to heritage, to articulate claims of inclusivity. This use of corporeality is most usefully and dramatically deployed at the ACWM in Richmond. Alex Wise, Christy Coleman, and John Motley combine highly varied and distinguished backgrounds to serve as the public faces of the museum in the roles of founder, president, and chairman of the board respectively. Confederate *bona fides* are often necessary when navigating the political terrain surrounding the opening and early years of a transformational Civil War museum, particularly one marshaling the discursive power of Richmond as a symbolic place. Wise's credibility in this regard is quite compelling, as his lineage would suggest an orientation toward the status quo when it comes to historical narratives. It was his great-great grandfather, as governor of Virginia, who determined that John Brown was mentally competent and could therefore be hanged after his failed raid on Harper's Ferry in 1859. Known for his attempt to incite an armed insurrection of slaves and free blacks, Brown, like Lincoln, remains an antihero in dominant southern mythology. Thus, though there were doubts at the time with respect to Wise's loyalty to the interests of planter elites, his condemnation of Brown may be positioned as a sort of redemptive act within southern memory. The construction, by his descendent, of a museum that displays all three perspectives on the war may then be positioned as part of a transformational process. Furthermore, Wise's tenure with the Museum of the Confederacy, founded in 1896 by prominent society matrons and seen as one of the premier "shrines" to the Lost Cause, further strengthens his credibility. His ancestral and professional backgrounds, along with his public service, provide a significant aspect of the identification and credibility necessary for the critique of dominant history offered by the ACWM.[67]

Coleman and Motley provide the other aspects, in different but perhaps more important ways. For Civil War museums with missions involving the incorporation of African American memory and identity into their displays, the rhetorics of the body and identification form a crucial element of their strategy, as their goal is to include black constituencies alienated from and wary of dominant memory. Coleman is an African American woman with an extensive background in the practice of public history, having begun her career performing as a "slave" in Colonial Williamsburg and gone on to management positions at several other institutions, including the Urban Museum in Baltimore, the Charles H. Wright Museum in Detroit and the Peale Museum and the H. L. Mencken House, both in Baltimore. "These opportunities to educate the public ... you don't get this in school," she said of her experiences. "None of this was part of the learning when I was growing up. We've built a bunch of social, historical narratives." She views her work with the ACWM as an even greater opportunity within a "different kind of museum" that is attempting to grow its African American audience. Her background provides many important points of identification with African Americans wary about the assumed one-sidedness of Civil War museums: "One of the things intriguing about the Center, [is that] I have been asked if being a black woman changes the mission of the center—it does not."

The Chairman of the Board of the ACWM is John Motley, an African American businessman who lives in Connecticut. Motley began collecting Civil War memorabilia upon developing an intellectual fascination with African American military history while serving in Vietnam, a fascination that intensified with the popularity of the 1970s television miniseries *Roots*. He eventually amassed a substantial collection of lithographs, paintings, weapons, canteens, military order, and other objects. Because these items were the property of USCT, they are extremely rare with a historical significance undervalued in the African American community. In the late 1990s, Motley received a cold call from Wise, who had learned of his collection and invited him to become involved in the ACWM's formation. Upon traveling to Richmond and meeting with Wise and with local black legislators, he donated his entire collection to the museum and agreed to serve as the chair of its Board of Directors. In this capacity, Motley has delivered lectures on black participation in the Civil War to many African American institutions and social groups, and this exposure, along with his military background, has afforded him significant credibility with African Americans distrustful of Civil War displays.

Both the AASCWM in Selma and the AACWM in DC use corporeality as a discursive strategy, but do so as a means of building connections between the Civil War-era history on display and the civil rights movement. Toure and Smith have served as highly visible community activists and have marshaled the credibility gained from their civic engagement to represent Civil War memory to communities whose orientation toward it may be described as circumspect at best. They do so in a way that frames it, along with civil rights, as an indisputable part of their heritage. Smith emphasized the importance of these connections in forging black interest in Civil War history when he constructed the museum's theme as "From Civil War to Civil Rights."

The use of corporeality extends to museum staff as well. Annie Pearl Avery, who volunteers at the AASCWM in Selma, describes herself as one of the "foot soldiers" of the civil rights movement. She has a long history of activism in the South, including multiple arrests during the sixties. She brings this personal history to the forefront when conducting tours and interacting with museum visitors and uses it to help them see both eras as part of the same struggle. Hari Jones, the curator of the AACWM, is frequently called upon to serve as a consultant or to present lectures on African American involvement in the war at colleges, museums, symposia, and other public forums, and has appeared on the *History Channel*.

Museum exhibits, along with space, place, performance, and corporeality function effectively as separate elements in the construction of inclusive memories and identity. However, it is their collaboration with each other that renders them powerful elements of a transformational rhetoric. These features are more than just strategies in the rhetorical repertoires of each museum; they function as discourses (and, in the case of performance, discursive representations) that play a part in producing knowledge, memories, and identities. Moreover, they also produce social relations and organize and challenge the power relationships implicit in them. Therefore, it is their interaction—their *interdiscursivity*—that produces these elements. When articulated together in unconventional ways, these discourses serve to contest the dominant order, constructing transformational rhetoric crucial to the effective interrogation of hegemonic history.[68] In the final sections of this chapter, I use my visits to these museums to look specifically at the ways in which these different discourses are articulated interactively and unconventionally at each site.

Space, Place, and Performance in the African American Civil War Museum

When I called on the AACWM in DC, I noted that most of my fellow visitors did not head directly for its exhibits (which include a bill of sale for an eleven-year old female slave, a newspaper ad for a runaway slave, an engraving featuring the "First Reading of the Emancipation Proclamation," and other artifacts). While there were a few school-age children perusing these objects, most of the visitors—many of whom were members of a pre-formed group from a local youth organization—were gathered in a medium-size auditorium situated to the immediate left of the museum's entrance. They were there to hear a lecture by Hari Jones, the chief curator. Jones began his presentation, titled "The Glorious March to Liberty," with a first-person narrative from the perspective of a drummer boy from the *Corps d'Afrique*, along with the following admonition to those present: "You will not hear about this anywhere." He then continued by lamenting the marginalization of black Civil War history while emphasizing its place as part of American history.[69] "This story is one of the best-kept secrets in the US—that a disenfranchised group freed themselves," he exclaimed in the distinct rhythmic cadence characteristic of a preacher. "Our soldiers enforced the Emancipation Proclamation and liberated themselves and their families. This is the story we share here at the museum. It is an American story."

Throughout the presentation, Jones emphasized the importance of consulting primary sources for African American history, suggesting that most of official academic history is propaganda designed to silence memories of black historical contributions. Upon closing the approximately twenty-five-minute lecture, Jones took questions from the assembled visitors. Most of the inquiries were not about the specific history he had just detailed but rather focused on its erasure from dominant narratives. The following exchange between a middle-aged black male visitor and Jones is illustrative:

Visitor: As a historian, which do you think is the hardest to combat—knowledge from movies or from school itself?

Jones: Most difficult are the victims of propaganda. You want to take them out, but you have to remember they're victims. Even African American scholars, from Harvard, Yale—they didn't do it on purpose. They're victims of disinformation, or propaganda, over a hundred-year period. I won't quote James McPherson or Benjamin Quarles. I look at primary sources.

Once the visitors dispersed to look at the exhibits, Jones used the social space in the exhibition hall to encourage them to converse with him and each other about the displayed history, including its legacy in historical and contemporary public policy debates over issues such as residential segregation and affirmative action. This space was also mobilized to stimulate conversations about the exhibits and enabled him and other museum staff to direct the interpretation of the objects. Much like the questions during the presentation, these conversations also veered toward the marginalization of African American Civil War history, with visitors taking the opportunity to discuss their experiences in this vein. The following conversation, between Jones and a pair of African American visitors from Texas, exemplifies the instrumentality of social space:

> Visitor A (looking at the displayed copy of the Emancipation Proclamation): So that's how they freed the slaves.
> Visitor B: Everybody wasn't freed at the same time.
> Visitor A: So they (freed) us as last resorts.
> Jones: Juneteenth is the day we whooped Texas's butt and brought them back into the Union. We didn't sit around.
> Visitor A: I kind of heard that too, but they sort of kept that quiet.
> Visitor B: The problem with school is when it comes to African American history, it's not history.
> Jones: It's propaganda.
> Visitor B: Anything that makes us look good, you don't hear. So we have to educate ourselves.

A significant aspect of the museum's production of memory is its use of a combination of performance, space, and place to articulate themes of community. The interdiscursivity of these elements functions in two ways. The first involves using the interactive performances conducted within the museum's social space to promote the idea that visitors are part of a community that extends beyond the organizations sponsoring their visit. When it comes to discourses of community constructed in opposition to hegemony, the sharing of experiences relies upon cultural understandings that signify one's membership in the community in question. In this case, sharing occurs along the contours of critical historiography. "When the story of the Civil War is told accurately, it is a community story," Jones told one group of visitors. "There is no reason for you to believe you did nothing. You are your own emancipator. African Americans worked in league with the Constitution and the federal government—a community effort."

During my fieldwork at the AACWM, I noticed that the discourse of community often entailed discussion of the duties of African Americans to share these revised narratives. On one occasion, an African American woman said to Jones, "we need to sit down with people like you and share what we know and what you know." Additionally, in response to the exhibits and Jones's presentations, visitors made comments such as, "they never give us credit for [anything]," "they're still short-changing us," or "I don't think I'll be able to look at *Glory* the same way again," to knowing agreement from other members of their groups. Small groups of visitors also engaged in such exchanges with Jones:

Visitor A: The youth can become advocates of these stories.
Visitor B: Why is Lincoln here?
Jones: Lincoln was the great facilitator . . .
Visitor A: . . . not the emancipator.

In the second interdiscursive formation, the museum uses its interactive performance and social space to construct a sense of community that advances a discourse of place, implicating the museum's geographical community as part of its exhibits. The museum is located in the historic Shaw neighborhood in northwest Washington, DC, often referred to as the U Street Corridor. It is approximately two-and-a-half miles off the standard tourist "beaten path" of the National Mall and offers an alternative to the celebratory narratives of American Exceptionalism characteristic of the iconic monuments situated there, as well as of others scattered throughout the District cityscape. This was part of Smith's goal in locating the museum in a part of the city where "average" people live and work, and the location has indeed served as an attraction for many of the visitors. A woman and her son visiting the capital from Reading, Pennsylvania, told me that they wanted to go to places in DC that were "nontraditional." A trio of graduate students from Texas said that they wanted to have a museum experience that was different from those offered by the institutions that make up the Smithsonian. Another visitor, a schoolteacher, said that he makes it a point to take a week off every year to see "nonstandard" tourist attractions. There were also several tour groups whose members expressed their desire to see the "real" or the "non-Smithsonian" DC.

Additionally, the museum's staff uses its social space to facilitate conversations in which they promote the little-known role of the Shaw community in the struggle for emancipation. Named for Robert Gould Shaw, the commander of the famous Fifty-Fourth Massachusetts regiment of the United States Colored Troops, the area was originally populated as a freed slave encampment. These were referred to as contraband camps, and the museum uses this history to put forward a critique of dominant history, particularly the one associated with the more tourist-centered areas of the city, such as the monument to Abraham Lincoln on the National Mall. Fielding a question from a visitor about the encampments, Jones responded, "people say Lincoln didn't want to commission black officers.

Pay attention to what [Lincoln] did, versus what they *say* he did." In addition, many of the area's churches served as stops on the Underground Railroad, a history the museum touts on its website.

In addition to using the Shaw/U Street area's Civil War history, the AACWM uses its location to construct black memory and identity in another important way: it promotes the neighborhood as symbolic of the achievements African Americans have made upon securing freedom in the war. It is here that the museum's production of cultural syncretism becomes most explicit, as it situates its narratives within a discourse of place in which location functions as a source of affirmative notions of blackness. The museum is housed in the historic Grimke Building, named for activist and intellectual Archibald Grimke, one of the early leaders of the NAACP. The first chartered African American bank—formerly known as the Penny Savings Bank of the True Reformers—financed the building that housed the museum until it moved in 2011. The True Reformers was an organization founded by William Brown, a USCT veteran. According to a placard displayed on the building, it was constructed as a means of presenting "the achievement of the race since the War of Rebellion." Every person involved in the construction was African American. Howard University, historically perceived as the most prestigious institution for African American higher education and aspiration, was founded in the area in 1867. In the decades that followed, the community developed a rich history as the center of middle-class black Washington.

The contemporary entrepreneurial vitality of U Street is an important part of the place discourse the museum constructs. The neighborhood experienced decades of blight after becoming one of many urban areas that were scenes of civil unrest shortly after the King assassination in 1968. City officials initiated a process of regeneration in the early 1990s, and Smith situates the museum as a crucial element of the area's revitalization. The majority of the businesses operating in the area are black-owned, with many currently in their second or third generation of family ownership. The museum emphasizes and positions this data as the economic and cultural results of the Civil War. It thus positions U Street as an example of community empowerment, neighborhood pride, and social identity. Smith put it this way: "After people visit the museum and the monument, they walk out into the community and see Howard University, Vermont Avenue Baptist Church, the Masonic Temple—all historic places made possible because of the guys whose names are listed on that memorial."[70] Moreover, the museum's use of place represents a reconciliation of two types of community typically served by museums: those defined by location and those defined by shared historical experience. It thus operates as part of a broader strategy of reframing the Civil War in terms of African American historical agency and freedom through asserting the conflict's continued relevance to the present.

Exhibits, Place, and Corporeal Agency at the ACWM

The ACWM combines its exhibits with discourses of place and corporeality as part of a broader project of reconciliation. The museum was founded after a period of racial conflict centered on Richmond's historical identity as constructed through its memorial landscape. As a "reparative" institution, it uses its displays and public face to reorder the discourse of place implicit in the cityscape and fashion a set of memories conducive to a more inclusive sense of southern identity. As the birthplace and "mecca" of the Lost Cause interpretation of history, for more than one hundred years after the end of the war Richmond was "the central site for the production and maintenance of the Confederate version of the causes of the Civil War, the nature of African American enslavement, and the postwar sufferings of the southern people."[71] As a result, the city is home to the densest concentration of memorials to the Confederacy.[72]

Demographic shifts during the immediate post-civil rights years initiated a dramatic transformation in political power: as Richmond's white residents fled the city for the suburbs in the 1960s, the political winds began to shift in favor of its African American population. In 1977 black candidates won a majority of seats on the city council for the first time. These developments have produced a contemporary urban milieu in which a new New South sociopolitical regime operates in the midst of a landscape celebratory of the Old South. This latter is most strikingly visible on Monument Avenue, one of the more notorious streets of Richmond's racialized cityscape; an oak tree-lined residential street located just west of the downtown area, the neighborhood came into being at the height of the Lost Cause era in the 1890s as the preferred address of the local wealthy. From 1890 to 1929 many stately mansions were built here, while large statues of five Confederate generals (Robert E. Lee, Jefferson Davis, J. E. B. Stuart, Stonewall Jackson, and Matthew Fontaine Maury) were erected in the grassy area separating east- and west-bound traffic.

The increased political power wielded by the city's black residents resulted in challenges to the white hegemony that sustained the dominion of the Lost Cause on the landscape and reified the city's traditional Confederate identity. The resulting tensions led to the eruption of three civic battles near the turn of the twenty-first century. These conflicts, in turn, set the development of the ACWM in motion. The first, in 1995, concerned the erection of a statue of tennis great and Richmond native Arthur Ashe on Monument Avenue as a means of "integrating" the neighborhood. While the city's African American citizens believed the statue deserved a more appropriate location, many of its white residents felt that it would disrupt the historic integrity of the street. A few years later, a second civic conflict occurred in 1999 over a waterfront history display erected by a private organization called the Richmond Historic Riverfront Foundation. The display featured a walkway decorated with a rotating gallery of twenty-nine murals depicting Richmond's historic events and figures, including Robert E. Lee. The removal of the Lee image after a complaint from an African American city council member initiated a backlash among the city's white residents and resulted in threats of a boycott by the SCV. The resulting compromise featured the return of Lee's image, albeit in civilian clothing and standing alongside a USCT soldier and Abraham Lincoln. The third battle occurred in 2003 when the National Park Service took the initiative to erect a statue of Abraham Lincoln at its Richmond Battlefield visitor center at the historic Tredegar Ironworks building. This action again angered Confederate heritage groups, who saw a monument to Lincoln as an affront to the location's symbolic value as a historically significant Confederate munitions plant. The public response in each of these cases hinged on issues of race, identity, and power.[73]

The ACWM came into existence as a solution to these conflicts. Alex Wise proposed an institution that would commemorate the war but would do so in a way that would ease—rather than exacerbate—the ongoing tensions. "One of the things we sought to achieve with the Civil War Center was to tell everybody's story in one place which could be a safe place for discussion and dialogue, even disagreement about it," said Wise. "Perhaps thereby we could reduce the temperature and increase the civility of the discussion. We wanted to have more light than heat." Beyond this, the public tensions over the memorialization campaigns mentioned above revealed the extent to which African American agency in the war had been erased in order to privilege images consistent with the Lost Cause. "That subject is the elephant in the room," said Wise. Keen to end the neglect of Civil War blacks, he would work in conjunction with the Riverfront Development Corporation to plan a museum that would be a draw for downtown area tourists interested in viewing Civil War battlefields, including African Americans.

The museum's location within the city further strengthens its use of place: the construction and marketing of the ACWM as a new New South

Figure 8. The remains of the old Tredegar Ironworks on the grounds of the American Civil War Museum in Richmond. Photo by Patricia G. Davis.

museum is contingent not only upon its position in Richmond but also on the historical significance of the actual physical space it occupies. The ACWM is housed on an eight-acre campus that encompasses the old Tredegar Ironworks building and cannon factory on the riverfront. The strategic utility of the site, on the north bank of the James River, was instrumental in the decision to move the Confederate capital from Montgomery, Alabama, to Richmond in 1861. The factory made iron railroad tracks, locomotive components, and cannon for the US Army and Navy. When the war broke out, it became a major munitions production center for the Confederacy and is best known for producing the iron plates that turned the USS Merrimack into the warship CSS Virginia.[74] As the structure was once the industrial heart of the Confederacy, the museum's location within enables it to further mobilize rhetorics of space and place, imbuing the exhibits with greater meaning. During the time of my visit to the museum in the fall of 2007, it was embroiled in yet another heated conflict with the SCV over its donation of a statue of Jefferson Davis intended to provide "balance" to the Lincoln statue erected in 2003. Christy Coleman spoke about the attachment neo-Confederate groups have to the site. "Museums have the ability to provide the details. The rest of us will continue to take comfort in myths," she said. "People are upset that this is not a shrine. The presence of the museum speaks volumes about the evolution of Richmond. I was amazed, especially at Tredegar, [to see] an honest and accurate statement of [slavery]."

The ACWM's restructuring of Richmond's place identity is strengthened through its use of corporeality and its exhibits. In her capacities as the museum's president, Coleman serves as its public face in the media and at Civil War roundtables, symposia, workshops, and other events in and well beyond Richmond. As part of this work, she represents the museum at Black History Month events, effectively embodying to multiple publics the incorporation of Civil War memory into black history.

This integrative function is performed even more explicitly through the museum's exhibits. The very first exhibit features the Declaration of Independence and the US Constitution and details the ways in which slavery was enshrined within these founding documents. In offering the explanation that the Declaration was "never intended to be an official challenge to slavery," it reveals the contradictions inherent in the fact that Thomas Jefferson and many of the other founding fathers were slave owners. In addition to displays featuring a variety of artifacts representing Union and Confederate combat in the war, the museum also commemorates the efforts of black men to enlist in the Union army in the face of political opposition. A film on the Emancipation Proclamation is featured, along with the contention that the enlistment of black men into the Union army was its most controversial provision. The rise of these "armies of liberation" is chronologically displayed in the "Fighting for Freedom" exhibit, featuring a combination of photographs, document copies, and objects such as weaponry, epaulets, and cartridge cases donated by John Motley. The story of the war is displayed in a chronological progression; the narrative ends with two exhibits on the effects of the war. One of the exhibits, "The War for Freedom, 1866–1876," focuses on Reconstruction, detailing black priorities such as education, voting rights for men, representation in government, and employment. This lies in stark contrast to popular depictions of the era as a failure, particularly in films such as *The Birth of a Nation*. More importantly, the inclusion of Reconstruction marks a unique turn for Civil War history museums in the South, which typically begin and end with combat itself. In displaying the immediate postwar years, the ACWM resurrects forgotten narratives of African American historical agency and belonging to both the region and the nation.

Before exiting the exhibit area, visitors are invited to share their thoughts on the displays by answering questions centered on the museum's themes and articulating connections between the war and its contemporary legacy. There is a partition near the exit for guests to write their opinions on stick-it notes, as well as to indicate where they are from. They then attach these notes to the wall. This enables guests to play an active role in influencing the interpretations of future visitors who might read the notes upon exiting the museum. One of the questions posed prompts visitors to think about how America would be different today had the Union not won the war. Interestingly, when I visited most of the responses revealed an ability to couch the consequences of the continuation of slavery in terms suggesting harm to all: "We would all be slaves raddling [*sic*] our chains," "we might all be slaves if we were not rich," and "the US would have dissolved and been taken over by stronger, more unified powers, or the US would have reconnected later; in a growing world you can't stop progress." On another section of the wall, the Gettysburg Address is invoked to ask visitors if all Americans are "treated equally today." The majority of the responses that I witnessed indicated "no," with one person adding the opinion that "the rich legislate to break down the middle class, keep poor people poor, and fatten their wallets. That's why GREED is a [*sic*] deadly," and another suggesting that "no, but all Americans should be treated equally no matter the race, gender, or color." These responses, which indicate the ability of visitors to connect slavery and the Civil War to contemporary racism, sexism, and classism, suggests the vital role of these museums in facilitating the interrogation and revision of dominant historical narratives. It also demonstrates the evolution of the modern museum from an institution facilitating the *othering* of subjugated populations to one that acts as a potential agent of change.

Place, Space, Corporeal Agency, and Affective Performance at the AASCWM in Selma

Selma as a place poses a strong contrast to the global cosmopolitanism of DC and the genteel urbanism of Richmond. The drive along historic US Highway 80 from Montgomery—across the iconic Edmund Pettus Bridge over the Alabama River and into Selma—suggests a difference between the town and the two cities that is quite striking in its intensity: semirural, deindustrialized, and still racially segregated, it appears to have changed very little from the Selma depicted in the black-and-white "Bloody Sunday" file footage from the violent battles over voting rights in the 1960s. With no dynamic city center appealing to tourists, the AASCWM has had to rely almost exclusively on the municipality's voting rights history to draw in visitors, most of whom are in large preformed groups put together by community and church organizations, black family reunion tours, middle- and high school students and college students. Moreover, though the museum has engaged efforts to attract visitors from the local community, most guests are from out of town. Many, according to museum staff, come to the museum looking for hidden gems in the community.

Indeed, the tourists who travel here from afar have different goals from those who visit the other two museums: they come in search of civil rights landmarks. Every March the city hosts a Bridge Crossing Jubilee, in which participants reenact the crossing of the Pettus Bridge, a commemoration in which the AASCWM and its sister institution, the National Voting Rights Museum (also founded by Toure), take the lead. In an illustration of the temporal trajectory represented by the two eras, the museums are located on opposite ends of the bridge, which has "taken on the meanings and features of a venerated public place."[75] Its value as a historically symbolic place was part of Toure's strategy in locating the museum, as she sought a large space for it near the bridge in order to advance visitors' ability to perceive the continuity of the two eras. In fact, many of the AASCWM's visitors perform a ceremonial walk across the bridge after exiting the museum and then proceed to visit the other museum. Most tourists travel to Selma to visit the Voting Rights Museum and are offered a tour of the AASCWM as part of a package. They are then invited to make historical connections between the two. As one visitor said, "[We] came here for voting and civil rights history. [The] slavery stuff was unexpected, but it enabled me to see what the civil rights stuff was for."

The museum is located on Water Avenue, an area with significant historic value as a Civil War munitions and shipping center, second only to Tredegar in terms of its productivity.[76] "Selma is a historical place, so it's great to have a museum here," said museum volunteer Sister Yomi. "This building was a Confederate factory. This is the birthplace [of the voting rights movement], makes it more powerful; definitely draws a lot of people here."

In spite of the district's history, it is currently vulnerable to the blight characteristic of other Black Belt towns sharing Selma's racial geography: According to the 2010 census, the city of Selma is 79.3 percent African American, with 19.2 percent of its population identifying as white.[77] As was the case in Richmond and many other parts of the country, Selma's white residents fled for the suburbs in 2000 once the racial composition of its governmental power structure flipped from majority white to majority black. The precipitating event was the election of the town's first black mayor, who prevailed in a controversial contest in which he unseated long-time incumbent Joe Smitherman, who had presided over the "Bloody Sunday" beatings in 1965. As was the case in Richmond, this sociopolitical context has produced a number of striking juxtapositions as well as conflict in a town in which the overwhelming majority of residents are African American. These have been particularly salient because of Selma's position as a symbolic place for both Civil War and civil rights memories. There is an annual reenactment of the Battle of Selma held in late April, which includes an antebellum ball at Sturdivant Hall. In 2000, shortly before leaving office, Smitherman approved the efforts of a group called the "Friends of Forrest" to erect a bust of Confederate General Nathan Bedford Forrest in the city's historic Live Oak Cemetery, a move which prompted protests from black residents that the monument would constitute an affront to Selma's civil rights history.[78] After the bust was repeatedly vandalized and finally stolen in 2012, "Friends of Forrest" and other heritage organizations attempted to erect an even more prominent monument to Forrest, an effort that Toure was able to halt with threats of a lawsuit. These tensions render Selma a uniquely symbolic place as its African American residents work to preserve its well-known civil rights memory amid the efforts of white locals to preserve its lesser-known Civil War history.

It is within this context that the AASCWM, which combines black Civil War and civil rights memories, operates. The museum's rhetorical strategy integrates Selma's symbolic power as a historically significant place in civil rights memory with a construction of slavery and Civil War history that mobilizes corporeality, performance, and space. Some of the museum's volunteer staff were "foot soldiers" of the civil rights movement and interweave stories of their experiences into the museum's narratives. They use the power of these discourses to encourage guests to envision—through experience—the horrors of slavery and to connect these understandings to the violent battles over voting rights that took place over one hundred years later. In their use of affective and interactive performance, the staff members employ the southern tradition of storytelling.

The tour of the museum takes visitors to Ancient African civilization, along the transatlantic slave trade, and through the Jim Crow era. The excursion begins outside the building, where all visitors are directed to line up against the wall of its physical structure, with men on one side and women on the other. I participated in the tour with a visitor group of approximately fifty college students who had traveled from southern Ala-

Figure 9. Visitors lined up before embarking on the "transatlantic voyage" at the Ancient Africa, Slavery, and Civil War Museum in Selma. Photo by Patricia G. Davis.

bama as part of an African American Studies course. Three quarters of the members of the group (including the instructor) were African American, with the rest being white. Sam Walker, the tour guide, assumed the role of "plantation overseer" and ordered everyone to turn off their cell phones and to refrain from talking or making eye contact with him. Referring to the men in the group as "bucks" and "sambos," Walker ordered the group to walk into the building and to do so while assuming a subservient posture, with shoulders hunched and knees bent. The first stop was the museum's "Africa Room." The room features artifacts displaying the wealth and sophistication of Ancient Africa, particularly that of the Kingdom of Timbuktu, and a timeline representing African progress from this period to the modern era, with the election of Nelson Mandela representing the endpoint. Describing this timeline to the group as depicting the African culture "before it was interrupted," Walker explained that "this room is where Africans come to lose their history. We know history didn't start with slavery." He then returned to "overseer" mode, exclaiming to the "enslaved" that their illustrious history as educators and inventors will become irrelevant upon arrival in America, and that only their labor will be considered to have any value. "We don't need niggers who can do science and math, but who can do cotton," he told the assembled "slaves." According to one staff member, the Ancient Africa room makes visitors more comfortable about seeing, hearing, and experiencing the slavery exhibits that follow.

The group was then directed to enter the "Boat Room," where the women were ordered to get into a slave ship replica, while the men stood against the wall and watched. As the lights were turned off and the transatlantic "journey" began, Walker continued his performance of dehumanization by constantly referring to the women in the boat as "wenches" while the men stood by, powerless to intervene. After this part of the performance concluded, everyone was ordered to exit the room through the "Door of No Return," a 4 × 2 slave door, whereupon the group was once again lined up, this time in the hallway connecting the "Boat Room" to the next exhibit space. "Overseer" Walker inspected everyone and delivered a lecture on "good niggers" versus "bad niggers," picking four or five "good niggers" out of the lineup. He then instructed them to select several others from among the remaining "slaves." Walker informed the selected group that they are in fact the "bad niggers," as true "good niggers" would never sell out their fellow slaves. Walker led this group into a room out of sight of the remaining visitors, where a simulation of a beating took place, with "hitting" and "screaming" sounds translated back into the exhibit room. The remaining members of the group were then directed to enter the next space, the "Lynching Room," where Billie Holiday's recording of "Strange Fruit" played in the background and the visitors' gaze was directed toward a lynching noose and other post-Civil-War artifacts, including images of Emmett Till, the Mississippi teen whose murder in 1955 is considered one of the catalysts of the civil rights movement.

Upon completion of the performance, the visitors were led into the Hall of Resistance, where, surrounded by large pictures of prominent twentieth century African American activists, Walker led a group discussion of the experience. Asked to describe how the performance made them feel, visitors volunteered responses such as "terrifying," "loss of control," humiliated [at] not having a name," "angry and degraded," and "ashamed that our country, [that] white people could do this." Other responses hinged on the potency of experiencing—rather than viewing—the trauma associated with slavery, with visitors describing it as "powerful" and, in the words of one, "a lot more powerful than reading about it." Another visitor suggested that, "It's important to know how our ancestors felt, even if it was just a little taste." Other visitors discussed the limitations of the performative narratives but did so within a dialogue centered on the acknowledgement that a truly authentic replication of the lived experiences of the enslaved was a privileged result of the freedom for which blacks had fought during both the war and the voting rights movements. "[It was] powerful, but I knew it wasn't real," one visitor explained. "It gave me an out psychologically, because I felt the privilege of knowing it would end."

After the twenty-minute discussion, the visitors were free to peruse the exhibits in the museum, which showcase the election of President Barack Obama as the endpoint of the historical arc it advances. During a catered lunch served in one of the exhibit halls, many of the visitors spoke in more detail about the experience. "This stuff broke my heart, and made me so angry. I could not take the pain that this made me feel but this is good because our generations need to know how it felt back then when all of this was around," one woman shared. When asked to describe his overall impression of the museum, one visitor offered this response. "[I] wanted to come to Selma for history. [I] learned about Selma [in school], wanted to do 'Footprints to Freedom,' led by local folks," he said. "I wanted the whole experience; really glad we started there. [The museum] added a dimension, a narrative arc to what we see here. Having the slavery context makes this more than an intellectual experience, but an intellectual exercise."

Conclusion

On May 25, 2009, on his first Memorial Day as president, Barack Obama continued a tradition—begun by Warren Harding in 1922—of sending a wreath commemorating the nation's war dead to the Confederate Monument at Arlington National Cemetery. The monument, funded by the UDC and dedicated in 1914, advances memories of the Civil War era steeped in Lost Cause sentimentalism, including Latin phrases describing the Southern "cause" as noble and asserting the opinion that the "wrong" side was victorious in the war. It also contains a sculpture of a loyal mammy handing off a white child to his father, a soldier returning from war. Given its origins as part of the UDC's memorial campaign for Confederate vindication and its display of many of the most archetypical symbols of the Old South, the monument has been described by historian Karen L. Cox as "no less than a pro-southern textbook illustrated in bronze."[79] Obama's wreath-sending was not without controversy. Critics pointed to the ironies of the first African American president honoring what many consider to be a tradition initiated during the "nadir" of American race relations, profoundly implicated in reconciliationist sentiment and white supremacy, and used by contemporary neo-Confederate groups to claim state legitimation for their promotion of the Lost Cause version of Civil War memory.[80] A group of sixty academics sent a letter to Obama urging him to discontinue the tradition.[81] In spite of these concerns, Obama sent the wreath. However, in a gesture of "compromise," he started a new tradition by sending an identical wreath to the Spirit of Freedom Memorial at the AACWM. While the implied positioning of both monuments as historically and morally equivalent is problematic, the episode presents an illustration of the critical public role African American slavery and Civil War museums play in the twenty-first century.

The AACWM, ACWM, and AASCWM are all disruptive of the hegemonic memories advanced through the hundreds of Confederate monuments situated on the southern landscape. Their very existence suggests that there are other stories to tell, and the representational strategies they employ reflect the ways in which the sharing of those stories constitutes a rhetoric of consciousness raising and resistance. Discourses of space, place, corporeal agency, and affective and interactive performance all come together within this transformational rhetoric. They involve locating museums in places historically and symbolically important to either Lost Cause or twentieth-century civil rights memory, and using the spaces within them to facilitate dialogue between museum personnel and visitors. They also involve rhetorically positioning bodies in various ways, particularly in the integration of visitors in affective and interactive performances and the strategic exploitation of the public face associated with the museum. It is the interaction of these elements—their interdiscursivity—that performs the identity/cultural work necessary for the transformation of the landscape from one on which racial hegemony is etched to one on which the region's complex history and memories are acknowledged, ensuring a measure of justice.

The combination of the resistant power embedded in these interdiscursive elements with the identity-producing capacities of museums constructs black southern subjectivity. Museums use their locations, architecture, material displays, and other features to supply the meanings foundational to identities—be they ethnic, local, regional, or national. African American vernacular producers, in the forms of both personnel and visitors, exploit the rhetorical powers of museums to build culturally syncretic themes that transform what many African Americans perceive as the burdens of history and affirm positive ways of being black and southern. The next chapter explores this work in the context of interactive cybermuseums, with special attention to the identity-producing capacities that emerge from the intersection of digital media and participatory culture.

3
From Old South to New Media

Museum Informatics, Narrative, and the Production of Critical History

It is precisely in order to do away with misunderstandings, to restore an incomplete or deformed truth that the autobiographer himself takes up the telling of his story.

  Georges Gusdorf, "Conditions and Limits of Autobiography" (1956)

Oppressed people resist by identifying themselves as subjects, by defining their reality, shaping their new identity, naming their history, telling their story.

  bell hooks, *Talking Back: Thinking Feminist, Thinking Black*

The narrative begins with a photograph of six people standing in a beautifully decorated parlor at Mount Vernon, the plantation home of George Washington, on December 14, 1999. The occasion was the ritual commemoration of the evening of Washington's death. Present at the ceremony were descendants of Washington and his wife Martha, a descendant of Tobias Lear, Washington's personal secretary, and a medical researcher who had written an account of Washington's illness and death. The narrator herself is included in the picture, for one of her ancestors also had a close personal connection to the Washingtons. Identifying as "zsunlight," she is a descendant of Caroline Branham, Martha Washington's personal maid. Writing about the event ten years later, on January 19, 2009, "zsunlight" shares the photograph—along with an account of her personal experience of that night—on a website on which hers is but one in a substantial collection of many such stories. She writes about Caroline, her "grandmother to the seventh generation":

> In 1799, there were the enslaved, the masters, and those who knew them well. They say my Caroline practiced resistance, a common practice among slaves to keep Masters aware that the things they enjoyed, their way of life, was dependent on the labor of enslaved people. That night, as I stood in my grandmother's place, I became a wit-

ness to 100 years of history. . . . The Americans Experience was born anew in me that night. I dedicated my life to the preservation of intercultural histories in America and around the world. I love sharing my family history with children and watching them 'catch the spirit of healing with history'. . . . The stories I continue to spin will be gifts to my children and grandchildren and will become my legacy to them. . . . That night still haunts me and gives me hope that one day, all of the stories will finally be told at every historic site. Our children need to know.

"Zsunlight" is a member of an online social networking community called *Memory Book*, a website created by the Smithsonian Institution as part of its newest museum, the National Museum of African American History and Culture (NMAAHC). Established by Congress in 2003, the NMAAHC is the only national museum devoted exclusively to the documentation of African American life, art, history, and culture.[1] The institution's physical structure is scheduled to open to the public on the National Mall in Washington, DC, in 2016. In anticipation, the NMAAHC has constructed an online community in which members post photographs of personal historical artifacts, create written or audio narratives about them, and engage in conversations with others about the memories created through the stories.[2] The historical narratives constructed through *Memory Book* are part of NMAAHC's first oral history collection.

Memory Book is the result of a partnership between the Smithsonian and IBM, which provided a $1 million grant in technology and expertise to develop the online museum using social networking technology. While the site allows for technological monitoring of the content for racist and obscene language (as well as inaccuracies), the visitors assume nearly complete agency over the presentation of information. Contributors upload photographs, narratives, or audio recordings, and create their own "tags"—or keywords—describing their entry. A navigable online map at the top of the webpage shows how the individual memories are linked to each other and to the content of the future museum. Visitors to the site are invited to engage in conversations with community members about both the artifacts and the narratives. NMAAHC staff regularly mine the site for objects with potential to become part of the physical museum's displayed collections.

Memory Book is representative of the increasingly transformative role of digital media in the vernacular production of cultural memory. As sociologist Andrew Hoskins has suggested, the various technologies included in the term "new media" have "seized, ransacked and made visible the past" through increasing its fluidity, enhancing the forms and nature of the communal influences to which it is subject, and making possible the bridging of the personal and the collective.[3] Digital museums in particular are instrumental in producing grassroots memory through facilitating greater access to archival institutions and increasing the mobility of objects from the private to the public sphere. These capacities are proffered through museum informatics, which, at its most basic level, refers to the use of technology to create and share information in museums. On a broader level, it encompasses the relationships and issues ensuing from the interaction of technology, information, and people.

The combination of museum informatics and social networking technology is an especially productive site for the reconstruction of marginalized African American memory. According to media theorist Dara Byrne, civic engagement and social action have long been central activities within traditional black social networks. This is especially the case for black social networking sites on the Internet.[4] These technologies allow for a more egalitarian relationship between producers and consumers, providing both with opportunities to influence and to be heard. This is in contrast to the one-to-many communication style found on traditional websites and media forms. The ability of citizens to move private artifacts into the public sphere, and to view and discuss them without leaving their homes represents an upending of the traditional power structures that gave rise to hegemonic history. For those committed to the recovery of silenced memories, this is an important means of giving voice to the otherwise voiceless.

For African Americans, thought of both as consumers and source communities, interactive cyber-museums are becoming important alternative knowledge systems for the preservation of their heritage. *Memory Book* provides them with a structure for the production of cultural representations within an institutional setting, combining the intellectual resources and cultural authority of a traditional museum with the access and interaction enabled by digital media and social networking technologies. Dr. Lonnie Bunch, the museum's founding director, confirmed the advantages of online museums in presenting African American history. "Because we're the Smithsonian, we're able to introduce this culture to those who can't be reached through other institutions," he said. "We want to cross racial lines. Technology sometimes brings out the worst, but this allows a non-threatening, 'safe' community." The contributors to the site marshal the discursive power of narratives—which are essential elements in the creation of a sense of communal belonging—and oral history, which has served as an important alternative knowledge system for marginalized groups. The rhetorics intrinsic to both have been mobilized through the use of museum informatics and social networking technologies to construct a sense of southern identity through Civil War memory.

This chapter is concerned with the *Memory Book* cybermuseum as a technology in mediating public discourse about the Civil War era and constructing African American southern identity through the virtual presentation of familial memories. As a site for the production of Civil War memory, *Memory Book* shares the goals of battle reenactments and traditional museums. It is similar to these other modes of representation in the sense that it exploits the power of interaction in the construction of alternative narratives. However, it is markedly different in that the centrality of new media technologies ensures that the participants are much more temporally and geographically diffuse than those drawn to battle reenactments and brick-and-mortar museums. While the use of technology inside museums has enhanced the visitor experience in general, the ways in which new media technologies have brought the museum experience to multiple publics engages broader discussions about the uses of these technologies in society, specifically the cultural changes they have initiated. In order to address these transformations, this chapter is divided into three sections. In the first section, I discuss the role of computer-mediated biographical narratives in the vernacular production of resistant memory and identity. The second section foregrounds a detailed analysis of *Memory Book's* role in this production, with particular attention to the enabling capacities of participatory cyber-museums in advancing oral histories. The third section focuses on the particular narratives the community constructs in its production of southern identity. Finally, as no mode of representation functions completely free of constraints on the identity/cultural work it performs, I conclude with a discussion that situates *Memory Book's* many strengths within its limits.

Biographical Narrative, Resistant Memory, and Cyber-Identities

Approximately one hundred entries were posted to the site from 2007 to 2011. In addition to museum director Bunch, well-known African Americans—such as former San Francisco mayor Willie Brown (who described both his childhood in segregated Mineola, Texas, and his education in California), and United Negro College Fund President Michael

Lomax (who described his life in Alabama)—have uploaded narratives. The typical poster, however, is not a high profile civic leader but rather an "average" person. While the narratives assume different forms, the majority of them are stories that have been part of family oral histories. As such, they perform the identity work characteristic of biographical narratives. Sociologist Anthony Giddens highlighted the centrality of stories in the production of identity when he noted that "[a] person's identity is not to be found in behavior, nor—important though this is—in the reactions of others, but in the capacity to keep a particular narrative going. The individual's biography, if she is to maintain regular interaction with others in the day-to-day world, cannot be wholly fictive. It must continually integrate events which occur in the external world, and sort them into an ongoing 'story' about the self."[5]

Invoking a concept first elaborated by historian Pierre Nora, literary scholar Nellie McKay has situated African American (auto)biographical narratives as *lieux de memoire*, or memory sites, that extend the privileges of authenticating memory to everyone. Vernacular producers use their life stories to make claims about the significance of their lives and to advance powerful interventions in the functioning of hegemonic history. Personal accounts of slavery are particularly significant for their capacities to reveal the humanity of those who "knew it best."[6] Similarly, they are also powerful for the potential to become primary documents of enduring significance that highlight the tensions between official versions of history and local memories. The use of "grassroots" narratives to present alternative versions of Civil War history is not new, as there have been many published diaries, journals, letters and other memoires documenting the lived experiences of "ordinary" white men and women during the era. However, when the stories of the antebellum (as well as the wartime and post-bellum) past are of those who, as McKay suggests, are its most intimate witnesses—the enslaved—the meaning of the narratives changes, mobilizing an epistemological frame centered on a much different historical experience.[7]

Biographical narratives are productive means of building cultural syncretism and hold a position of priority among the narrative traditions of African Americans. According to literary scholar DoVeanna Fulton, family histories invoke the tradition of the African griot and are "related among the various forms of oral traditions that emerge from syncretic cultural productions and practices of African legacies within the American historical context."[8] The social impact of these stories is of great import to a number of constituencies, with their tropes of triumph over adversity serving as a mobilizing device for both black and white interlocutors, as well as a mode of selfhood and identification for the former.[9] Community members use familial narratives as a means of redeploying Civil War memory in a way that undermines superficial notions of black victimhood in favor of a more affirmative discursive focus on resistance and resilience.

The identity/cultural work implicated in the production of *Memory Book's* biographical narratives represents the contemporary iteration of a tradition of African American resistance writing and shares a technology-enabled continuity with the slave narratives of the past. Though the number varies according to the definition of "slave narrative," there are estimates of more than six thousand works so labeled in existence.[10] They were composed during the eighteenth and nineteenth centuries, as well as during the 1930s as part of the Depression-era Works Progress Administration. They performed significant political work, using stories of violence, familial separation, and escape to help build abolitionist sentiment in the decades before the Civil War. During the post bellum period, the narratives shifted focus, advancing the integration of blacks into the national community by emphasizing stories of individual and racial progress. While the importance of the goals associated with the earlier narratives was quite substantial, it is the broader objectives implicated in the stories recorded and constructed during the twentieth century that is most closely aligned with the identity/cultural work the *Memory Book* community performs. Narratives emphasizing resistance to dehumanization and perseverance within a hostile social, political, and economic context are particularly powerful forms of discourse and function in a way that uses experience to construct and assert subjectivity.

It is tempting to conceptualize the resistant power implicated in *Memory Book's* texts in a way that privileges slave narratives, as the narratives the site produces represent a continuity of the same culturally syncretic themes of resistance and resilience in the face of adversity. However, it is more productive to situate the site's identity/cultural work within a broader set of African American autobiographical writing, a category of representation characterized by the blurring of traditional genre distinctions. In her analysis of black women's autobiographical writing, Johnnie M. Stover has suggested that such stories take on a "hybrid" character that draws from both literary writing and personal history.[11] The narratives that result from this mixture perform the work of upending hierarchies of knowledge production. As Fulton has suggested, the passing down of family history thus functions as a form of historiography, resistant to the dominant culture's efforts to negate black identity.[12] As "zsunlight" and many of the other posters to *Memory Book* remind us, part of the identity/cultural work the site carries out involves informing the reader about the importance of sharing the stories and making suggestions about how the reader might assign useful meanings to them. These social actions refocus history in ways that suggest to contemporary audiences that their identities are not narrowly defined by narrations centered on degradation and suffering, and that more expansive notions of southernness and blackness—as delineated through Civil War memory—are empowering.

Moreover, the biographical narratives featured on the site perform the resistant work of shifting the focus of African American history to lesser-known or unknown figures, putting forward a vernacular production of memory in which it is the community members—rather than professional historians—who are the arbiters of which "heroes" might serve as figures of inspiration. In other words, rather than focusing on well-known historical figures such as Frederick Douglass, Ida B. Wells, and Martin Luther King, the site enables community members to privilege narratives in which a great-grandfather survived a lynching in Mississippi at the turn of the twentieth century, or an aunt refused to sit at the back of the bus in Alabama five years before Rosa Parks, or a great-great grandfather managed to escape slavery and build a successful business in Louisiana during Reconstruction.

In analyzing the resistant nature of these narratives, it must be noted that the earlier texts cannot be divorced from the sociohistorical context in which they were created. This is an important point, as the differences in the memories constructed through them and those constructed within a new media format form part of the basis for the work that *Memory Book* performs. Slaves needed to prove not only their ability to write, to develop knowledge, and to reach valid conclusions about their condition based on that knowledge but also to relay their stories in a social context in which their very humanity was not a preordained assumption.[13] Emancipation and Jim Crow brought on a new set of challenges in relaying these stories to a public that perhaps grudgingly accepted the fact of black humanity but remained wary of assertions of black citizenship. Historian Paul D. Escott has described the trepidation displayed by many former slaves during the collection of stories about their lives, in keeping with the racial etiquette and economic practicalities of the time. The fear of economic retribution often negatively impacted the candor with which the subjects expressed their feelings about their experiences as slaves. Additionally, as Escott reminds us, the primarily white interviewers often held their own prejudices that affected their mediation of these stories, for which the audience was also primarily white. However, he contends, the former slaves did want their stories to be told and for future generations to know what slavery was like.[14]

The community members who post their narratives to *Memory Book* have concerns that are both similar to and different from those of the past. In addition to the expressed importance of passing down their memories to future generations, the primary motive in sharing them remains the same: in presenting stories about their experiences, they mobilize discourses used to construct both regional and national identities. Though this similarity is significant, the identity/cultural work these newer narratives perform is delineated by a major difference. The contemporary cultural environment, defined by the proliferation of new media technologies, has dramatically transformed the construction and representation of memory and identity online. While the *Memory Book* community derives much of its ability to construct black southern identity from the discursive power of biographical narratives, its also draws its capacities to transform notions of regional belonging from the role of digital media technologies in the production of identity. The Internet has transformed the ways in which we build, maintain, question, and change our identities. Online communities are often virtual spaces for individuals from widely different backgrounds to coalesce over one or two common interests. In contrast to the closed confines of the movie theater or living room, cyberspace offers sets of social spaces in which users can transcend geographical boundaries to build community centers within which to engage in conversations. Additionally, unlike the one-sided nature of traditional media venues, consumers can engage in interactive discussions with media producers about content. In this regard, the *Memory Book* community is like the millions of other online communities.

However, as is the case with other social arenas, the introduction of racial identities complicates the analysis of cyber-communities. There has been much debate within studies of new media on the subject of racial identity. In the past, some scholars contended that the anonymity of cyberspace, with its absence of visual and aural markers of race, renders racial identities irrelevant. The underlying assumption in these studies was that users shed their offline identities in online interaction, making the Internet a "raceless" space.[15] Such studies did not explicitly argue that race ceases to exist once one logs in online, they simply positioned the disembodied subject as a starting point in their analysis. That said, many scholars now contend that race does indeed "matter" in cyberspace because our online activities are very much shaped by the knowledge, experiences, and values we bring to our interactions from an offline world in which race matters very much.[16] A more productive area of inquiry, these analyses suggest, would provide a focus on various sites in which racial identity is not merely visually represented online but actively constructed, reinforced, and deployed. In her studies of three of the most popular social networking sites for African Americans, Latinos, and Asian Americans, media theorist Dara Byrne contends that "the dissolution of racial identification in cyberspace is neither possible nor *desirable.*" In providing a forum for members to discuss globally relevant and racially specific topics such sites facilitate "'nation' (and movement) building, identity formation, belonging, and ownership."[17] In enabling African Americans to build agency in telling their stories—a level of self-definition unavailable in other media forms—these sites have become media for the production of resistant identities.

Identity is constructed through these sites via the creation of a set of publics and, especially, counterpublics, in which members build community through the production and wide dissemination of counterhegemonic interpretations of local and global events. As such, cyberspace becomes an African American public sphere, one with emancipatory potential for those who have access to it.[18] Digital media technologies have blurred the distinctions between the private and the public, enabling users to perform the identity work of extending the influence of family narratives to a much broader "family," one created through shared historical experience. Specifically, the richer fluidity of personal texts has enabled individual and family memories to become part of public archives in which collective identities are forged and maintained through sharing.[19] *Memory Book* performs this function, as it offers a space for individuals to build a community with like-minded others through discussions in which personal stories are used to offer critiques of dominant memories, as well as of the social structures through which particular versions of history have become hegemonic.

However, the site's construction of identity is more complicated than the mere provision of a subaltern space in which to upload artifacts and create narratives. It involves a combination of rhetorical influences, particularly visual and oral discourses. This work is reflected in the photos community members have uploaded. For example, an entry to *Memory Book* posted by "sherillfamily" consists of a photograph of an elderly black man holding a young white child. The child, a girl of about six years old, touches the man's beard, perhaps in youthful fascination with its woolly texture. The entry is described simply as a "photograph dated 1890 [that] has been in the family for years," and poses the question, "what was slavery

[to] Uncle Tom?" While the photograph invokes an iconic image easily recognizable to anyone who has seen a pre-civil rights Hollywood film set in the Old South, it enables the poster and the community at large to engage in discussions of its meaning in both the past and present. The image of the "Tom" is an archetype of emasculated blackness and, as such, represents a significant point of tension in African Americans' memories of slavery and concomitant regional identification. In this sense, it represents an important private memory that is at the same time a public text, and from which the tensions implicit in black southern subjectivity are teased out through conversation.

The identity-producing capacities of photographs uploaded to the Internet are further advanced in the case of *Memory Book* through the site's photo-tagging function. Tagging involves the organization of large amounts of shared content into descriptive data. The tags enable the uploading user—as well as other community members and visitors to the site—to organize, search for, and share the images. The social activities embedded in tagging allow site members even greater agency in developing shared, inferred understandings about the role each photograph plays in history, an identity-producing process Thomas Vander Wal has referred to as "folksonomy."[20]

More broadly, with respect to its position as a subaltern public sphere, the capacities to mobilize the rhetorics embedded in images makes the site what Nicholas Mirzoeff has called a countervisual archival space. Countervisuality, according to Mirzoeff, refers to the "revolutionary work" of images that transcend their potential as mere illustrations, bringing into view alternative ways of imagining and modes of becoming. These, he contends, constitute an active rejection of the authority assigned to dominant regimes.[21] In the case of *Memory Book*, this serves to further highlight the resistant nature of black southern identity.

In addition to the visual rhetorics the site produces, the written discourse—specifically the language the contributors employ in creating narratives around the photos—further advances the construction of identity. Language is a prominent marker of identity, and its function in constituting subjectivity in other communicative contexts is replicated online.[22] In the case of *Memory Book*, however, its role departs from the more conventional conception of this function, which entails the use of non-dominant language and dialect as means of expressing and identifying membership in a marginalized group. Social identity through language, according to Elinor Ochs, reflects the role of linguistic interactions in the production of ways of knowing and behaving. A group's language is implicated in

the development of cultural norms reflective of particular values and beliefs representative of a shared system of communication.[23] This function
of language carries even greater emancipatory potential for groups whose
histories have been relegated to the margins, as the commonality of linguistic references frees its members from the more formal structures associated with the production of dominant memory. In this case, it is the
development of syncretic language rooted in African American discursive values, particularly those employing traditional narratives of uplift.

Specifically, the *Memory Book* community deploys language in a manner that constructs particular meanings through the photographs and biographical narratives and situates them as lenses through which community members and visitors may forge a sense of belonging to the South.
Site members perform the identity work of developing a communal discourse that blends the old with the new in order to reconfigure the stereotypes imbricated in hegemonic memories of slavery and reorder them
into affirmative conceptions of the era. For example, many of the narratives are peppered with words such as "pride," "spirit," and "resilience" in
describing the experiences of those featured in them. One poster, "beandeary," uses the word "chattel" in describing his great-great-grandfather's
life as a slave in Texas, before describing the post-emancipation lives of his
and others' ancestors as characterized by "Texas stoicism," a term that invokes a form of masculinity typically reserved for white men. In this case,
the way that members speak about the history of their families is culled
from the syncretizing thematics implicit in the political work performed
by black biography and serves as linguistic markers of group solidarity—
not only as African Americans but as a historically conscious community.

All of these ways of producing racial identity online—biography and
visual and linguistic discourses—coalesce in the construction of black southern identity in the *Memory Book* cybermuseum. They do so in ways that
extend beyond the mere provision of a subaltern space for the production of countermemories, mobilizing place as an additional discursive element of the identity/cultural work they perform. In order to envision the
collaboration of all of these elements in the production of regional belonging within an online archive, we can, ironically, borrow from neo-
Confederate groups. As part of their own identity work, these organizations have exploited new technologies to construct what Tara McPherson
calls "Dixiefied" utopias in cyberspace in which overt discussions of race
are conspicuously absent. These sites feature photographic and biographical narratives centered on images evocative of the Old South—such as
personal stories about the Confederate battle flag—and are peppered with

linguistic cues signaling group membership (such as references to "federal tyranny"). Similarly, on the *Memory Book* site, photographs of enslaved ancestors, quilts, and family artifacts created during slavery combine with language evocative of the violence, terror, and familial separation to construct the cybermuseum as a memory place. But they do so in a way that foregrounds the collaboration of these discourses with an intersecting southernness and blackness. Another aspect of this intersection, that of the African griotic tradition, operates as an invocation of homeplace, though perhaps more implicitly invoking Africa as the "true" home. As such, *Memory Book* functions both as a museum and, metaphorically, as the southern front porch on which family stories are handed down.

While the Internet presents a unique and powerful forum for vernacular discourse and identity production, it also presents challenges. One of the primary concerns lies with uneven access to these technologies. Literary scholar Lisa Yoneyama has contended that, in terms of the recovery and accumulation of historical knowledge, what we know about the past is less important than our structural access to that knowledge, combined with the "personal, social, and historical conditions [within which] we come to an awareness about it."[24] While access issues are an important aspect of any discussion centered on new media technologies, they become particularly salient with respect to the abilities of disenfranchised groups to exploit them for their own purposes. This suggests the need for an analysis of access issues centering on what one does with knowledge obtained through the use of these technologies, including the ways in which they help build identity. Scholars of digital media and ethnicity contend that, in contrast to earlier research focusing strictly on access and consumption—which has limited applicability to analyses of the experiences of racial and ethnic minority groups and women—contemporary concerns with the digital divide should more properly focus on a "digital difference" in the ways in which these groups create visual cultures on the Internet. The level of black online participation in particular, they suggest, is substantially influenced by the availability of race and/or community-centered content, with cultural production and interactivity as central to the successful exploitation of these technologies.[25]

This conceptualization of access is particularly relevant to the specific identity/cultural work *Memory Book* advances. Adam Banks has argued for a scholarly focus on online African American discourse, examining the connections between communication technologies, black rhetorical traditions, and questions of access and has suggested that the standard definition of access is incompatible with the unique needs of African Americans. The transformative ideals that unify black rhetorical traditions, he argues, necessitate an understanding of technological access that includes the "systems of knowledge [required] to use any particular tool and the networks of information, economics, and power relations that enables that tool's use."[26] Institutional actors such as the Smithsonian have utilized the resources of the federal government—often in public-private partnerships with corporations—to enable African Americans and other groups with otherwise limited access to shape content on the Web. NMAAHC director Bunch has suggested that there is indeed a "shrinking" divide, but that it occurs along the lines of class rather than race. He detailed the efforts of the Smithsonian to remedy the disparity. For example, the NMAAHC sponsors a "Save Our Treasures" program in the Anacostia neighborhood of southeast Washington, DC. The program allows children to be part of the process of identifying artifacts in their homes and discussing them with others. "If you can begin where the kids are you can get them to see history as more about today and tomorrow than it is about yesterday," he said. According to Bunch, the typical *Memory Book* member is in his or her late-thirties, though a "fair" number of them are school-age children and older retirees. "Most," he claimed, "are interested in connecting with history, want to learn more, and better understand who they are."

Another challenge concerns the memories themselves. The more general African American discomfort with memories of slavery and alienation from Civil War memory that complicate participation in reenactments and traditional museums are replicated in the cybermuseum context. While a fairly significant number of the entries to *Memory Book* reflect memories of slavery, the majority are reminiscences of the Jim Crow era and the civil rights movement. When I asked Bunch about the disparity in the number of entries between the two eras, he pointed to to African Americans' ambivalence about memories of slavery: "Sure, I have noticed differences, big differences in the way people perceive the two histories. [The] civil rights movement is seen as concrete, positive, accomplished, intimate, and immediate. For many, [slavery] was a defeat, something to be ashamed of. [I] met a guy who criticized me for wanting to interpret slavery in a national museum; [he] felt it devalued African kings and queens. I want to use this technology to help people reclaim their slave past."

As Bunch's experiences indicate, the narratives of slavery posted to the site face many of the same challenges that those constructed through reenactments, traditional museums, and other discursive arenas must overcome in attempting to restructure dominant narratives and recover traumatic memories. In a society in which Hollywood versions of American history inform most people's views of African American memory—including those of slavery, Jim Crow, and the Civil War—the importance of representational agency, and of the alternative knowledge systems it upholds, is paramount. The identity-forming capacities found in the combination of biographical narratives and digital media technologies work to advance these systems.

The *Memory Book* community expands the parameters of southernness by presenting memories and identity that stand in contrast to those promoted through neo-Confederate websites. In her study of the large number of websites concerned with "preserving southern heritage," media scholar Tara McPherson has noted that the construction of identity advanced through these sites is reliant upon a vision of Civil War memory in which race is carefully elided. Dixienet, Dixieland Ring, and the hundreds of other sites that make up what she has called the "cyber-Confederacy" invoke the language and imagery of the Old South as a means of "transforming the 'unrooted' realms of cyberspace into particular 'cyberplaces' that correlate to real and imagined landscapes of gentility." A comprehensive reading of the visual and verbal discourse on these sites reveals a nostalgic preoccupation with this vision of history, though not through an explicit sense of longing for it. The nostalgia instead takes the form of resentment of contemporary cultural shifts that have led to non-European immigration, greater acceptance of gay rights and, most importantly, changes to the ways in which Civil War history is taught and the increasing disappearance of Confederate symbols from public spaces. The solution to these "problems," according to the sites, is another attempt at secession. These themes represent the understandings site members and visitors have of their regional subjectivity and inform many of the broader discourses constitutive of traditional southern identity. *Memory Book* cultivates a historically conscious cyberpublic that engages a similar transformation but does so in a way that constructs a much different southern "cyberplace," one tied to the historical experiences of those whose exploitation made possible the genteel landscapes of the neo-Confederates' vision.[27] As such, it offers an alternative definition of southern heritage and identity.

The resistant nature of *Memory Book* and other digital media sites works in ways distinct from those of traditional museums and battle reenactments. Unlike a Civil War battlefield or memorialized landscape—which represent the exploitation of public spaces to advance racially exclusionary historical narratives—these sites operate within a vast cyberscape that, though subject to significant concerns about the lingering digital divide, is relatively accessible. Therefore, the *Memory Book* community constitutes less of an appropriation of space and ritual as means of interrogating and reordering dominant memory and more of a cultivation of a self-sustaining, historically conscious cyberpublic committed to inserting its own stories into an internationally recognized public sphere. The social actions implicated in posting artifacts and narratives constitute resistance, but in a less direct, more subtle way than more traditional means: it is entirely possible, perhaps even probable, that members of "opposing" communities (*Memory Book* members and online neo-Confederate community members, for instance) will never experience any sustained, or even perfunctory, contact with each other online. Nevertheless, the relative insularity of the consumers of these narratives works to frame them, using community-specific discourses to perform identity/cultural work that is narrower and more focused than that of traditional, brick-and-mortar museums. Thus, the primary mode of resistance the site offers is through the creation of a subaltern counterpublic for marginalized memories and an oppositional identity, one that represents a critique of assumptions of whiteness and neo-Confederate values as constitutive of normative southern heritage in cyberspace.

The destabilization of normative assumptions of southern identity is advanced through the combination of biographical narratives and the creation of an online public. However powerful this relationship may be, it alone is insufficient to the task of overturning hegemonic history in the creation of African American-centered memory. In order to construct a counterhegemonic historical narrative, biographies and online community spaces work in tandem with yet another element crucial to the functioning of *Memory Book*. The third aspect of this work involves museum informatics, which refers to the "sociotechnical interactions that take place at the intersection of people, information, and technology in museums."[28] It is the combination of the three that empowers site participants as agents in the production of dissonant history. In the next section, I look at the ways in which this third feature, specifically in the form of participatory cybermuseums, functions together with biography and online identity to enable *Memory Book* members to navigate a complex discursive terrain and build southern identity through the virtual display of artifacts.

Museum Informatics, Interactivity, and the Production of Vernacular Memory

Information technologies have become crucial elements of what many museum studies scholars perceive as the decades-long transition of museums from repositories of objects to repositories of knowledge.[29] Exhibitions have assumed a significant degree of mobility through the ability of museums and other knowledge communities to transition from strictly physical institutions with limited constituencies to virtual institutions with vastly expanded visitor bases. These transformations have instigated profound challenges to traditional ways of compiling and representing museum collections, and, more broadly, to creating and distributing knowledge. The resistant opportunities enabled by new media technologies for the construction of racial identity through the sharing of stories within the *Memory Book* community would be inaccessible without these changes.

Paul Marty and Katherine Burton Jones have located the beginning of the transformation of museum information to electronic format to 1963, when the Smithsonian's National Museum of Natural History (NMNH) and the Institute for Computer Research in the Humanities (ICRH) developed systems that led to the introduction of data processing systems in museums. In 1966 a network of "pioneer" museums in New York successfully sought funding for the installation of a Museum Computer Network for the creation of a trial databank. By the early 1970s this system had begun to be used in museums outside of the New York network. According to Jones, the development of professional standing committees during the 1970s was instrumental in the technical transformation of museums. This development—enabled through the creation of the American Association of Museums (AAM)—facilitated innovation at each level of the division of labor in the display process. Through the efforts of the AAM, the registration area, which provides the information on the objects in the exhibits, first made efforts toward the digitization of museum collections. Throughout the 1980s and early 1990s, there was increased use of technologies in exhibits, from slide projectors to digital images.[30]

It was during this time period that museum professionals began to explore the possibilities offered by the emerging Internet. Beginning with the use of email and listservs, museum professionals quickly saw the potential in the World Wide Web to transform the ways in which museums operate. From 1994–1998, a few museums began to take steps toward establishing their presence online. These early sites, according to Jones, were essentially "short informational flyers."[31] Later advances included the Smithsonian National Museum of American Art HELIOS American photography site, which allowed visitors opportunities to email comments about the photographs they viewed. By the late 1990s new media had become ubiquitous in the museum community. Jones pinpoints the year 1999 as the "Slope of Enlightenment" for museum use of Internet technologies.[32] While few would predict that virtual museums will take over as substitutes for physical museums, visitors have come to value them for making immediately accessible a wide variety of digital museum resources that are useful in their daily lives, including images of artifacts and research materials.[33]

The benefits these technologies bring to museums are pragmatic. As NMAAHC director Bunch explained to me, because they are inexpensive to use, monitor, and change, museum technologies supply financial benefits to museums in various stages of change and stability, enabling them to better compete with each other. "These technologies really allow a good museum with a good critical eye to compete with other museums," he said. This is a particularly salient advantage for museums struggling financially. For example, America's Black Holocaust Museum—a virtual museum with a mission to educate the public about the historical struggles of blacks in America—was launched in 2012 after the physical museum in Milwaukee was forced to close in 2008.[34] Relocating the museum to cyberspace enables it to continue its operations, as well as to reach more numerous and diffuse visitors.

The cultural transformations advanced through virtual museums are even more profound. Information technologies have enabled museums to construct a greater diversity of stories through the virtual presentation of their artifacts. This has served a democratizing function within the museum source and visitor communities, linking a multiplicity of publics and advancing greater social integration. Through these activities, cybermuseums have transformed the cultural work performed by history museums and other archival institutions, creating a broader field of contributors and a more comprehensive scope of narratives imbricated in individual, group, and national identities.

Moreover, according to media scholar Henry Jenkins, the proliferation of these technologies has empowered vernacular actors to intervene in traditional archival processes. Participatory culture has thus upended hierarchies of historical knowledge production in two very important ways. First, it fosters an access culture in which average consumers may "archive, annotate, appropriate, and recirculate media content in powerful new ways."[35] Second, it enhances the role of oral histories, invoking and extending the ancient African griotic tradition of storytelling as a primary tool in the intergenerational transfer of memory. Oral history is a very important part of postmodern understandings of historical narratives, and for groups whose memories have been marginalized from mainstream document-based knowledge infrastructures, the ability to deploy oral traditions in the creation of a substantial and diffuse public is central to the ability to construct dissonant histories. The resistant power implicit in the digitally mediated production of these narratives, in which one's ancestors become archives, presents an accessible alternative to more traditional systems of knowledge production. Indeed, as some scholars have argued, conventional memory institutions have traditionally privileged the histories of the powerful at the expense of those of the marginalized.[36] Moreover, when the historical experiences of non-dominant groups have been acknowledged, the relationship has been defined by appropriation, with traditional structures creating archives *about*, rather than *of*, these communities.[37] A related issue concerns access. While archival institutions have relatively recently experienced a significant surge in interest in the collection of African American materials, many minority populations remain underserved as consumers and underutilized as source communities.[38]

These concerns reflect the failure of traditional methods of archiving to serve the particular needs of African Americans and other minority groups and raise the stakes implicated in the goals of alternative archival bodies in preserving histories that are contested and under constant threat of erasure. *Memory Book* and other digital institutions have been created to address these concerns, increasing the significance of both oral traditions and their delivery systems in the construction of group identity. According to Bunch, a much broader community responds to virtual museums than traditional ones, which enriches their sense of cohesiveness. This has extended the emancipatory potential of the Internet to vaunted memory institutions and serves to promote a reconsideration of "some of the most fundamental tenets of archival authority."[39] This more critical orientation effectively "decentralizes official knowledge production" and "changes not only the way we interact, but our very identities."[40]

The introduction of interactivity into the museum experience has even more dramatically enriched the potential for cybermuseums to serve as vernacular spaces. Certainly, the rise of participatory culture during the last two decades, of which interactivity is a crucial element, has facilitated the production of agency for audiences who seek not only to consume history but to actively construct it. The nature of participatory culture, along with its importance as context for the work of the *Memory Book* community, may be seen in Jenkins's description: "A participatory culture is a culture with relatively low barriers to artistic expression and civic engagement, strong support for creating and sharing one's creations, and some type of informal membership whereby what is known by the most experienced is passed along to novices. A participatory culture is one in which members believe their contributions matter, and feel some degree of social connection with one another."[41]

The level of interactivity enabled through social media technologies has transformed museums in ways that go beyond the digital display of artifacts, affecting the very narratives they construct. Museum studies scholar Katherine Burton Jones discussed the benefits of enabling dialogue between and among individuals, and between individuals and museum personnel. "[Technology] customizes the museum experience," she said. "Involving the community represents a great leap forward for museums. It optimizes the stories they can tell."[42] She also suggested that the unlimited "gallery space" within cybermuseums allows a greater number and diversity of stories to be told in potentially transformative ways. Jones pointed to the example of holocaust museums to demonstrate how the interactivity enabled by social networking technology often expands the very definition of the subjects of museums. She suggested that the physical space of the Holocaust Museum in Washington, DC, allows relatively limited narratives—and thus definitions—of *holocaust*. In 2007, in partnership with Google Earth, the museum launched "Crisis in Darfur," an online initiative featuring stories of the genocide in Sudan. Since then, the physical museum has included exhibits detailing genocide in places like Syria and Cambodia, as part of its commitment to ending such atrocities. These activities, according to Jones, provide an example of the ways in which technology enables the museum to feature exhibitions that not only foreground recollections of the Holocaust but also implicitly critique popular conceptions of the term "holocaust" itself. The expanded narratives of *Memory Book* emerging from the vast expanse of cyberspace thus build cultural syncretism through redefining the Civil War era away from dominant notions of victimhood toward an emphasis on resistance and resilience.

Moreover, while Jones acknowledged the logistical difficulties of managing continuous access to information and cautioned against technological determinism, she suggested that the vastly expanded accessibility and visitor-centeredness of virtual museums represents a shift in the locus of agency in the production of museum narratives. "Museums have evolved," she suggested, "from being organizations that focused on the objects to being those that focus on audiences and experiences, with the collections still in the forefront but made more approachable." This evolution in the location of agency from museum funders, officials, and personnel to cybercommunity members, when combined with the discursive powers of autobiographical narratives and online identity, has situated *Memory*

Book as a site for an alternative, African American-centered southern subjectivity. In the next section, I analyze the specific ways in which its oral and visual narratives perform this identity/cultural work.

Memory Book's Virtual Slave Narratives

The entries posted to the site mobilize memories of slavery to build culturally syncretic themes of resistance, resilience, and belonging to the national community. These tropes are particularly salient to the identity work the site performs. Stories of resistance to the physical and psychological degradations of slavery—as well as of resilience in the face of this oppression—signal to African Americans that the era is not defined by memories of suffering but may instead be thought of as a period of strength through and from adversity from which they may draw inspiration in the contemporary moment. Narratives foregrounding national belonging resist the "ghettoization" of African American history by emphasizing its place and importance as part of American history, a role that involves serving as a critical lens on its triumphalist frames. While the discourse of racial uplift underlying these themes is not free from controversy, it is particularly useful in the project of upending the core assumptions of dominant history and enabling African Americans to construct affirmative notions of southern blackness from the emergent memories.[43]

The themes of resistance and resilience are often intertwined. For example, the *Memory Book* posting dated June 4, 2007, is one of the few entries in which the contributor (Kevin B. Fowler) used his full name. The entry, titled "Traveling South to Freedom," features a drawing of a young girl sitting on her grandfather's lap, imagining him as a boy slave. In the imaginary image, the sparsely dressed boy is tearing himself loose from his shackles as he escapes his plantation. In the narrative that follows, it emerges that the girl in the picture is Fowler's grandmother, Rosetta Riddick, who, according to the author, often told stories of slavery passed down to her during her childhood in segregated Norfolk, Virginia. Her grandfather Lewis Foster was the original source of the narratives, having lived the early years of his life as a slave in King and Queen County, Virginia. Fowler offers a vivid description of his great-great grandfather's journey:

> Papa Foster remembers seeing the humiliating sight of his mother, brother, and sister sold on the auction block in King and Queen. It is not known who his father was or the name of his mother or sister.

The details aren't given, but Papa Foster escaped slavery as a teenager prior to the end of the Civil War. As an escaped slave, Papa Foster talked about seeing his brother still in bondage. He desperately wanted to talk to him, but he never did for fear of being recaptured. Papa Foster proceeded to leave the King and Queen County area. He would sleep during the day in the woods. He traveled during the night, smartly avoiding the Confederate and Union soldiers. Papa traveled several months in the southern direction to his eventual freedom. Papa Foster settled in the Titustown section of Norfolk, Virginia across the railroad tracks from Brownstown. Titustown is one of the few black towns in [the] United States. Starting in the early 1900s a white farmer parceled his land and sold the lots only to black families. The stipulation was that the houses couldn't be built until the land was paid for in full. My parents bought one of those lots too. As many escaped slaves traveled north to freedom, traveling south proved to have been a very beneficial route for my family.

For Fowler, posting his ancestor's story provides a cathartic moment in which he can share a family narrative with others. More importantly, it enables a critique of many common assumptions with regard to slavery, such as the notion that the North was seen as the land of salvation for all escaped slaves and that post-Reconstruction southern blacks were, by definition, completely dispossessed. It is also a story of black self-determination in the presence of overwhelming obstacles.

Another poster calling himself "Andre_46817" shares a similar story, accompanied by a photograph of "Cousin Emma," in which a young African American woman dressed in dark clothing stares unemotionally into the camera. Emma was a distant cousin of the contributor, and lived to the age of 109. In his narrative, he recounts his childhood fascination with the woman's age and with the stories of her youth in South Carolina. He describes his amazement at hearing tales of her girlhood as a slave, including her horror at seeing her mother tied to a tree and whipped. "My time with Cousin Emma, almost forty years ago, has been a lasting memory," he writes. "Remembering how Mother took care of Cousin Emma reminds me of the love and commitment to family that filled our home at 902 Anderson Road. Reflecting on Cousin Emma's life experiences along with the peace and serenity she embodied is a reminder of just how strong, resilient, and enduring we can truly be."

A personal family story uploaded on October 22, 2008, by "marchfish" details the Bronston family history as it has been "verbally passed down through the generations." The writer begins his narrative with a description of his family origins in the east African island nation of Madagascar and ends with his great grandfather's heroic tale of escape from Kentucky to Ohio. According to family lore, Lafayette Bronston feared for his life after murdering a slave master who had attempted to sell Bronston's wife to another plantation owner. "Marchfish" describes the narrative as the subject of conversation at reunions, funerals, and other family events. The story is a typical depiction of black sacrifice, resilience and agency, rather than victimhood, amid the trauma of slavery. Indeed, each of the narratives described here advances a sense of African Americans not as historical objects but as historical subjects.

In situating African American history within American history, the posters attempt to reinsert black agency into national stories and culture in a pattern similar to that of the story I described at the beginning of this chapter. On January 19, 2009, "ekramer" posted a narrative on black participation in the Revolutionary War. In addition to briefly describing the relatively well-known story of Crispus Attucks, the author details the efforts of Peter Salem, a freed slave who served in the battles of Lexington and Concord. He also describes the conflicts that arose over the question of conscription of both free and enslaved blacks. An entry titled "Black Ice," by "RonLevi," uses the story of the poster's sons' interest in ice hockey to reveal the history of black participation in what is commonly regarded as a "white" sport. He references "oral and written family history" to describe the life of his ancestor John Wesley Levi, who was born in Virginia in 1815 and who may have fled to Canada from Virginia in the aftermath of Nat Turner's rebellion. "I remember the day I learned that there was a long history of participation in the sport of ice hockey by people of African heritage who were, to my amazement, the sons and grandsons of American slaves who arrived in Nova Scotia via the Underground Railroad," "RonLevi" writes.

Many of the personal narratives in this vein are presented as explicit prescriptions for the importance of preserving African American cultural memories. In a post dated October 10, 2007, titled "An Ordinary Life," "beandeary" recounts "over 120 years" of his Texas family's history. "Beandeary" describes himself as having inherited many treasured family possessions and expresses a desire to share the narrative of the page from the family album he has uploaded to the website:

My great-great grandfather, King Bean, was born in 1850. On July 11, 1859, he was listed, along with other chattel, in his slave owner's will. His owner listed his worth as $700. My great-grandfather,

Wesley Bean, was born free in 1869. And my grandfather, Tom Bean, was born at the turn of the century in 1899. My grandfather died in 1981. Because of my grandfather, I have my family's collective memories. Memories told through possessions. My grandfather, great-grandfather, and great-great-grandfather were ordinary men who lived ordinary lives in a rural Texas community on the Fayette-Bastrop county line. They were stoic Texas men who never talked much about the past because it never occurred to them that the past or themselves [*sic*] could be of much consequence. But yet, these tough Texas stoic men managed to leave behind their life stories, not in words, but in possessions. These possessions have allowed me to take walks through history, any time I please, to get a glimpse into their lives.

Here "beandeary" fuses several discourses concerning race, gender, and memory. He suggests the importance of keeping these memories alive for future generations and foregrounds the significance of material culture as a means of doing so. The reference to his great-great grandfather as "chattel," along with the price his life and labor were worth, is striking in that it personalizes the banality with which human beings offered other humans up for sale. The display of bills of sale for slaves is common in traditional museums. However, its inclusion in online personal narratives invokes an even greater appeal to modern sensibilities about the intrinsic worth of human lives. Additionally, "beandeary" engages gendered discourses by implicitly invoking the popular conception of women as keepers of memory, particularly with respect to the scrapbook-like entry he uploaded. The references to "Texas stoicism" deploy the "triumph over adversity" theme common in slave narratives while engaging in an underlying discourse of African American masculine toughness. The poster uses his personal story to present a stark contrast to the emasculated "coons" and "Toms" of southern mythology.

Many of the posters to *Memory Book* utilize cherished family artifacts to tell their stories. For example, "23jayhawk" uses an iconic artifact to talk about the importance of remembering African American history. She uploaded a photograph of a quilt and discusses the role of quilting in preserving memory. In her entry, she recounts the story of a quilter in Kansas who made her quilts based on stories from slavery passed down from her great-grandmother. She urges visitors to see quilting and other artistic activities as a means of capturing the "pride, spirit, pain, and joy of the African American experience" and to honor ancestral heroes for the "great sacrifices they made for us all." Similarly, "jandersonsoli" uploaded a photograph of pieces of pottery, describing the objects' place in "Texas' first black-owned business." Though the relationship of the contributor to the subjects is unclear from the text, it is reasonable to guess that they are ancestors who have become a source of family pride. The provided description of the pottery's significance informs *Memory Book* visitors that the creation of these objects was an anomaly in an era in which cotton was the standard commodity. Thus, after emancipation, the former slaves' ability to produce the pottery resulted in a very early example of successful black entrepreneurship. As such, it provides a classic example of black people's ability to turn adversity into art or opportunity. The objects themselves are beautiful, but unremarkable in an objective sense. Their symbolic power thus comes not from their presentation but from their role in bringing to the fore the historical endurance of African Americans. Neil Cummings and Marysia Lewandowska contend that we use artifacts as means to negotiate a relationship between a transitory and contradictory present and a profound, continuous, and stable individual and collective past.[44] One assumes that these urns have, over the years, been objects of great pride in this particular family, leading the poster to share them with the *Memory Book* community.

The combined themes of black resilience, resistance, and national belonging are sometimes situated within a romantic view of Africa. The following excerpted audio file, posted by "Rajnii" and described as "a tribute to our ancestors for all those who lost their lives and those that survived," references the Middle Passage:

There should be oceans of tears (sung twice); this ink is not my blood; what right have I to speak; what right have it to speak . . . mother's one perfect tear for her children; there were children; in that small cramped space; giving birth in fetal position; to still born [*sic*] cosmos tiny infinities with mayhem as midwife; below deck below death; below breath was hope hidden in heart beat rhythm; now I see our children are below deck; crammed into small cramped space; but the wooden planks are blocks, and stoops, and streets; but our heart beating hope tells me, we don't have to live that metaphor; for we are the lineage of stars and suns; look at the sky and see your reflection; forgetfulness would have us think the oceans dreamt them, but galaxies do little the seafloor; no one can ever take away our *before*; they sunk *so that we soar*; the [*sic*] hung *so that we soar*; they sung and sung with tears in their lings [*sic*] lungs *so that we soar*.

The entry directly confronts the erasure of black history, references the idea of a glorious African past, and highlights the sacrifices made by ancestors who survived slavery and Jim Crow. In invoking these discourses, "Rajnii" brings to the site intellectual conversations over black cultural memory that have taken place over more than a century. All of the stories discussed here are reminiscent of the slave narratives of previous eras; however, the fact of self-mediation in an online public sphere dramatically changes the narratives, empowering contemporary *memory entrepreneurs* to construct a usable past.

Conclusion

Memory Book is a transformative site because it provides a space for representations of history not found in other arenas. Through a combination of technology, visual culture, and biographical narratives, the contributors become historical producers as well as consumers. This, in turn, enables African Americans to attain a greater sense of historical agency. In uploading an artifact to the site and constructing a narrative to explain its personal and cultural significance, the contributors implicitly critique dominant history by asserting the cultural authority of their personal narratives. This leads to new possibilities for the role of nineteenth century cultural memories in the shaping of black identification with and belonging to the South in the contemporary era.

While participatory culture and interactivity have forged a transformation in the relationships among museums and their visitors, they have also presented challenges. The first of these concerns the primary way it produces cultural syncretism. With a significant discursive focus on themes of resilience and uplift in the face of adversity and subjugation, the triumphalism that underwrites many of the narratives the site produces is vulnerable to privileging a positive view of the era and its aftermath. This may run the risk of promoting a "moral boosterism" that obscures the systemic and interpersonal violence, familial separation, sexual coercion, insurmountable economic burdens, and social death characteristic of enslavement and its legacy. The result of this is that the site, at times, advances the same celebratory orientation toward history it implicitly critiques, albeit from the perspective of the silenced memories of the disenfranchised.

Moreover, the presentation of images online imposes limitations at the same time that it opens up possibilities in terms of access. Viewing an image of object online does not proffer the same emotional impact that the ability to view it in material form does and carries a lesser emotional "punch" than the ability to touch artifacts—particularly those associated with atrocities. Similarly, though *Memory Book* constitutes an online public dedicated to sharing personal histories, the disembodied nature of cyberspace forecloses similar opportunities for the production of community facilitated through other modes of representation, such as traditional museums and reenactment, which rely more on interpersonal interaction among the various social actors engaged in those arenas. The power implicated in the work the site performs must be understood within these parameters.

Nevertheless, these concerns must be balanced with *Memory Book*'s ability to empower vernacular producers to construct memory "from below," producing an empowered culture in which average people are the driving force behind their own narratives. This phenomenon is gradually transforming the representation of dominant history, as private memories of lesser-known historical actors become represented in digital, democratized public spheres. Moreover, the site's members are able to use social media technology to build a historically conscious cyber-public through the continuation of a long tradition in the African American community of using social networking as a form of critical civic engagement. Through these activities, participants are involved in the social action of building communities of memory, while engaging in the more political project of exercising greater control over the representation of both African American and American history.

The work they perform with these narratives emphasizes the idea that an identity of tragedy—of suffering and victimization—does not define blackness. These narratives broaden the scope of representation of black historical experiences, deploying the African griotic tradition to privilege oral histories and undermine traditional archival authority, presenting an alternative narrative to dominant tropes of victimization and ultimately fostering an affirmative subjectivity predicated on—rather than opposed to—southernness.

Interactive technologies have provided frameworks for "the radical transformation of the social meaning of history."[45] According to NMAAHC director Bunch, *Memory Book* offers a means of creating new data that affords people opportunities to understand their past and get validation from their peers. "They see their history as legitimate, worthy of preservation, and validated," he told me. "When experiences are put online, there is a response from others sharing theirs, a cachet enabled by technology."

Conclusion

Southern Identities in the Twenty-First Century

On a cool, crisp early-winter afternoon in December 2013, I paid a visit to Monticello for the first time in more than thirty years. I understood that a number of developments during the late 1980s and early 1990s—social, cultural, and archeological—had led to the evolution of an official tourist narrative that was much different from the one I had encountered as a child and wanted to experience the results of this transformation. I arrived at the estate early so that I could observe other aspects of the tourist experience and reflect upon their meanings before boarding the shuttle bus that would take me and other visitors to the main house for the guided excursion. After strolling through the small slave cemetery located near the parking lot on the periphery of the five-thousand-acre estate, I settled in the visitor's center to watch a film on Jefferson's life, work, and legacy. Beginning with this film, titled "Thomas Jefferson's World," the stories of the enslaved people who lived and labored at Monticello are interwoven throughout the tourist narrative and, at times, even occupy a central place in the memories presented. The guided tour of the main house offers a comprehensive description of the daily activities of all those who had lived there, and includes language that explains the labor of the plantation's African Americans in terms that reflect their humanity: I heard no passive voice-descriptions of their work, nor did the guides refer to them as "servants." Indeed, instead of reproducing the traditional practice of narratively situating slaves as abstract figures, the docents at Monticello refer to them by their names, with Burwell Colbert, Edith Hern Fossett, Isaac Jefferson, and Frances Gillette-Hern serving as notable examples. Additionally, with some prodding from her descendants and the development of scientific DNA analysis, the story of Jefferson's exploitative sexual relationship with his young slave Sally Hemings has become a part of the narrative, though it is often qualified with the statement that "many historians now believe," implying that the evidence remains controversial. The site also offers an outdoor guided tour, titled "Slavery at Monticello," specifically focusing on African Americans, from mid-March to late October when the weather permits such activities. Moreover, Monticello's administrative body (the Thomas Jefferson Foundation) sponsored the 2012 restoration of Mulberry Row, the principal street, residential quarter, and industrial hub of Monticello that was home to as many as 130 slaves and is described as the "nerve center" of the plantation.[1]

The gift shop and museum, located on the grounds near the visitor's center and away from the main house, offer further illustrations of the narrative's transformation. Among the souvenir mugs, plates, cookbooks and other memorabilia one finds a significant number of books detailing the lives of Monticello's enslaved denizens. Laurence Pringle's *American Slave, American Hero*, B. Bernetiae Reed's *The Slave Families of Thomas Jefferson*, Annette Gordon Reed's *The Hemingses of Monticello*, and for the children, Kadir Nelson's *Heart and Soul* are but a few examples. The museum also offers comprehensive descriptions of the labors of the slaves, detailing the specific duties they performed and implicitly suggesting that it was they, and not Jefferson, who employed the required skill and ingenuity to keep the plantation running smoothly.

Just as importantly, Monticello's new narrative does not treat Jefferson's roles as the father of American democracy and slave owner as discrete concerns. Nor are these facts of his biography positioned as existing beyond critical scrutiny in the contemporary era. In both the film "Thomas Jefferson's World" and the guided tour of the main house, the contradiction inherent in Jefferson's stated ideals and his practices is described as the "central irony" of Jefferson's life. The fact that Jefferson freed only two of his slaves during his lifetime and one in his will is also mentioned, perhaps foreclosing any potential depictions positioning him as a "benevolent" slaveholder. The articulation of these concerns as part of the tour demonstrates that the desire to separate Jefferson and his legacy from the country's "original sin" is no longer operative within the narratives proffered at Monticello.

The stories of Jefferson's slaves and the critical interventions these perspectives offer in the memories advanced at Monticello are illustrative of the evolution of southern identity from a narrowly defined subjectivity centered on whiteness to a multitude of identities that acknowledges all contributions to the region's history and culture. The discussions of the lives African Americans endured, coupled with the critical reflections on the contradictions inherent in Jefferson's ideals and his realities, shatters the illusion of gentility previously advanced at Monticello and other sites. The allure of conventional representations of antebellum life relies on a blackness that is at once there and not there—a necessary element for its role in defining whiteness through serving as its polar opposite, yet servile, one-dimensional, hidden in the background, and silenced. It is this nostalgic imagery that provides the backbone for traditional southern identity. As African Americans have gained increased political, economic, and social power, they have mobilized this influence to demand the insertion of their historical experiences into the dominant narratives that constitute conventional notions of southernness. The central role memories play in the construction of group identities helps make these interpositions assertions of communal belonging.

In the particular case of Monticello, the identities at stake are both regional and national (and, as the estate, in tandem with the University of Virginia, was designated a UNESCO World Heritage Site in 1987, perhaps even global). Still, the plantation's transformation stands as synecdoche for the changing landscape of southern memory and identity. Public demands for historic sites to afford more attention to slavery and to the lives of individual slaves, of which Monticello provides a particularly striking example, are part of the much broader project of redefining and expanding southern belonging through the construction of more comprehensive memories. The identity/cultural work intrinsic to this project is not yet complete, as the relative paucity of African American officials, staff, and visitors to the Monticello estate strongly suggests. Nevertheless, I introduced this book with a description of the one-sided memories advanced at Monticello in the past; it is fitting that I end with the new ones presented there in the second decade of the millennium. I therefore offer the evolution of its narrative as an exemplar of the argument I build in this book.

The twenty-first-century South is increasingly marked not by a singular, fixed, racially delineated regional identity but by the emergence of fluid, decentered, and fragmented *identities*. These are often antagonistic, yet remain intrinsically interdependent. By referring to identities in the plural, I do not suggest the existence of multiple subjectivities that hinge on a competitive, "separate-but-equal" dynamic. What I have argued is that the region's changing political, economic, and social dynamics have precipitated a cultural shift that has facilitated the evolution of the South from a region defined by what Rebecca Bridges Watts refers to as a rhetoric of division to one characterized by a rhetoric of identification.[2] In turn, this transformation has helped foster a milieu in which southernness is no longer defined by the assumption that some aspects of the region's often troubled past are more salient than others.

While it may seem, at first glance, that this provides for a decreased role for Civil War memory in this new New South, the conflict's centrality remains intact. Historian James McPherson has observed that the Civil War is the war that never goes away, because the issues underlying the war have never gone away.[3] Thus, approximately 150 years after Appomattox, it continues as a culturally binding force, though the breadth of its cohering narratives has changed. The new elements inherent to southernness incorporate a more expansive set of parameters for Civil War memory, acknowledging the importance of slavery to notions of sectional distinctiveness, integrating the social and economic relations that led to the rebellion, and fostering a recognition of its many legacies. Though much work remains to be done, the new memories also challenge African American notions of Civil War history and their place in it: the recovery and restructuring of memories of slavery, war, and Reconstruction work to destabilize assumptions of the urban North as the central site of resistant blackness and resituate the South as the primal scene for black subjectivity. Representation is the key to the production of these memories.

Black Vernacular Production of Civil War Memory

African American Civil War memories and the identity on which they are centered is constructed and articulated through carefully selected vernacular communicative practices cemented by a set of strategically deployed African American rhetorical traditions. As the trauma associated with slavery may only be experienced through representation, and as its expression in a variety of public spheres is part of the resistant nature of the memories and identity, communication is a crucial aspect of the grassroots cultural work those invested in this emergent identity perform. As John Nerone and Ellen Wartella have suggested, contest is positioned at the heart of all communicative practices invested in retelling the past.[4]

The early decades of the twenty-first century pose a particularly compelling context for the execution of practices of contestation in the South, illustrating both how far the region has progressed in acknowledging multiple readings of history and identity, and how much work is yet to be done. Conventional interpretations of history—on the part of both black and white southerners—remain very powerful and continue to inform many areas of civic and cultural life. This is particularly the case in the political arena. Political rhetoric in the Obama era has been characterized by a resurgence of neo-Confederate discourse, with the language of "secession" and "nullification" becoming rhetorically powerful means of political mobilization in the South. Moreover, right-wing racial discourse has increasingly included blithe references to slavery, with both implicit and explicit suggestions that African Americans—who are at times described in mainstream political rhetoric as having "slave" or "plantation" mentalities—were better off during the antebellum period. This discourse, when coupled with rhetoric equating the duties of citizenship—such as paying taxes—with slavery, performs the ideological work of conjuring up stereotypical images of black contentedness during the slaveholding era, minimizing the misery inflicted upon those who were subject to the practice and trivializing the damage wrought by its legacy.[5] More importantly, these simplistic renderings of the past obscure its complexities, which include resistance in its many forms, including war service in the USCT. These political discourses, according to *New York Times* columnist Charles Blow, "do violence to the memories of those who endured it, or were lost to it, and to their descendants."[6]

These historical distortions of black Southern subjectivity are incomplete without romantic notions of Southern white participation in the war. The rhetorical power of such imagery is perhaps best illustrated with a case in Chattanooga, Tennessee, where a battle over an attempt at worker organization at a Volkswagen plant was described as "ground zero" in halting the momentum for unionization in the South. In May 2013 Matt Patterson, a consultant hired by antiunion groups, penned an op-ed in which he situated the unionization drive as an opportunity for southerners to refight the Civil War. Invoking the Battle of Chickamauga, Patterson wrote:

> One hundred and fifty years ago an invading army was halted at Chattanooga by the Confederate Army of Tennessee under General Braxton Bragg. The Battle of Chickamauga was one of the bloodiest days of the entire Civil War, and a resounding defeat for the Northern forces. Today Southeastern Tennessee faces invasion from another union—an actual labor union, the United Auto Workers (UAW). The UAW has its heart set on organizing Chattanooga's Volkswagen plant, which employs several thousand and supports thou-

sands more throughout the Southeast. . . . No wonder Hamilton County Commissioner Tim Boyd warns that unionization 'will be like a cancer on [Chattanooga's] economic growth.' Indeed it would be, though perhaps an infection is a more apt metaphor, an infection borne by an invading union force from the North. One hundred and fifty years ago, the people of Tennessee routed such a force in the Battle of Chickamauga. Let their descendants go now and do likewise.[7]

While the ultimate defeat of the unionization effort may be attributed to a variety of factors, the invocation of nostalgic memory and identity indicates its continuing currency as a rhetorical strategy in the South. More importantly, it is illustrative of the lingering potency of assumptions equating Civil War memory and identity with whiteness. African American claims of belonging to the South, and the Civil War memories on which they are based, are still very much contested.

These assumptions also operate, though to a lesser extent, in the arena of popular culture. In September 2012 Gary Rossington, the lone surviving original member of the southern rock band Lynyrd Skynyrd, told a national news organization that the band would stop using the Confederate battle flag at concerts promoting its new album. In explaining the decision, he cited its offensive and racist undertones and suggested that its true symbolic meaning lay with the "tradition and heritage of the soldiers" but had been "kidnapped by hate groups." After an outcry from the group's fans, which included derogatory suggestions that the band's cultural significance was now more closely aligned with "Massachusetts," "Yankeeland," and "Barack Obama," Rossington clarified his position one day later. "Myself, the past and present members (that are from the South), are all extremely proud of our heritage and being from the South," he wrote on the band's website. "We know what the Dixie Flag represents and its [sic] heritage; the Civil War was fought over States [sic] rights. The Confederate flag means something more to us, Heritage not Hate." After assuring angry fans that Lynyrd Skynyrd was and would always be a "Southern American Rock band," Rossington indicated that the band would continue to display the flag at its concerts.[8]

Another example from the realm of popular culture focuses an even sharper lens on the ways in which hegemonic Civil War memory, particularly its erasures of the complexities of slavery, continues to operate: the 2013 release of the film *12 Years a Slave*. Based on the 1853 memoir by Solomon Northup, a free-born African American who was kidnapped and sold into slavery, the film is notable for several features that represent significant departures from previous filmic portrayals. Chief among these are its exclusive focus upon an African American protagonist in Northup and its unflinching depiction of the physical and psychological violence of slavery. It thus stands as a substantial counternarrative to more than a century of romantic characterizations of the antebellum period. It is also noteworthy that both the director and screenwriter are black and that the film garnered Academy Awards for Best Picture and Best Adapted Screenplay. However, at the same time that modern sociocultural conditions enabled the making of such a film, its mixed reception among African Americans is reflective of the persistent ambivalence with which they hold memories of slavery. Evocative of the intellectual debates in the late nineteenth century about the utility of memories of slavery in the project of black advancement, the critical and commercial success of the film initiated a discussion in the black community about the place of these memories within broader issues of mass mediated representation. While there were many who praised the film for its realistic depiction of slavery, others suggested weariness with films that, in their eyes, portray African Americans in conditions of subservience and victimization rather than in more productive, uplifting historical contexts. Others, particularly those in the academic community, criticized the film for adhering to Hollywood convention and not going far enough in portraying the breadth of black resistance.[9] Both sets of concerns pointed to the erasure of black agency in popular representations of the era and highlighted the challenges still inherent in situating its memories as sites for contemporary black subjectivity.[10]

These concerns, voiced in the broader political and cultural spheres implicated in official histories, both inform the grassroots projects analyzed in this book and reflect the work that still needs to be done. Vernacular practices are productive means of constructing and expressing dissonant memories, both because of their accessibility and because of the opportunities they contain to create dialogue with dominant structures of historical production. They may also exploit the dialogic relationship between official and dissonant histories or complete the work of these structures. The dialogic relationship that characterizes the vernacular practices described here delineates the nature of black southern identity while offering resistance to the parameters of the conventional identity it seeks to upend.

The vernacular production of black southern identity, with its emphasis on critical grassroots social action, represents an interrogation of traditional southern identity as well as a complete rejection of the very power dynamics inherent in its establishment as the norm for notions of regional belonging. It is drawn from the same set of memories as the ones at the core of the hegemonic narrative, which are then reconstructed in a way that mobilizes the principal features of vernacular discourse: cultural syncretism and pastiche. These two features come together in a set of cultural practices designed to produce memories centered on affirmative notions of blackness and southernness. We *know* slavery happened. The goals of the cultural producers studied here are not limited to merely bringing these stories out or countering dominant narratives. Instead, their ultimate rationale for engaging in their cultural work involves both agency and responsibility—agency in the sense that they control the production and representation of their own historical narratives, responsibility in the sense that they perform their work in ways that facilitate sharing their knowledge with others, particularly youth.

As identities are constructed through negotiation, the emergent black southern subjectivity is created through the strategic deployment and redeployment of communicative practices and institutions central to the production of dominant memories. The three sets of practices and institutions analyzed here—reenactments, history museums, and cybermuseums—are reflective of this process of negotiation, with each mobilizing the rhetorical powers implicit in the particular forms as discursive "bargaining chips." The resulting narratives constructed through performance, visual culture, and digitally mediated communication have worked to transform a variety of spaces from sites in which hierarchical social relations are reified to spaces of negotiation. These new spaces, in turn, reflect the changing social relations and practices of the South.

The negotiation may take place on the hallowed ground of the Civil War battlefield where, as discussed in chapter one, discourses of masculinity, citizenship, and historical agency are constructed through battle—both metaphorical and actual—and shift the meanings traditionally ascribed to the sites on which they are waged. Though much of the most meaningful identity/cultural work is negotiated in these spaces, it is a testament to its power that African American reenactment is increasingly being utilized in conjunction with other sites of negotiation, such as museums, and that these spaces are often located outside of the South. For example, as part of its commemoration of the 150th anniversary of the Emancipation Proclamation, held in June 2013, the DuSable Museum in Chicago hosted two battle reenactments centered on the actions of the USCT.[11] In so doing, it demonstrated the mobility of black-centered battle reenactment, relocating a cultural practice traditionally associated with southern identity to the urban North, a place more conventionally associated with black subjectivity. This further demonstrates the fluidity of both southernness and blackness.

As chapter two illustrates, these processes of negotiation may also take place in a historically significant southern city hosting a slavery/Civil War museum, in that institution's interactions with a variety of publics—both supportive and oppositional—and in the interdiscursive display strategies deployed to address them. The existence of these museums represents the integration of African American memory into notions of southern identity; in addition to the exhibits themselves, the discourses of space, place, corporeality, and performance advance the identity/cultural work necessary for this integration. The processes of negotiation central to these discourses may be seen in a small but growing proliferation of museums located in historically and symbolically significant southern places, institutions that foreground the experiences of the enslaved and use alternative strategies utilized to tell their stories. The Old Slave Mart Museum, opened in Charleston in 2007 is a particularly notable example. In its stated goals, the museum has indicated the importance of unique display strategies that extend beyond its exhibits, including narratives delivered by its staff and interactive digital displays.[12] An additional museum, the Whitney, located in Wallace, Louisiana, represents one of the more overtly resistant forms these negotiations may produce. This slavery museum is situated on the premises of a former plantation in an area famous for numerous tourist-oriented house museums offering romantic visions of the pre–Civil War era. Among the numerous memorials constituting its grounds is a granite wall, modeled after the Vietnam Veterans Memorial in Washington, DC, listing the names of the 107,000 slaves who lived in Louisiana before 1820. Approximately half of the visitors who attended its opening in December 2014 were African American.[13] These institutions are part of a broader cultural shift from division to identification, a transformation that has brought further changes to the landscape, including the renaming of public buildings and parks that had previously honored prominent Confederate figures.[14]

Moreover, many Deep South urban areas are revising their cityscapes to reconcile their Confederate and civil rights memories with their histories of slavery, constructing monuments which—much like the AASCW in Selma—exploit the discursive power of material structures to forge connections among the three. Montgomery, Alabama, serves as a notable example. In December of 2013, the Equal Justice Initiative, a legal advocacy organization, unveiled three markers in the city describing in detail its role in the domestic slave trade. In commemorating the experiences of the more than twenty thousand slaves held in pens and depots in Montgomery, the group positioned their activities as crucial to understanding the Confederacy and the civil rights movement, which are prominent elements of the city's memorial cityscape.[15]

Even the most vaunted symbol of regional identity, the Confederate Battle flag, is disappearing from the southern landscape. On July 10, 2015, in a highly ritualistic six-minute ceremony performed before a cheering crowd of thousands and a television audience of millions, the flag was removed from the Capitol grounds in South Carolina. It had been raised in 1961 both as a civil rights-era act of defiance against the changing times and as part of the Civil War's centennial and had withstood an attempt to remove it in 2000 as well as an economic boycott by civil rights organizations and corporations. The 2015 legislative vote in favor of removal of the flag was a reaction to the racially motivated mass killing of nine members of the historically significant Emanuel African Methodist Episcopal Church in Charleston. Images of the killer celebrating the flag surfaced online shortly after he was arrested. The event represented the culmination of national media deliberations over the meaning of the flag—as well as its appropriateness as a publicly sanctioned icon—and prompted additional calls for its removal from a multitude of governmental and commercial venues.[16]

The most notable aspect of this latest and most momentous battle in the flag wars was that it catalyzed significant public discussion of the meaning of southern identity itself. The attention focused on the declarations of "southern heritage" for which the flag purportedly stood and that formed the basis for opposition to its removal revealed much stronger resistance to the authority of the dominant narratives it symbolized than had been offered in the past. The racially motivated nature of the Charleston church shootings undermined claims that the flag's meaning was limited to an innocuous "heritage" detached from slavery and its Jim Crow legacy and provided a critical foundation for interrogating the role of state institutions in legitimating the white-centered memories the banner represents. For example, in highlighting the erasure of African American history signified by the display of the flag and the broader concerns over memory and identity underlying its removal, an editorial in the *Richmond Times-Dispatch* contended that "the half remains untold" and suggested that the time had come for a process of truth and reconciliation.[17]

Another event that had taken place a year earlier offered an even more explicit rejection of the flag's symbolism in favor of a more inclusive vision of Civil War memory and southern identity. In July 2014 the Confederate flag was removed from Lee Chapel at Washington and Lee University in Virginia. Accompanying the removal was a promise to "study [the university's] historical involvement in slavery."[18] While this relatively quiet occasion lacked the dramatic impact of both the violent context and the pomp-and-circumstance of the events in South Carolina, it stands as a particularly compelling illustration of the processes implicated in the geographical production of multiple southern identities, occurring as it did at Robert E. Lee's burial site. Generally speaking, in bringing discussions of slavery and its centrality to the Old South to the fore, both events upended assumptions about shared history, memory, and regional belonging etched upon the southern landscape.[19]

Yet another meaningful space of negotiation is that of the cyber variety discussed in chapter three, where a cyberpublic of historically-conscious individuals traverses boundaries of space and time to create alternative memories of both slavery and the Civil War. The *Memory Book* community members and site visitors engage in storytelling and the sharing of visual images and deploy conversation—along with dominant cultural themes of resistance and resilience—to negotiate the meanings of their narratives. *Memory Book* represents the future of museums, enabling them to become additional spaces where racial and regional identities are constructed online.

Finally, the processes of negotiation may—and do—take place in any number of discursive arenas not detailed in this study. Yet, reenactments, brick-and-mortar museums, and cybermuseums present particularly compelling sites for the production of new memories. They inform us about the ways in which they are used to advance hegemonic historical narratives and, more importantly, offer us lessons on the ways they may be (re) deployed in the production of dissonant histories. This role, in turn, provides us with alternative frameworks with which to analyze them as identity/cultural practices. In broader terms, they demonstrate the mutability of memory, the fluidity of identities, and the centrality of representational systems—both official and vernacular. All of these practices and institutions have combined to construct a regional southern "we" that is much more inclusive than the identity that preceded it. In the final section, I offer a brief example that further illustrates the future direction these practices and institutions proffer for the production both of new Civil War memories and twenty-first-century southern identities.

Fort Monroe and the Negotiation of
Twenty-First-Century Southern Identities

The processes of negotiation characteristic of the new regional identities may be seen in the emergent narratives at many other historic sites besides the ones already mentioned in this book, including those more aligned with official historical institutions. Fort Monroe National Monument presents a particularly interesting example of the reconstitution of the new New South's landscape as a space of negotiation.[20] Located at the tip of the Virginia Peninsula in the city of Hampton, the area encompassing Fort Monroe was designated a National Historic Landmark in 1960. The fort was an army base under federal management until 2011, when it reverted back to the control of the Commonwealth of Virginia. On November 2, 2011, President Obama signed a proclamation creating the monument, placing it under the purview of the national park system.[21] At Fort Monroe, the NPS works with the Fort Monroe Federal Area Development Authority (FMFADA), which serves as the local authoritative body on the project, to develop the site into a new, 325-acre national park. The involvement of the NPS indicates that the park's interpretation of history will fall under the 1989 congressional mandate that the agency offer multiple readings of the history presented at the sites under its oversight. Notwithstanding the regulatory context, Fort Monroe offers a compelling illustration of these processes of negotiation in action.

The area was the place where slavery first took root in 1619 with the establishment of the Virginia Colony. For more than a century afterward, the site's location as the entry point for the entire Chesapeake Bay rendered it the home of a series of forts designed as first lines of defense for the colonists. Fort Monroe was built in 1834 to protect the Hampton Roads Waterway from potential enemy attacks. Shortly after the beginning of the Civil War, it had become the lone Union outpost in Confederate territory. On May 23, 1861, Frank Baker, Shepard Mallory, and James Townsend—three field hands pressed into service building a Confederate battery nearby—stole a boat, crossed the harbor and arrived at the fort, seeking refuge. It was here that Union General Benjamin Butler made his pivotal declaration that enslaved African Americans who had escaped behind Union lines were no longer slaves but rather contraband of war. Fort Monroe thus became the site of the Union's first contraband camp where, ultimately, nearly one thousand formerly enslaved people resided. By the end of the war, approximately ten thousand African Americans had settled there, living in the fort and in houses they had built on the ruins of Hampton, which had been burned by the Confederates. It eventually came to be known as the "freedom fort" and has been described by contemporary historians as the place where slavery began to die.[22] This history has rendered the site as a significant place within African American Civil war history and memory.

However, Fort Monroe is also a historically significant place for other reasons. A young Lieutenant Robert E. Lee was stationed here from 1831–1834. Lee occupied Quarters No. 17, his home on the site in 1832. Fort Monroe is also the current location of the Casemate Museum, which opened in 1951 and displays the military history of the fort. Notably, the museum features the room where Jefferson Davis was briefly held as a prisoner after the close of the war.[23] A memorial park bearing Davis's name was opened on the site in 1956. For these reasons, its place symbolism is appealing to Confederate heritage groups, particularly the United Daughters of the Confederacy (UDC).

All of these factors make Fort Monroe a uniquely situated place. The NPS has thus had to navigate the concerns of multiple constituencies by addressing the question posed by Eola Dance, the former chief of visitor services at Fort Monroe: "How will we talk about the complex history of it being both a Union fort and [home of] the Casemate Museum?" In recognition of the African American history of Fort Monroe, the Historic Preservation Advisory group of the FMFADA organized the African American Culture Working Group, whose members include ACWM President Christie Coleman. The group made visits to other historical sites, such as Gettysburg National Park in Pennsylvania, and Freedom's Frontier National Heritage Area in Kansas and Missouri as "fertile ground" for an interpretive strategy that engages the multiplicity of perspectives inherent in Fort Monroe's history. In December 2009 the group issued its final report. It recommended that the site's historians conduct research on the initial arrival of Africans, that its presentation should emphasize the details of the lives and statuses of freeborn, enslaved, "contrabanded," and freed people, that its narratives should include attention to the nearby sites to which African Americans migrated, and that its interpretation should incorporate data on the evolution of race and gender roles in the seventeenth, eighteenth, and nineteenth centuries as part of the stories of the lives of the "ordinary and extraordinary people" who lived and labored there. Interestingly, the report also recommended that the site's interpretive lens be extended to include the story of Chief Black Hawk's imprisonment there as part of its place symbolism in the "continued struggle for freedom."[24] This recommendation was advanced as a means of positioning Fort Monroe as a site where universal themes of human rights may be explored.

Around the same time, a letter circulated by a local official of the UDC revealed the group's concerns that the proposed interpretation of Fort Monroe would foreground its role as a contraband camp at the expense of its Confederate history. The group expressed the view that the Casemate Museum should remain at Fort Monroe, that Lee's Quarters No. 17 be turned into a museum, that the Museum of the Confederacy (MOC) be involved in the interpretation at the site, and that Jefferson Davis Park be revitalized. The language used to articulate these recommendations is quite revealing of the group's deeper concerns, as it positions Confederate history at the site as under threat from "revisionist" history, and refers dismissively to academics, "some of the followers of the National Park Service concept," and other advocates of the contraband narrative as "revisionist groups." The letter urged UDC members to attend a scheduled town hall meeting to voice these concerns to Fort Monroe officials.[25]

The deployment of a victimization trope in describing the decline in the status of the Lost Cause narrative and the attendant assumption of other perspectives as "revisionist"—with the negative connotations associated with that word in popular discourse—was not new. However, it is indicative of the remarkable evolution from the social context that gave the UDC and other Confederate heritage groups nearly unfettered power to determine the interpretations advanced through historic sites to one in which these groups constitute one of multiple perspectives subject to negotiation within public institutions. Fort Monroe is thus illustrative of both the tensions and promises that arise when bodies previously involved in the construction of hegemonic history navigate the conflicting yet intersectional memories central to the new New South narratives.

The NPS has undertaken these negotiations by engaging in what Dance referred to as a "'facilitated dialogue" in which input is solicited from multiple communities. The agency has partnered with a wide range of groups. These have included the Contraband Historical Society, the National Trust, the City of Hampton, the National Collaborative for Women, various Civil War and battlefield organizations, and an interdisciplinary team of academics from a number of universities, including from two local institutions, Hampton and Norfolk State Universities. The agency hosted public meetings, presentations, workshops, roundtables, and surveys in conjunction with these partners. It began developing a Foundation Document for Fort Monroe National Monument based on a "shared un-

derstanding of what is most important about the park." The intended result of this project will include a narrative that incorporates a variety of
perspectives. This includes that of a collectivity outside of the assumed
black–white binary of Civil War memory: a partnership with a representative from the John Smith Trail is charged with serving as a consultant
on the Native American history of the site. Moreover, unlike many other
Civil War memorials, Fort Monroe will offer tours highlighting the war's
impact on the local community. This will include narratives detailing
the Reconstruction era, particularly the influx of northern missionaries
and educators to assist the contrabands' transition to citizenship, and the
founding of Hampton Institute, now Hampton University. The ultimate
goal, according to Dance, is to cast a wide net relevant to four hundred
years of history, one that enables diverse visitors and community members
to see Fort Monroe as a place for inclusive conversations about history, one
where they may see themselves in the history presented.

Dance credited these partnerships to the relative smoothness of Fort
Monroe's transformation from yet another Confederate monument to Lee
and Davis to a site where a broader set of memories is represented. The
high level of public participation pulled in to constructing the interpretation constitutes Fort Monroe as more than just a historically significant
site, transforming it into as a place of negotiation and a space for civic engagement. The cultural work advanced here, much like that performed in African American-centered reenactments and museums both traditional and
virtual, represents only the beginning of an emergent new New South,
as delineated through the contemporary construction, contestation, and
representation of the region's history. According to Dance, Fort Monroe
marks the direction in which Civil War-era parks, museums, monuments,
and other sites of memory are headed. "This collaborative relationship is
becoming the new normal," she told me. "We are setting the mold."

Though Fort Monroe is a work in progress, it joins Civil War battlefields, museums, and online spaces as a site of negotiation disruptive of
traditional hierarchies of historical knowledge production. The effectiveness of these grassroots institutions and practices, combined with the South's
changing demography means that the question of what it means to be
southern will remain fluid and dynamic. Given these developments, we
can also see—more broadly—how history, memory, and culture have con-
spired to initiate the emergence of more expansive notions of southernness, creating a multitude of intersecting identities for the twenty-first
century.

Notes

Introduction

1. Throughout the book, I use the term "Civil War" interchangeably with the antebellum, war, and Reconstruction eras.

2. This encompasses the period from the 2000 census to the 2010 census. For data on general migration to metropolitan areas in the South, see Paul Mackun and Steven Wilson, "Population Distribution and Change: 2000–2010," 2010 Census Briefs, the website of the United States Census Bureau, March 2011, accessed July 14, 2013, https://www.census.gov/prod/cen2010/briefs/c2010br-01.pdf.

3. For data on African American migration to the South, see Sonya Rastorgi et al., "The Black Population: 2010," 2010 Census Briefs, the website of the United States Census Bureau, September 2011, accessed July 14, 2013, https://www.census.gov/prod/cen2010/briefs/c2010br-06.pdf.

4. William W. Falk, Larry L. Hunt, and Matthew O. Hunt, "Return Migrations of African Americans to the South: Reclaiming a Land of Promise, Going Home, or Both?" *Rural Sociology* 69, no. 4 (2004): 490–509; William H. Frey, "The New Great Migration: Black Americans' Return to the South, 1965–2000," The Living Cities Census Series, The Brookings Institution, Center on Urban and Metropolitan Policy, May 2004, accessed September 12, 2008, http://www.frey-demographer.org/reports/R-2004-3_NewGreatMigration.pdf; John B. Cromartie and Carol B. Stack, "Reinterpretation of Black Return and Non-Return Migration to the South, 1975–1980," *Geographical Review* 79, no. 3 (1989): 297–310.

5. C. Vann Woodward, "Look Away, Look Away," *Journal of Southern History* 59, no. 3 (1993): 496; Thadious M. Davis, "Expanding the Limits: The Intersection of Race and Region," *Southern Literary Journal* 20, no. 2 (1988): 6–7.

6. Toni Morrison, "The Site of Memory," in *Inventing the Truth: The Art and Craft of Memoir*, ed. William Zinsser (Boston: Houghton Mifflin, 1995), 110.

7. Emile Durkheim, *The Elementary Forms of Religious Life*, trans. Karen E. Fields (New York: Free Press, 1995); Maurice Halbwachs, *On Collective Memory* (Chicago: University of Chicago Press, 1992).

8. Edward Casey, "Public Memory in Place and Time," in *Framing Public Memory*, ed. Kendall R. Phillips (Tuscaloosa: University of Alabama Press, 2004), 17–44.

9. Marita Sturken, *Tangled Memories: The Vietnam War, the AIDS Epidemic, and the Politics of Remembering* (Berkeley: University of California Press, 1997), 3.

10. Joan M. Schwartz and Terry Cook, "Archives, Records, and Power: The Making of Modern Memory," *Archival Science* 2, nos. 1–2 (2002): 1.

11. Ibid., 3.

12. W. Stuart Towns, *Enduring Legacy: Rhetoric and Ritual of the Lost Cause* (Tuscaloosa: University of Alabama Press, 2012).

13. Ibid.

14. For a productive discussion of symbolic annihilation, see Jennifer L. Eichstedt and Stephen Small, *Representations of Slavery: Race and Ideology in Southern Plantation Museums* (Washington, DC: Smithsonian Institution Press, 2002), 10, 105–46.

15. Carole Blair, Greg Dickinson, and Brian L. Ott, "Introduction," in *Places of Public Memory: The Rhetoric of Museums and Memorials*, eds. Carole Blair, Greg Dickinson, and Brian L. Ott (Tuscaloosa: University of Alabama Press, 2010), 6.

16. David R. Goldfield, *Still Fighting the Civil War: The American South and Southern History* (Baton Rouge: Louisiana State University Press, 2002), 42.

17. See, for example, Goldfield, *Still Fighting the Civil War*; James C. Cobb, *Away Down South: A History of Southern Identity* (Oxford, UK: Oxford University Press, 2005); Rebecca Bridges Watts, *Contemporary Southern Identity: Community through Controversy* (Oxford, MI: University Press of Mississippi, 2007).

18. Gloria L. Cronin and Ben Siegal, eds. *Conversations with Robert Penn Warren* (Oxford, MI: University Press of Mississippi, 2005), 40.

19. Norman R. Yetman, ed., *Voices from Slavery: 100 Authentic Slave Narratives* (Mineola, NY: Courier Dover publications, 2000), 140.

20. David Blight, *Race and Reunion: The Civil War in American Memory* (Cambridge: Harvard University Press, 2009).

21. Friedrich Wilhelm Nietzsche, *The Use and Abuse of History* (New York: Cosimo, Inc., 2006), 21.

22. Eichstedt and Small, *Representations of Slavery*, 10. I use the term "symbolic annihilation" to denote an emphasis on the cultural and representational arena. I employ Eichstedt and Small's conceptualization of the term as practices that "ignore the experience and institution of slavery altogether or treat them in a perfunctory way." Symbolic annihilation signifies the white/black power dynamic operative at all of the sites I analyze. However, there are cases described in this book in which other terms may be applicable. For example, the tendency of many African Americans to engage in practices erasing their own memories of slavery would constitute "forgetting" rather than symbolic annihilation.

23. A Pew survey conducted in 2011 found that a majority of Americans of all races and ethnicities (56 percent) agreed that the era still has relevance to contemporary politics and public life. The same survey also found that 62 percent of

respondents admired the leaders of the southern states "some" or "a great deal," and that 48 percent of whites Americans and 39 percent of African Americans believed the war was fought over "state's rights." For details, see "Civil War at 150: Still Relevant, Still Divisive," Pew Research Center, April 8, 2011, accessed July 26, 2013, http://www.people-press.org/2011/04/08/civil-war-at-150-still-relevant-still-divisive/.

24. I refer here most specifically to the work of Frederick Douglass, Alexander Crummell, and W. E. B. Du Bois. See Frederick Douglass, "I Denounce the So-Called Emancipation as a Stupendous Fraud," in *Frederick Douglass: Selected Speeches and Writings*, ed. Phillip Foner (Chicago: Chicago Review Press, 2000); Alexander Crummell, "The Need for New Ideas and New Aims in a New Era," in *Civilization and Black Progress*, ed. J. R. Oldfield (Charlottesville: University of Virginia Press, 1995), 121; and W. E. B. Du Bois, "Darkwater," in *The Oxford W. E. B. Du Bois Reader*, ed. Eric J. Sundquist (Oxford, UK: Oxford University Press, 1996), 481–623. Also see William M. Banks, *Black Intellectuals: Race and Responsibility in American Life* (New York: W. W. Norton and Company, 1996). For a discussion of categories of forgetting, see Paul Connerton, "Seven Types of Forgetting," *Memory Studies* 1, no. 1 (2008): 59–71.

25. W. E. B. Du Bois, *Black Reconstruction in America, 1860–1880* (New York: Simon and Schuster, 1935), 722.

26. As James McPherson notes, southern whites even perceived themselves to be of a distinct *race* from northern whites. See James McPherson, "Was Blood Thicker Than Water? Ethnic and Civic Nationalism in the American Civil War," in *Proceedings of the American Philosophical Society* 143, no. 1 (1999): 102–8. More recently, the *Atlanta Journal Constitution* reported in 2010 that the Southern Legal Resource Center embarked on a campaign to urge white southerners to declare their "heritage and culture" by checking "other" and writing in "Confederate Southern American" on the line that asks for "race" on the 2010 census. Rhonda Cook, "Declare 'Confederate Southern American' on Census Forms, Group Says," *Atlanta Journal Constitution*, March 26, 2010.

27. Ron Eyerman, *Cultural Trauma: Slavery and the Formation of African American Identity* (Cambridge, UK: Cambridge University Press, 2001).

28. Cobb, *Away Down South*, 5; Ed Guerrero, *Framing Blackness: The African American Image in Film* (Philadelphia: Temple University Press, 2012), 30.

29. Eyerman, *Cultural Trauma*; Alexander, "Toward a Cultural Theory of Trauma," in Jeffrey C. Alexander et al., *Cultural Trauma and Collective Identity* (Berkeley, CA: University of California Press, 2004), 1–30.

30. Sidonie Smith and Julia Watson, "Introduction" in Sidonie Smith and Julia Watson, eds., *Getting a Life: Everyday Uses of Autobiography* (Minneapolis, MN: University of Minnesota Press, 1996), 15.

31. Barbara Ponse, *Identities in the Lesbian World: The Social Construction of Self* (Westport, CT: Greenwood Press, 1978), 208.

32. This is in contrast to Lewis Killian's description of the prototypical white southerner, who is either "born and raised at least until young adulthood in the South and who thinks of himself as a southerner" or "a person who, no matter where he was born and raised, lives in the South and identifies himself as a southerner." This description advances a notion of southernness tied to geogra-

phy. Lewis Killian, *White Southerners* (Amherst: University of Massachusetts Press, 1985), 10–11. Also see Rebecca Watts, *Contemporary Southern Identity*, 4.

33. Stuart Hall, "Cultural Identity and Diaspora," in *Identity, Community, Culture, Difference*, ed. Jonathan Rutherford (London: Lawrence and Wishart, 2003), 222.

34. Eyerman, *Cultural Trauma*, 1.

35. Stephen Small, "Still Back of the Big House: Slave Cabins and Slavery in Southern Heritage Tourism," *Tourism Geographies* 15, no. 3 (2013): 405–23; Owen Dwyer, David Butler, and Perry Carter, "Commemorative Surrogation and the American South's Changing Landscape," *Tourism Geographies* 15, no. 3 (2013): 424–43.

36. Larry Griffin, Ranae Jo Evenson, and Ashley B. Thompson, "Southerners, All?" *Southern Cultures* 11, no. 1 (2005): 6–25; Ashley B. Thompson and Melissa M. Sloan, "Race as Region, Region as Race: How Black and White Southerners Understand their Regional Identities," *Southern Cultures* 18, no. 4 (2012): 72–95.

37. John E. Bodnar, *Remaking America: Public Memory, Commemoration, and Patriotism in the Twentieth Century* (Princeton, NJ: Princeton University Press, 1992), 13.

38. Mikhail M. Bakhtin, *The Dialogic Imagination: Four Essays* (Austin: University of Texas Press, 1981).

39. Kent A. Ono and John M. Sloop, "The Critique of Vernacular Discourse," *Communication Monographs* 62, no. 1 (1995): 19–46.

40. Mark C. Hopson, *Notes from the Talking Drum: Exploring Black Communication and Critical Memory in Intercultural Communication Contexts* (Cresskill, NJ: Hampton Press, 2011).

41. Houston Baker, preface to *The Black Public Sphere: A Public Culture Book*, ed. The Black Public Sphere Collective (Chicago: University of Chicago Press, 1995), 13.

42. Houston Baker, *Blues, Ideology, and Afro-American Literature: A Vernacular Theory* (Chicago: University of Chicago Press, 1987).

43. Gerard Hauser, *Vernacular Voices: The Rhetoric of Publics and Public Spheres* (Columbia: University of South Carolina Press, 1999).

44. Mark Lawrence McPhail, "A Question of Character: Re(-)signing the Racial Contract," *Rhetoric and Public Affairs* 7, no. 3 (2004): 397–98.

Chapter 1

1. For a broader discussion on the fusion of spiritual and militant elements within African American rhetoric, see Mark Lawrence McPhail, "Dessentializing Difference: Transformative Visions in Contemporary Black Thought," *Howard Journal of Communication* 13, no. 1 (2002): 77–95.

2. For an estimate of the number of participants in reenactment, see Gigi Douban, "Fewer People Participate in Civil War Reenactments," NPR.org, July 4, 2001, accessed February 11, 2014, http://www.npr.org/2011/07/04/137609367/fewer-people-participate-in-civil-war-reenactments. See also Jim Cullen, *The Civil War in Popular Culture: A Reusable Past* (Washington, DC: Smithsonian Institution Scholarly Press, 1995) and Cathy Stanton and Stephen Belyea, "Their Time Will Yet Come: The African American Presence in Civil War Reenactment," in *Hope and Glory: Essays on the Legacy of the 54th Massachusetts Regiment*, ed. Martin

Blatt, Tom Brown, and Donald Yacovone (Amherst: University of Massachusetts Press, 2001), 253–74.

3. James Oscar Farmer, "Playing Rebels: Reenactment as Nostalgia and Defense of the Confederacy in the Battle of Aiken," *Southern Cultures* 11, no. 1 (2005): 46–73; Will Kaufman, *The Civil War in American Culture*, Baas Paperpacks (Edinburgh: Edinburgh University Press, 2006); Mitchell D. Strauss, "Identity Construction among Confederate Civil War Reenactors: A Study of Dress, Stage Props, and Discourse," *Clothing and Textiles Research Journal* 21, no. 4 (2003): 149–61.

4. Craig Thompson Friend and Lorri Glover, *Southern Manhood: Perspectives on Masculinity in the Old South* (Athens: University of Georgia Press, 2004). Also see Eichstedt and Small, *Representations of Slavery*, 29–30 and Stanton and Belyea, "Their Time Will Yet Come."

5. The sutlers' area at reenactments is the space where vendors sell food and souvenirs.

6. Leigh Clemons, "Present Enacting Past: The Functions of Battle Reenacting in Historical Representation," in *Enacting History*, ed. Scott Magelssen and Rhona Justice-Malloy (Tuscaloosa: University of Alabama Press, 2011), 10–21. Clemons also offers a discussion of the functioning of the hardcore/farb binary in reenactment, as does Tony Horwitz in Tony Horwitz, *Confederates in the Attic: Dispatches from the Unfinished Civil War* (New York: Vintage, 1999).

7. Juneteenth, also known as Emancipation day, refers to June 19, 1865, the date on which the slaves were freed in Texas. It is formally recognized in twenty-nine states and the District of Columbia and is typically commemorated with festivals, picnics, symposia, and other events.

8. In addition to African American men, this includes white women, who were allowed to participate after the successful litigation of a sex discrimination lawsuit against the National Park Service hinging on historical accuracy. While women are allowed to participate as military reenactors, they must abide by each site's "impressions standards" which, at times, include the requirement that they be indistinguishable as members of "the female gender at not less than fifteen feet." For more on this, see Kent Courtney, *Returning to the Civil War: Grand Reenactments of an Anguished Time* (Darby, PA: Diane Publishing Company, 1997), 71–82; Robert Lee Haden, *Reliving the Civil War: A Reenactor's Handbook* (Mechanicsburg, PA: Stackpole Books, 1999), 92–93; Farmer, "Playing Rebels," 64; Cullen, *The Civil War in Popular Culture*, 192–93; Leigh Stein, "I Would Have Followed Them into Battle: Female Reenactors Portray Women Who Passed as Men to Fight," Slate.com, April 27, 2014, accessed April 29, 2014, http://www.slate .com/articles/news_and_politics/history/2014/04/female_civil_war_re_enactors _portray_women_who_passed_as_men_to_fight.html.

9. The notion of *communitas* was elaborated on by Victor Turner in his theory of ritual action. Turner described it as a condition in which adherence to conventional hierarchical relationships is suspended in favor of a higher-level principle in order to advance the effectiveness of the ritual. See Victor Turner, *The Ritual Process: Structure and Anti-Structure* (Chicago: Aldine Transaction, 1995).

10. E. Patrick Johnson, "'Quare' Studies, or (Almost) Everything I Know about Queer Studies I Learned from My Grandmother," *Text and Performance Quarterly* 21, no. 1 (2001): 11.

11. Diana Taylor, *The Archive and the Repertoire: Performing Cultural Memory in the Americas* (Durham: Duke University Press, 2003).

12. Richard Bauman, "Verbal Acts as Performance," *American Anthropologist* 77, no. 2 (1975): 290–311. Also see Turner, *The Ritual Process*, 129.

13. Antonio Gramsci, "Observations on Folklore," in *An Antonio Gramsci Reader: Selected Writings, 1916–1935*, ed. David Forgacs (New York: Schocken Books Inc., 1988), 362.

14. Kirt Wilson, "The Racial Politics of Imitation in the Nineteenth Century," *Quarterly Journal of Speech* 89, no. 2 (2003): 102. It is important to note that mimesis, as a category of resistant performance, has traditionally been received with some ambivalence. Wilson notes that the racial politics of mimesis in the late nineteenth century included the notion that—in keeping with the assumptions of black inferiority characteristic of pseudoscientific discourse at the time—imitation was a "natural" African American quality, with imitative performances perceived as markers of racial difference. African American elites were similarly ambivalent about its value, believing that imitative practices more broadly share a tendency to undermine black creativity and autonomy and therefore hold limited appeal as a resistant practice.

15. Fredric Jameson offered a critique of pastiche, arguing that it represents mere imitation stripped of the subversive elements inherent in other mimetic forms, such as parody. See Fredric Jameson, *Postmodernism or the Cultural Logic of Late Capitalism* (Durham: Duke University Press, 1992). While this concern is valid, I argue that in the context of destabilizing hegemonic history pastiche serves an exceptionally useful purpose, as African American co-optation and celebration of dominant memory practices from which they were previously excluded reveals the socially constructed nature of the dominant assumptions implicit in these practices. Moreover, the selection of these expressions is not random, but is instead the result of strategically co-opted elements of dominant memory, drawn from the very infrastructural sources involved in its power.

16. Ibid., 23–25.

17. Stanton and Belyea, "Their Time Will Yet Come," 253–74.

18. Cullen, *The Civil War in Popular Culture*, 184.

19. Mikhail M. Bakhtin, *Rabelais and His World* (Bloomington: Indiana University Press, 1984).

20. Ronald L. Jackson II, *Scripting the Black Masculine Body: Identity, Discourse, and Racial Politics in Popular Media* (Albany: State University of New York Press, 2006).

21. Gail Buckley, *American Patriots: The Story of Blacks in the Military from the Revolution to Desert Storm* (New York: Random House, Inc., 2001).

22. Buckley, *American Patriots*, 59. Buckley also notes that black men had always been allowed to serve in the Navy; in the nineteenth century, to be at sea was considered to be a "desperate" job. However, pressure from southern congressmen led to the imposition of a 5 percent quota on weekly or monthly black enlistment. For more on the attempts of black men to enlist, see Van Gosse, "'Beyond Glory,'" *New York Times*, November 29, 2011, accessed February 10, 2014, http://opinionator.blogs.nytimes.com/2011/11/29.beyond-glory/. Also see Terry L. Jones, "The Free Men of Color Go to War," *New York Times*, October 19, 2012, ac-

cessed January 15, 2014, http://opinionator.blogs.nytimes.com/2012/10/19/the -free-men-of-color-go-to-war/.

23. Bruce Levine, "In Search of a Usable Past: Neo-Confederates and Black Confederates," in *Slavery and Public History: The Tough Stuff of American Memory*, eds. James Horton and Lois Horton (New York: The New Press, 2006): 187–212.

24. James McPherson, *Battle Cry of Freedom: The Civil War Era* (New York: Oxford University Press, 1988), 354.

25. Joseph P. Reidy, "The African American Struggle for Citizenship Rights in the Northern United States During the Civil War," in *Civil War Citizens: Race, Ethnicity, and Identity in America's Bloodiest Conflict*, ed. Susannah J. Ural (New York: New York University Press, 2010), 215.

26. William C. Davis, Brian C. Pohanka, and Don Troiani, *Civil War Journal*, vol. 3, *The Legacies* (Nashville: Rutledge Hill Press, 1999), 345; Rick Beard, "Organizing Black Soldiers," *New York Times*, May 31, 2013, accessed January 30, 2014, http://opinionator.blogs.nytimes.com/2013/05/31/organizing-black-soldiers/; Tera W. Hunter, "A Mother's Letter to Lincoln," *New York Times*, August 1, 2013, accessed January 30, 2014, http://opinionator.blogs.nytimes.com/2013/08/01/a -mothers-letter-to-lincoln/. Approximately twenty thousand black men served in the Navy, bringing the total numbers of black Civil War military servicemen to more than two hundred thousand. See Scott Hancock and Alexandra Milano, "The Real Rebels of the Civil War," *New York Times*, October 15, 2013, accessed Janaury 30, 2014, http://opinionator.blogs.nytimes.com/2013/10/15/the-real -rebels-of-the-civil-war/.

27. William C. Davis, Brian C. Pohanka, and Don Troiani *Civil War Journal*, vol. 2, *The Battles* (Nashville: Rutledge Hill Press, 1998); Beard, "Organizing Black Soldiers."

28. James McPherson, *The Negro's Civil War: How American Blacks Felt and Acted During the War for the Union* (New York: Vintage, 2003), 246; Noah Andre Trudeau, *Like Men of War: Black Troops in the Civil War, 1862–1865* (New York: Little Brown and Company, 1998), 414.

29. James McPherson, *Marching toward Freedom: Blacks in the Civil War 1861– 1865*, Library of American History (New York: Facts on File, 1991), 247–48. It should be noted that the war ended before black Confederates could begin fighting.

30. Ibid., 248.

31. William C. Davis, Brian C. Pohanka, and Toiani (1999), 345. Davis states that the USCT were not issued regimental flags but rather had special flags designed especially for them. Many of these were made by the artist David Bustill Bowser. For the Malone quote, see Noah Andre Trudeau, "Proven Themselves in Every Respect to be Men: Black Cavalry in the Civil War," in *Black Soldiers in Blue: African American Troops in the Civil War Era*, ed. John David Smith (Chapel Hill: University of North Carolina Press, 2002), 300. For the Long declaration, see Jack Foner, *Blacks and the Military in American History: A New Perspective* (Santa Barbara: Praeger Publishers, 1974), 51.

32. Foner, *Blacks and the Military*, 45.

33. James McPherson, *Marching toward Freedom*, 101–2.

34. Reidy, "The African American Struggle for Citizenship Rights," 216.

35. For details on the Dred Scott case, see Don Fehrenbacher, *The Dred Scott Case: Its Significance in American Law and Politics* (New York: Oxford University Press, 2001).

36. A disappointed Douglass later qualified these views, stating that he and others had overestimated the capacity of the government to extend full citizenship status and inclusion to blacks. See Hancock and Milano, "The Real Rebels."

37. Ervin L. Jordan Jr., *Black Confederates and Afro-Yankees in Civil War Virginia*, Nation Divided: New Studies in Civil War History (Charlottesville: University of Virginia Press, 1995), 237.

38. Thomas J. Ward, "The Plight of the Black POW," *New York Times*, August 27, 2013, accessed January 30, 2014, http://opinionator.blogs.nytimes.com/2013/08/27/the-plight-of-the-black-p-o-w/.

39. See "U.S. Civil War Colored Troops Medal" description at the National Museum of American History at www.americanhistory.si.edu/collections/object.cfm?key=35andobjkey=184.

40. Trudeau, "Proven Themselves in Every Respect to be Men," 465.

41. Riché Richardson, *Black Masculinity and the U.S. South: From Uncle Tom to Gangsta*, The New Southern Studies (Athens: University of Georgia Press, 2007).

42. Ibid.

43. Bryant Keith Alexander, "Passing, Cultural Performance, and Individual Agency: Performative Reflections on Black Masculine Identity," *Cultural Studies-Critical Methodologies* 4, no. 3 (2004): 377–404.

44. Chad L. Williams, *Torchbearers of Democracy: African American Soldiers in the World War I Era* (Chapel Hill: University of North Carolina Press, 2010).

45. For a detailed analysis of black women's cultural work as Civil War reenactors, see Patricia G. Davis, "The Other Southern Belles: Civil War Reenactment, African American Women, and the Performance of Idealized Femininity," *Text and Performance Quarterly* 32, no. 4 (2012): 308–31.

46. Kirk Fuoss, "Performance as Contestation: An Agonistic Perspective on the Insurgent Assembly," in *Exceptional Spaces: Essays in Performance and History*, ed. Della Pollock (Chapel Hill: University of North Carolina Press, 1998), 98–120.

47. Levine, "In Search of a Usable Past," 187–89.

48. Both here and throughout the remainder of the book, I utilize a conception of the public sphere that predominately borrows elements from Gerard Hauser's model of a public that is dialogic—e.g. one that foregrounds its rhetorical nature—but is also suggestive of Nancy Fraser's conception of subaltern counterpublic spheres, in which identity constitutes the primary formative structure. The nature of the sites I examine, along with the work that is performed within them, suggests that the two conceptions of the public sphere are not in tension with each other but rather coalesce to form a set of publics and counterpublics that exploit opportunities for dialog with dominant memory as a means of constructing identity. See Hauser, *Vernacular Voices* and Nancy Fraser, "Rethinking the Public Sphere: A Contribution to the Critique of Actually Existing Democracy," in *Habermas and the Public Sphere*, ed. Craig Calhoun (Cambridge: Massachusetts Institute of Technology Press, 1992), 109–42.

49. Harold Scheub, "Performance of Oral Narrative," in *Frontiers of Folklore*, ed. William Russell Bascom (Boulder: Westview Press, 1977), 54.

50. Jill Dolan, *Utopia in Performance: Finding Hope at the Theater* (Ann Arbor: University of Michigan Press, 2005), 91.

51. Eric King Watts, "Cultivating a Black Public Voice: W. E. B. Du Bois and the 'Criteria of Negro Art,'" *Rhetoric and Public Affairs* 4 no. 2 (2001): 181–201.

52. J. Christian Spielvogel, *Interpreting Sacred Ground: The Rhetoric of National Civil War Parks and Battlefields* (Tuscaloosa: University of Alabama Press, 2013).

53. There is a rather significant community of individual collectors of these items; they can also be seen on display in museums and for sale in gift shops, with prices determined by—among other things—which side used them, whether or not they were spent, the type of gun from which they were fired, and their present condition.

54. Claude Lévi-Strauss, "Introduction à l'œuvre de Marcel Mauss," in Marcel Mauss, *Sociologie et anthropologie: Précedé d'une introduction à l'œuvre de Marcel Mauss* (Paris: Presses Universitaires de France, 1950), cited in David Chidester and Edward T. Linenthal, "Introduction," in *American Sacred Space*, eds. David Chidester and Edward T. Linenthal (Bloomington: Indiana University Press, 1995), 6.

55. Chidester and Linenthal, "Introduction," 7; David Harvey, *The Condition of Postmodernity: An Enquiry into the Origins of Cultural Change* (Malden: Wiley-Blackwell, 1989).

56. Edward Linenthal, *Sacred Ground: Americans and their Battlefields* (Champaign: University of Illinois Press, 1993), 89.

57. See the website of the National Park Service at http://www.nps.gov/history/hps/abpp/battles/tvii.htm#sites, accessed October 1, 2008.

58. Chidester and Linenthal, "Introduction," 26.

59. Linenthal, 69

60. Dwight T. Pitcaithley, "'A Cosmic Threat'": The National Park Service Addresses the Causes of the American Civil War," in *Slavery and Public History: The Tough Stuff of American Memory*, eds. James Oliver Horton and Lois Horton (Chapel Hill: University of North Carolina Press 2008), 172.

61. Ibid.

62. Jonathan Z. Smith, "The Wobbling Pivot," in *Map is Not Territory: Studies in the History of Religions* (Chicago: University of Chicago Press, 1995), 88–103, cited in Chidester and Linenthal, "Introduction," 6.

63. David Blight, *Beyond the Battlefield: Race Memory, and the American Civil War* (Amherst: University of Massachusetts Press, 2002), 178.

64. Chidester and Linenthal, "Introduction," 1.

65. The assault at Battery Wagner, which was led by the Fifty-Fourth Massachusetts on July 11, 1863, is considered by many reenactors to have been one of the most crucial battles in which the USCT had to prove their mettle. It is also the battle in which Robert Gould Shaw, the commander of the Fifty-Fourth, was killed.

66. See the United States Census Bureau demographic estimate for 2014. United States Census Bureau, "Petersburg City Quick Facts," accessed November 3, 2015, http://quickfacts.census.gov/qfd/states/51/51730.html.

67. For a detailed historical analysis of the Battle of the Crater, see Richard Slotkin, *No Quarter: The Battle of the Crater, 1864* (New York: Random House, 2009).

68. See the United States Census Bureau 2014 demographic estimate for Chattanooga. United States Census Bureau, accessed November 3, 2015, http://quickfacts.census.gov/qfd/states/47/4714000.html.

69. See "The Civil War Sites Advisory Commission Report on the Nation's Civil War Battlefields, Technical Volume II: Battle Summaries," Heritage Preservation Services, National Park Service, accessed October 29, 2008, http://www.nps.gov/hps/abpp/battles/tvii.htm.

70. Foner, *Blacks and the Military*, 45.

71. This is not to discount the discursive value of memories of defeat, which are also quite productive in forming societies' understandings of themselves. For the South in particular, memories emphasizing chivalry in defeat—with respect both to specific battles and to the broader war—helped lay the foundation for the emergence of the Lost Cause premise of a glorious civilization going down in defeat to a crass and immoral but better-equipped enemy and invoke the promise of regional redemption. As such, they are a crucial component of the rhetorical construction and maintenance of traditional southern identity. For a detailed analysis of the social value of narratives of defeat, see Wolfgang Schivelbusch, *The Culture of Defeat: On National Trauma, Mourning, and Recovery* (New York: Picador, 2004). For a detailed discussion of the utility of the redemption narrative in southern memory, see Goldfield, *Still Fighting the Civil War*.

72. Arthur W. Bergeron Jr., "The Battle of Olustee," in Smith, *Black Soldiers in Blue*, 136–37.

73. Ibid.

74. Lizette Alvarez, "Blue and Gray Still in Conflict at a Battle Site," *New York Times*, January 16, 2014, accessed on January 17, 2014, http://www.nytimes.com/2014/01/17/us/blue-and-gray-still-in-conflict-at-a-battle-site/; Margie Menzel, "Civil War Passions Still Run Deep as Union Supporters Propose Monument on Confederate Site," *Miami Herald*, December 3, 2013, accessed January 23, 2014, http://miamiherald.typepad.com/nakedpolitics/2013/12.civil-war-passions-still-run-deep-as-union-supporters/propose-monument-on-confederate-site/; Fred Grimm, "In Florida, When it Comes to Race and the Confederacy, the Past is Never Past," *Miami Herald*, December 31, 2013, accessed January 23, 2014, http://www.miamiherald.com/2013/12/31/v-print/3831619/in-florida-when-it-comes-to-race-and-the-confederacy-the-past-is-never-past/. More re-cently, HB 493, a bill designed to remove the decision on the proposed monument from local officials to the state legislature has passed two of the three committee votes it needs to advance to the governor. See Bruce Ritchie, "Bill Prompted by Outcry against Union Monument on Civil War Battlefield Narrowly Passes," The FloridaCurrent.com, March 24, 2014, accessed April 2, 2014, http://www.thefloridacurrent.com/article.cfm?id=36958041. Also see Margie Menzel, "House Bill Would Give Lawmakers Final Say on Park Monuments," *News Service of Florida*, March 24, 2014, accessed April 2, 2014, http://www.news4jax.com/politics/house-bill-would-give-lawmakers-final-say-on-park-monuments/25146156; "Florida Civil War Battle on the 'Back Burner,'" accessed November 3, 2015, http://wusfnews.wusf.usf.edu/post/fl-civil-war-battle-conflict-back-burner#stream/0.

75. The League of the South, founded in 1994 by former college professor Michael Hill, is a self-proclaimed "southern nationalist" organization. Leaders of the organization have produced written material and made numerous public pro-

nouncements attempting to erase slavery as a cause of the war. It is listed by the Southern Poverty Law Center as a neo-Confederate hate group.

76. K. Michael Prince, "Neo-Confederates in the Basement: The League of the South and the Crusade Against Southern Emasculation," in *White Masculinity in the Recent South*, ed. Trent Watts (Baton Rouge: Louisiana State University Press, 2008), 146–71.

77. For details, see "The Stonewall of Forks Road," Cape Fear Historical Institute Papers, accessed January 15, 2014, www.cfhi.net/TheBattleofForksRoad .php.

78. William G. Robertson, "From the Crater to New Market Heights: A Tale of Two Divisions," in *Black Soldiers in Blue*, 169–73. Also see Richard M. Reid, *Freedom for Themselves: North Carolina's Black Soldiers in the Civil War Era* (Chapel Hill: University of North Carolina Press, 2008), 162.

79. It should be noted that Turner, one of the most influential African American leaders of his day, served many public roles, including serving as the first southern bishop of the AME Church. For more on his role during the war, see Edwin S. Redkey, "Henry McNeal Turner: Black Chaplain in the Union Army," in *Black Soldiers in Blue*, 345–46.

80. The Buffalo Soldiers were an army unit of USCT veterans, freedmen, and former slaves who served in the American west during the peacetime period after the Civil War. Many would later serve in the Spanish-American war.

Chapter 2

1. It is important to note that the website for the plantation does include a discussion of the slaves whose labor was critical to its functioning. However, Internet tourist descriptions and face-to-face tourist descriptions are distinct discourses—inclusions and exclusions in one have little bearing on those in the other.

2. Eichstedt and Small, *Representations of Slavery*. Eichstedt and Small borrow the term "social forgetting" from Iwona Irwin-Zarecka, *Frames of Remembrance: The Dynamics of Collective Memory* (New Brunswick: Transaction Publishers, 1994).

3. Michael S. Bowman, "Performing Southern History for the Tourist Gaze: Antebellum Home Tour Guide Performances," in *Exceptional Spaces: Essays in Performance and History*, ed. Della Pollock (Chapel Hill: University of North Carolina Press, 1998), 148.

4. Derek Alderman, "Introduction to the Special Issue: African Americans and Tourism," *Tourism Geographies* 15, no. 3 (2013): 375–79.

5. See Paul A. Shackel, *Memory in Black and White: Memory, Commemoration, and the Post-bellum Landscape* (Lanham: AltaMita Press, 2003), 16 and Craig Barton, "Foreword," in *Sites of Memory: Perspectives on Architecture and Race*, ed. Craig Barton (New York: Princeton Architectural Press, 2001), xiv.

6. Richard Hoelscher, "The White-Pillared Past: Landscapes of Memory and Race in the American South," in *Race and Landscape in America*, ed. Richard Schein (New York: Routledge, 2006).

7. Kirk Savage, *Standing Soldiers, Kneeling Slaves: Race, War, and Monument in 19th Century America* (Princeton: Princeton University Press, 1997), 3.

8. For a detailed historical account of the UDC Confederate memorial cam-

paigns, see Karen L. Cox, *Dixie's Daughters: The United Daughters of the Confederacy and the Preservation of Confederate Culture* (Gainesville: University Press of Florida, 2003).

9. Shackel, *Memory in Black and White*, 39, 86–94.

10. W. Fitzhugh Brundage, *The Southern Past: A Clash of Race and Memory* (Cambridge: Belknap Press of Harvard University Press, 2005).

11. Barry Schwartz, *Abraham Lincoln and the Forge of National Memory* (Chicago: University of Chicago Press, 2003), 15.

12. On the 150th anniversary of the start of the Civil War, a 2011 Pew Center survey found that 22 percent of self-identified southern whites react positively when they see the Confederate flag displayed, compared with just 4 percent of whites who do not consider themselves southerners. See "Civil War at 150." See also Steve Suitts, "Voting Rights, the Supreme Court, and the Persistence of Southern History," *Southern Spaces*, June 4, 2013, accessed February 20, 2014, http://southernspaces.org/2013/voting-rights-supreme-court-and-persistence-southern-history#sthash.qBGrR5Gf.dpuf. For a detailed history of the twentieth- and twenty-first-century public battles over state-sanctioned displays of the flag, see John Coski, *The Confederate Battle Flag: America's Most Embattled Emblem* (Cambridge: Harvard University Press, 2005).

13. Geoffrey Cubitt, Laurajane Smith, and Ross Wilson, "Introduction: Anxiety and Ambiguity in the Representation of Dissonant History," in *Representing Enslavement and Abolition in Museums*, eds. Laurajane Smith et al. (New York: Routledge, 2011).

14. For more on "humiliated silences" and other types of "forgetting," see Connerton, "Seven Types of Forgetting."

15. Jacqueline Trescott, "African American Civil War Museum Celebrates Reopening in Larger Location," *Washington Post*, July 8, 2011, accessed May 13, 2013, http://www.washingtonpost.com/lifestyle/style/african-american-civil-war-museum-celebrates-reopening-in-larger-location/2011/06/30/gIQApPjb1H_story.html.

16. Ivan Karp, "Introduction: Museums and Communities: The Politics of Public Culture," in *Museums and Communities: The Politics of Public Culture*, eds. Ivan Karp, Christine Mullen Kreamer, and Steven D. Lavine (Washington: Smithsonian Institution Press, 1992), 6.

17. Spencer Crew, "African Americans, History, and Museums: Preserving African American History in the Public Arena," in *Making Histories in Museums*, ed. Gaynor Kavanagh (New York: Leicester University Press, 1996), 80.

18. Ibid., 80.

19. Ibid., 83.

20. Brundage, *The Southern Past*, 302.

21. James Oliver Horton, "Slavery in American History: An Uncomfortable National Dialogue," in Horton and Horton, *Slavery and Public History*, 37.

22. Ira Berlin, "Coming to Terms with Slavery in Twenty-First Century America," in Horton and Horton, *Slavery and Public History*, 1–18.

23. Jeffrey Stewart and Faith Davis Ruffins, "A Faithful Witness: Afro-American History in Historical Perspective, 1828–1994," in *Presenting the Past: Essays on History and the Public*, eds. Susan Porter Benson, Stephen Brier, and Roy Rosenzweig (Philadelphia: Temple University Press, 1986); James Oliver Horton and Spencer

Crew, "Afro-Americans and Museums: Towards a Policy of Inclusion," in *History Museums in the United States: A Critical Assessment*, eds. Warren Leon and Roy Rosenzweig (Champaign: University of Illinois Press, 1998), 217.

24. John Michael Vlach, "The Last Great Taboo Subject: Exhibiting Slavery at the Library of Congress," in Horton and Horton, *Slavery and Public History*, 57–74.

25. George Fredrickson, *The Black Image in the White Mind: The Debate on Afro-American Character and Destiny, 1817–1914* (New York: Harper and Row, 1971), 61.

26. In December 1862 Fredericksburg and its surrounding areas were the sites of the Battle of Fredericksburg between the Army of Northern Virginia (led by Robert E. Lee) and the Union Army of the Potomac (led by Ambrose Burnside).

27. See Stephen P. Hanna, "A Slavery Museum: Race, Memory, and Landscape in Fredericksburg, Virginia," *Southeastern Geographer* 48, no. 3 (2008): 316–37.

28. As of March 2013, though the city had taken steps to sell the land on which the museum was supposed to be built, the attorneys for its organizers maintain that the project will proceed. In 2014 founder Wilder published an editorial in the *Richmond Times-Dispatch*, in which he revealed his tentative plans to locate the museum in Richmond (which was one of the initially proposed sites before Fredericksburg was ultimately chosen). For details, see L. Douglas Wilder, "Wilder: Locate the Slavery Museum in Shockoe," *Richmond Times-Dispatch*, February 26, 2014, accessed March 27, 2014, http://www.timesdispatch.com/opinion/their -opinion/columnists-blogs/guest-columnists/wilder-locate-the-slavery-museum -in-shockoe/article_fcbe76a9–586c-5d13–8b98–95b8f7579876.html.

29. Berlin, "Coming to Terms with Slavery," 3.

30. Ibid., 2.

31. See for example Flora Kaplan, "Exhibitions as Communicative Media," in *Museum, Media, Message*, ed. Eileen Hooper-Greenhill (New York: Routledge, 1995), 37–58; Kevin Heatherington, "Manchester's Urbis: Urban Regeneration, Museums, and Symbolic Economies," *Cultural Studies* 21, nos. 4–5, (2007): 630–49; Laura Peers and Allison K. Brown, "Museums and Source Communities," in *Museums and Their Communities*, ed. Sheila Watson, (New York: Routledge, 2007), 519–37 and Gaea Leinhardt and Karen Knutson, *Listening In on Museum Conversations* (Walnut Creek: AltaMira Press, 2004).

32. Richard Sandell, ed. *Museums, Society, Inequality* (New York: Routledge, 2002). Also see Richard Sandell, *Museums, Prejudice, and the Reframing of Difference* (New York: Routledge, 2006).

33. Roy Rosenzweig and David Thelen, *The Presence of the Past: Popular Uses of History in American Life* (New York: Columbia University Press, 1998), 43.

34. Karp, "Introduction: Museums and Communities," 1, 4.

35. Elizabeth Crooke, "Museums, Communities, and the Politics of Heritage in Northern Ireland," in Watson, *Museums and their Communities*, 300–312.

36. Sheila Watson, "Introduction to Part Three," in Watson, *Museums and Their Communities*, 269.

37. Salome Kilkenny, "Travel and Tourism," *The Network Journal: Black Professionals and Small Business News*, accessed March 12, 2014, http://www.tnj.com /departments/industry-focus/travel-and-tourism-1; Angela da Silva, "African American Heritage Tourism," *Preservation Issues* 7, no. 3 (1997), accessed March 12, 2014, http://law.wustl.edu/staff/taylor/preserv/v7n3/afamtour.htm. For more on the integration of the experiences of slaves into southern heritage tourism,

Stephen Small offers an excellent discussion of the ways in which tours of ante-bellum slave cabins have either been incorporated or are still marginalized from plantation tours. See Small, "Still Back of the Big House." For a more general discussion on the reordering of southern heritage tourism to include the histories of African Americans, see Dwyer, Butler and Carter, "Commemorative Surrogation"; Owen Dwyer and Derek Alderman, *Civil Rights Memorials and the Geography of Memory* (Athens: University of Georgia Press, 2008); Owen Dwyer and Derek Alderman, "Memorial Landscapes: Analytic Questions and Metaphors, *GeoJournal*, 73, no. 3, (2008): 165–78; Renee C. Romano and Leigh Raiford, *The Civil Rights Movement in American Memory* (Athens: University of Georgia Press, 2006).

38. Mary Foster, "Civil War Museums Changing as View on War Changes, "*The Grio*, January 8, 2012, accessed January 18, 2014, http://thegrio.com/2012/01/09/civil-war-museums-changing-as-view-on-war-changes/.

39. Cubitt, Smith, and Wilson, "Introduction: Anxiety and Ambiguity."

40. Carole Blair, "Contemporary U.S. Memorial Sites as Exemplars of Rhetoric's Materiality," in *Rhetorical Bodies*, eds. Jack Selzer and Sharon Crowley (Madison: University of Wisconsin Press, 1999), 18. Also see Blair, Dickinson, and Ott, "Introduction," 2 .

41. Kenneth Zagacki and Victoria Gallagher, "Rhetoric and Materiality in the Museum Park at the North Carolina Museum of Art," *Quarterly Journal of Speech* 95, no. 2, (2009): 172.

42. See for example Victoria Gallagher and Margaret LaWare, "Sparring with Public Memory: The Rhetorical Embodiment of Race, Power, and Conflict in the Monument to Joe Louis," in Blair, Dickinson, and Ott, 87–112 and Gregory Clark, "Rhetorical Experience and the National Jazz Museum in Harlem," in Blair, Dickinson, and Ott, "Introduction," 113–39.

43. Kaplan, "Exhibitions as Communicative Media," 59–71.

44. Geoffrey Cubitt, "Atrocity Materials and the Representation of Transatlantic Slavery," in Smith et al., *Representing Enslavement*, 229.

45. See Derek H. Alderman and Rachel M. Campbell, "Symbolic Excavation and Artifact Politics of Remembering Slavery in the American South," *Southeastern Geographer* 48, no. 3, (2008): 352. Also see Don Mitchell, *Cultural Geography: A Critical Introduction* (Malden, MA: Blackwell Publishers, 2000).

46. For more on "compassion fatigue" and other risks associated with the display of "atrocity materials," see Cubitt, "Atrocity Materials," 230. For a more detailed discussion of the potential of these objects to inspire in visitors a sense of African American resilience, see Alderman and Campbell, "Symbolic Excavation," 350–51.

47. Garry Wills, *Lincoln at Gettysburg: The Words That Remade America* (New York: Simon and Schuster, 1992).

48. Alan Radley, "Artefacts, Memory, and a Sense of the Past," in *Collective Remembering*, eds. David Middleton and Derek Edwards (Thousand Oaks: SAGE Publications, 1990), 47.

49. Hadwig Krautler, "Observations on Semiotic Aspects of the Museum Work of Otto Neurath: Reflections on the 'Bildpadagogische Schriften,'" in Hooper-Greenhill, *Museum, Media, Message*, 64.

50. Sheldon Annis, "The Museum as a Staging Ground for Symbolic Action," *Museum* 151 (1987), 168–71. Also see Gaynor Kavanagh, *Dream Spaces: Memory and the Museum* (New York: Leicester University Press, 2002), 2.

51. Tamar Katriel, "Our Future is Where Our Past is: Studying Heritage Museums as Ideological and Performative Arenas," *Communication Monographs* 60, no. 1 (1993): 69–75. Also see Tamar Katriel and Aliza Shenhar, "Tower and Stockade: Dialogic Narration in Israeli Settlement Ethos," *Quarterly Journal of Speech* 76, no. 4 (1990): 359–80.

52. Deborah F. Atwater and Sandra L. Herndon, "Cultural Space and Race: The National Civil Rights Museum and MuseumAfrica," *Howard Journal of Communication* 14, no. 1 (2003): 15–28.

53. Brian L. Ott and Greg Dickinson, "Visual Rhetoric and/as Critical Pedagogy," in *The Sage Handbook of Rhetorical Studies*, eds. Andrea A. Lunsford, Kirt H. Wilson, and Rosa A. Eberly (Los Angeles: SAGE Publications, 2009), 391–406.

54. David Glassberg, "Public History and the Study of Memory," *The Public Historian* 18, no. 2 (1996): 17.

55. Les Back, "Home from 'Home': Youth, Belonging, and Place," in *Making Race Matter: Bodies, Space, and Identity*, eds. Claire Alexander and Caroline Knowles (New York: Palgrave MacMillan, 2005), 19.

56. Barton, "Foreword."

57. Stephen Legg, "Sites of Counter-Memory: The Refusal to Forget and the Nationalist Struggle in Colonial Delhi," *Historical Geography* 33, (2005): 180–201, quoted in Derek Alderman, "Surrogation and the Politics of Remembering Slavery in Savannah, Georgia," *Journal of Historical Geography* 36, no. 1 (2010): 90.

58. Urban centers, with their dense populations and complex economic and social forces, are storehouses for the production of shared memory and time, as the landscapes connecting the streets, buildings, and patterns of settlement frame the lives of many different people. See Dolores Hayden, *The Power of Place: Urban Landscapes as Public History* (Cambridge: Massachusetts Institute of Technology Press, 1999). For more on the co-dependence of museums and cities, please see Eric Gable, "The City, Race, and the Creation of a Common History at the Virginia Historical Society," in *Museums, and Communities: Curators, Collections, and Collaboration*, eds. Viv Golding and Wayne Modest (London: Bloomsbury, 2013).

59. Blair, Dickinson, and Ott, "Introduction," 27.

60. Katriel, "Our Future is Where Our Past is," 69–75. Also see Alderman and Campbell, "Symbolic Excavation," 348–49 and Scott Magelssen, "Living History Museums and the Construction of the Real through Performance," *Theatre Survey* 45, no. 1, (2004): 61–74.

61. Taylor, *The Archive and the Repertoire.*

62. Susan Evans, "Personal Beliefs and National Stories: Theater in Museums as a Tool for Exploring Historical Memory," *Curator: The Museum Journal* 56, no. 2 (2013): 189–90.

63. A. Susan Owen and Peter Ehrenhaus, "The Moore's Ford Lynching Reenactment: Affective Memory and Race Trauma," *Text and Performance Quarterly* 34, no. 1 (2014): 86. Also see Dwight Conquergood, "Ethnography, Rhetoric, and Performance," *Quarterly Journal of Speech* 78, no. 1 (1992): 80–81.

64. Carel Bertram, "Housing the Symbolic Universe in Early Republican

Turkey: Architecture, Memory, and the 'Felt Real,'" in *Memory and Architecture*, ed. Eleni Bastea (Albuquerque: University of New Mexico Press, 2004): 165.

65. For more detailed analyses on corporeality, narrative, representation, and rhetoric, see Daniel Punday, *Narrative Bodies: Toward a Corporeal Narratology* (New York: Palgrave MacMillan, 2003) and Jack Selzer and Sharon Crowley, eds., *Rhetorical Bodies* (Madison: University of Wisconsin Press, 1999).

66. See Jackson, *Scripting the Black Masculine Body*, 54.

67. Having served as sister institutions for many years, the two museums merged in late 2013. The combined institution is now called The American Civil War Museum, with the Tredegar and Confederate White House located in Richmond, and the Museum of the Confederacy located in Appomattox.

68. Here I use the definition of discourse articulated by Patricia Hill Collins as well as the definition of discourse and interdiscursivity delineated by Louise J. Phillips and Marianne W. Jorgensen. See Patricia Hill Collins, *Black Sexual Politics: African Americans, Gender, and the New Racism* (New York: Routledge, 2005) and Marianne W. Jorgensen and Louise J. Phillips, *Discourse Analysis as Theory and Method* (Walnut Creek: SAGE, 2002).

69. The Corps d'Afrique was a USCT unit formed in New Orleans and comprised primarily of free men, many of whom were of creole descent.

70. See Courtland Milloy, "African American Civil War Museum Dedication Honors Black Soldiers," *Washington Post*, July 17, 2011, accessed March 15, 2014, https://www.washingtonpost.com/local/african-american-civil-war-museum-dedication-honors-black-soldiers/2011/07/17/gIQA5IAZKI_story.html.

71. Marie Tyler-McGraw, "Southern Comfort Levels: Race, Heritage Toursim, and the Civil War in Richmond, " in Horton and Horton, *Slavery and Public History*, 153. Historian Charles Reagan Wilson described Richmond as the "Mecca of the Lost Cause." See Charles Reagan Wilson, *Judgment and Grace in Dixie: Southern Faiths from Folklore to Elvis* (Athens: University of Georgia Press, 2007).

72. Jonathon Leib, "Separate Times, Shared Spaces: Arthur Ashe, Monument Avenue, and the Politics of Richmond, Virginia's Symbolic Landscape," *Cultural Geographies*, 9, no. 3 (2002): 286–312.

73. For details on the political conflict over the Ashe statue on Monument Avenue, see Leib, "Separate Times." For more on the tensions over the Lee mural, see Carrie Johnson, "Put Lee on Floodwall, Panel Says, General's Image is Revised, El-Amin's Opposition," *Richmond Times Dispatch*, July 1, 1999, Area/State.

74. Carrie Johnson, "Tested in War, Preserving the Past; Tredegar Iron Works to Play Another Role in History," *Richmond Times Dispatch*, April 20, 2000, Area/State, B-1.

75. Allen Tullos, "Selma Bridge: Always under Construction," *Southern Spaces*, July 28, 2008, accessed May 4, 2014, http://southernspaces.org/2008/selma-bridge-always-under-construction. It is also notable that Edmund Pettus, the man for whom the bridge was named, was a prominent Confederate general. In June 2015, a grassroots campaign was initiated with the goal of changing the name of the bridge. For more on this, please see "Proposal to Rename Edmund Pettus Bridge Dies in House," accessed November 1, 2015, http://www.montgomeryadvertiser

.com/story/news/politics/southunionstreet/2015/06/05/proposal-rename-edmund
-pettus-bridge-dies-house/28537757/.

76. See "Selma Ordnance and Naval Foundry," in *Encyclopedia of Alabama*, accessed April 18, 2014, http://www.encyclopediaofalabama.org/face/Article.jsp?id=h-2331.

77. See the United States Census Bureau, "American Factfinder," accessed March 12, 2014, http://factfinder2.census.gov/faces/tableservices/jsf/pages/productview.xhtml?pid=ACS_12_5YR_DP05.

78. Nathan Bedford Forrest is a controversial historic figure, and not only because of his role as a Confederate general and later, as one of the founders of the Ku Klux Klan. He is also alleged to have presided over the massacre of a group of surrendering African American Union soldiers at Fort Pillow, Henning, Tennessee, on April 12, 1864, although some historians continue to dispute the veracity of this account. For details on the controversy over the monument, see "Nathan Bedford Forrest Monument—Selma, Alabama," ExploreSouthernHistory.com, accessed April 26, 2014, http://www.exploresouthernhistory.com/selmaforrest.html.

79. Karen L. Cox, "The Confederate Monument at Arlington: A Token of Reconciliation," in *Monuments to the Lost Cause: Women, Art, and the Landscape of Southern Memory*, eds. Cynthia Mills and Pamela H. Simpson (Knoxville: University of Tennessee Press, 2003), 158.

80. The term "nadir" as a descriptor for the period was first coined by historian Rayford Logan in *The Negro in American Life and Thought: The Nadir, 1877–1901*. It has been used to describe the era from the end of Reconstruction to the early- to mid-twentieth century during which white supremacist ideology in all areas of public life was sanctioned by social, cultural, and legal structures. The term has since been used by numerous academics to describe the period, with variations as to its range. See Rayford Logan, *The Negro in American Life and Thought: The Nadir, 1877–1901* (New York: Dial Press, 1954).

81. It should be noted that, though the tradition of sending a wreath to the monument on Memorial Day began with Harding, the structure itself was ceremonially dedicated beginning with Woodrow Wilson in 1914, with the wreath-laying ceremony—held on Confederate Memorial Day (Jefferson Davis's birthday) in June—also beginning with Wilson in 1919. Many thus attribute the beginning of the tradition to Wilson's 1914 ceremony. In the intervening years, several presidents, beginning with Harry S. Truman in 1949, have occasionally declined to send the wreath. For the full text of the letter, see "Text of Letter to President Obama," accessed April 30, 2014, http://abcnews.go.com/US/Story?id=7658404&page=1.

Chapter 3

1. See the NMAAHC website at http://nmaahc.si.edu/About/History.

2. The museum accepted and posted entries to the site from 2007 to 2011. Its success prompted administrators to temporarily suspend the acceptance of entries in order to create a new platform to enhance its capacities. According to its administrators, the site will resume accepting and posting entries in 2016, in an-

ticipation of the opening of the physical museum. For more, see the *Memory Book* website at http://nmaahc.si.edu/programs/memorybook.

3. Andrew Hoskins, "The Mediatisation of Memory," in *Save as . . . Digital Memories*, eds. Joanne Garde-Hansen, Andrew Hoskins, and Anna Reading (New York: Palgrave-Macmillan, 2009), 28–29.

4. Dara Byrne, "Public Discourse, Community Concerns, and Civic Engagement: Exploring Black Social Networking Traditions on Blackplanet.com," in *Journal of Computer-Mediated Communication* 13, no. 1 (2007): 16, accessed September 23, 2008, http://jcmc.indiana.edu/vol13/issue1/byrne.html. Also see Elizabeth Lindsay Davis, *Lifting as They Climb* (New York: G. K. Hall, 1996).

5. See Anthony Giddens, *Modernity and Self-Identity: Self and Society in the Late Modern Age* (Palo Alto: Stanford University Press, 1991), 54.

6. Nellie McKay, "The Journals of Charlotte L. Forten-Grimke: *Les Lieux de Memoire* in African-American Women's Autobiography," in *History and Memory in African American Culture*, eds. Genevieve Fabre and Robert O'Meally (New York: Oxford University Press, 1994), 262–63.

7. Ibid.

8. DoVeanna Fulton, *Speaking Power: Black Feminist Orality in Women's Narratives of Slavery* (Albany: State University of New York Press, 2006), 1–2.

9. William L. Andrews, *African American Autobiography: A Collection of Critical Essays* (Englewood Cliffs: Prentice Hall, 1993).

10. Marion Starling, "The Slave Narrative: Its Place in American Literary History," (PhD diss., New York University, 1946), cited in Frances Smith Foster, *Witnessing Slavery* (Madison, WI: University of Wisconsin Press, 1979), 21. Foster contends that the estimate of six thousand narratives is contingent upon a broad definition of "slave narrative" that includes court records and broadsides as well as interviews. She also suggests that if the number were to include only those narratives of those legally enslaved in the United States, it would be considerably smaller.

11. Johnnie M. Stover, *Rhetoric and Resistance in Black Women's Autobiography* (Gainesville: University Press of Florida, 2003), 4.

12. Fulton, *Speaking Power*, 3.

13. Frances Smith Foster, *Witnessing Slavery*, 9.

14. Paul D. Escott, *Slavery Remembered: A Record of Twentieth Century Slave Narratives* (Chapel Hill: University of North Carolina Press, 1979).

15. Sherry Turkle, *Life on the Screen: Identity in the Age of the Internet* (New York: Simon and Shuster, 1995). Also see Dara Byrne, "The Future of (the) 'Race': Identity, Discourse, and the Rise of Computer-Mediated Public Spheres," in *Learning Race and Ethnicity: Youth and Digital Media*, ed. Anna Everett (Cambridge: Massachusetts Institute of Technology Press, 2008): 15.

16. Beth Kolko, Lisa Nakamura and Gilbert Rodman, "Introduction," in *Race in Cyberspace*, eds. Beth Kolko, Lisa Nakamura and Gilbert Rodman (New York: Routledge, 2000), 5; Danah Boyd, "Sexing the Internet: Reflections on the Role of Identification in Online Communities" (paper presented at the Sexualities, Medias, Technologies conference, University of Surrey, June 21–22, 2001).

17. Byrne, "The Future of (the) 'Race,'" 15.

18. For a more in-depth discussion of the Internet as a set of spaces for a va-

riety of African American counterpublics and a consideration of the limits of the Habermasian model, see Anna Everett, *Digital Diaspora: A Race for Cyberspace* (Albany: State University of New York Press, 2009).

19. Daniel Palmer, "Emotional Archives: Online Photo Sharing and the Cultivation of the Self," *Photographies* 3, no. 2 (2010): 155–71.

20. See Thomas Vander Wal, "Folksonomy," Vanderwal.net, 2007, accessed May 5, 2014, https://www.google.com/search?q=thomas+vander+walandie=utf -8andoe=utf-8andaq=tandrls=org.mozilla:en-US:officialandclient=firefox-a.

21. Nicholas Mirzoeff, "On Visuality," *Journal of Visual Culture* 5, no. 1 (2006): 53–79.

22. Mark Warshauer, "'Language, Identity, and the Internet," in *Race in Cyberspace*, eds. Beth E. Kolko, Lisa Nakamura, and Gilbert B. Rodman (New York: Routledge, 2000), 151–70.

23. Elinor Ochs, "Constructing Social Identity: A Language Socialization Perspective," *Research on Language and Social Interaction*, 26, no. 3 (1993): 287–306.

24. Lisa Yoneyama, "For Transformative Knowledge and Postnationalist Public Spheres: The Smithsonian *Enola Gay* Controversy," in *Perilous Memories: The Asia-Pacific War(s)*, eds. T. Fujitani, Geoffrey M. White, and Lisa Yoneyama (Durham: Duke University Press), 331.

25. Dara Byrne, "The Future of (the) 'Race'." Also see Ellen Gay Detlefsen, "Where am I to go? Use of the Internet for Consumer Health Information by Two Vulnerable Communities," *Library Trends* 53 no. 2, (2004): 283–300 and Byron Burkhalter, "Reading Race Online: Discovering Racial Identity in Usenet Discussions," in *Communities in Cyberspace*, eds. Marc A. Smith and Peter Kollock (London: Routledge, 1999), 60–75.

26. Adam Banks, *Race, Rhetoric, and Technology: Searching for Higher Ground* (London: Routledge, 2006), 40.

27. Tara McPherson, "I'll take My Stand in Dixie-Net: White Guys, the South, and Cyberspace," in *Race in Cyberspace*, eds. Beth E. Kolko, Lisa Nakamura, and Gilbert B. Rodman (New York: Routledge, 2000), 123. The differences between black and white southern "cyberplaces" invokes the Foucauldian conception of "effective history," in which a historical sense contends with events not in terms of specific battles but rather in terms evocative of the "reversal of a relationship of forces, the usurpation of power, the appropriation of a vocabulary turned against those who had once used it" as means of disrupting the traditional foundations of the self. It is, essentially, the recovered history of the repressed. Foucault contrasts this to what he refers to as Platonic history, which may be thought of as the mythological history of the "winners" used to maintain their dominance over the repressed. The divergent cyberplaces may thus be positioned as African American effective history versus neo-Confederate Platonic history. See Michel Foucault, "Nietzsche, Genealogy, History," in *The Foucault Reader*, ed. Paul Rabinow (New York: Pantheon), 88.

28. Paul Marty, "Museum Informatics," in *Encyclopedia of Library and Information Science*, 3rd ed., eds. M. J. Bates and M. N. Maack (New York: Taylor and Francis, 2010), 3717–25.

29. Paul Marty and Katherine Burton Jones, *Museum Informatics: People, Information, and Technologies in Museums* (London: Routledge, 2008); Paul Marty,

"Museum Websites and Museum Visitors: Digital Museum Resources and Their Use," *Museum Management and Curatorship* 23, no. 1, (2008): 81–99; Fiona Cameron, "Digital Futures 1: Museum Collections, Digital Technologies, and the Cultural Construction of Knowledge," *Curator,* 46, (2003), 325–40; Peter Cannon-Brookes, "The Nature of Museum Collections," in *Manual of Curatorship: A Guide to Museum Practice,* eds. John M. A. Thompson and Douglas A. Bassett (Boston: Butterworth-Heinemann), 500–512.

30. Marty and Jones, *Museum Informatics.*

31. Ibid., 21.

32. Ibid.

33. Marty, "Museum Websites and Museum Visitors."

34. Sharif Durhams, "America's Black Holocaust Museum Closing After 20 Years in Milwaukee," *Milwaukee Journal Sentinel Online,* July 30, 2008, accessed May 15, 2014, http://www.jsonline.com/entertainment/29565784.html. Also see the museum's website at http://abhmuseum.org/.

35. Henry Jenkins, "Confronting the Challenges of Participatory Culture: Media Education for the Twenty-First Century," The John D. and Catherine T. MacArthur Foundation Reports on Digital Media and Learning (Cambridge: Massachusetts Institute of Technology Press, 2006), 216.

36. See, for example, Michel Foucault's discussion of the archive as generative discourse—or statements about what can and cannot be said—in Michel Foucault, *The Archeology of Knowledge,* trans. A. M. Sheridan Smith, (New York: Pantheon, 1972), 128–29. Also see Katie Shilton and Ramesh Srinivasan, "Participatory Appraisal and Arrangement for Multicultural Archival Collections," *Archivaria* 63 (2007): 87–101; Verne Harris, "The Archival Sliver: Power, Memory, and Archives in South Africa," *Archival Science* 2, nos. 1–2 (2002): 63–86; Schwartz and Cook, "Archives, Records, and Power," 1–19. For a more detailed discussion on the notion of African American ancestors as archives, see David Scott, "Introduction: On the Archaeologies of Black Memory," *Small Axe* 12, no. 2 (2008): v–xvi.

37. See F. Gerald Ham, "The Archival Edge," *American Archivist* 38, no. 1 (1975): 5–13; William T. Hagan, "Archival Captive—The American Indian," *American Archivist* 41, no. 2 (1978): 135–42, quoted in Shilton and Srinivasan, "Participatory Appraisal," 90.

38. Elvin Montgomery Jr., *Collecting African American History: A Celebration of America's Black Heritage through Documents, Artifacts, and Collectibles* (New York: Stewart, Tabori and Chang, 2001), 9. Also see Lila Teresa Church, "Documenting African American Community Heritage: Archival Strategies and Practices in the United States," (PhD diss., University of North Carolina at Chapel Hill, 2008).

39. Joy Palmer, "Archives 2.0: If We Build It, Will They Come?" *Ariadne* 60 (2009), accessed April 22, 2014, http://www.ariadne.ac.uk/issue60/palmer. Also see Bjarki Valtysson, "Access Culture: Web 2.0 and Cultural Participation," *International Journal of Cultural Policy* 16, no. 2 (2010): 200–214.

40. Valtysson, "Access Culture," 201.

41. Jenkins, "Confronting the Challenges of Participatory Culture," 3; quoted in Robert Stein, "Chiming in on Museums and Participatory Culture," *Curator: The Museum Journal* 55, no. 2, (2012): 216.

42. While Katherine Burton Jones is cited, along with her coauthor Paul Marty, as a secondary source via her book on museum informatics, the quotations attributed to her from this point on are the result of my interviews with her.

43. For a useful discussion on the limits of racial uplift ideologies in the twenty-first century, see Fredrick Harris, "The Rise of Respectability Politics," *Dissent*, Winter 2014, accessed August 12, 2014, http://www.dissentmagazine.org/article/the-rise-of-respectability-politics.

44. Neil Cummings and Marysia Lewandowska. *The Value of Things* (Berlin: Birkhauser, 2000).

45. Paul Thompson, *The Voice of the Past: Oral History* (New York: Oxford University Press, 1978), 248. Also see Margaret Anne Clarke, "The Online Brazilian Museu da Pessoa," in Garde-Hansen, Hoskins, and Reading, *Save as*, 152.

Conclusion

1. It is notable that an exhibit centered on six of Monticello's slave families was developed in collaboration with the National Museum of African American History and Culture (NMAAHC), the sponsor of the *Memory Book* website discussed in chapter three. The exhibit, "Slavery at Jefferson's Monticello: Paradox of Liberty," ran from January to October 2012 and was the first such exhibit to be featured on the National Mall in Washington, DC. For more on the exhibit, see http://www.monticello.org/slavery-at-monticello. For more on Mulberry Row, see http://www.monticello.org/mulberry-row. Also see Michael Aubrecht, (n.d.) "Race and Remembrance at Thomas Jefferson's Monticello," accessed July 15, 2014, http://www.pinstripepress.net/MonticelloPAR1-10.pdf.

2. Rebecca Watts, *Contemporary Southern Identity*. For a more detailed discussion of space as reproductive of social relations and practices, see Henri Lefebvre, *The Production of Space* (Malden: Blackwell Publishing, 1991), 416. Finally, for a further analysis of historic places as sites of negotiation, please see Steven Hoelscher and Derek Alderman, "Memory and Place: Geographies of a Critical Relationship," *Social and Cultural Geography* 5, no. 3 (2004): 347–55.

3. William R. Ferris, "The War that Never Goes Away: An Interview with Civil War Historian James M. McPherson," *Humanities* 21, 2 (March/April 2000), accessed May 13, 2014, http://www.neh.gov/humanities/2000/marchapril/conversation/the-war-never-goes-away.

4. John Nerone and Ellen Wartella, "Introduction: Studying Social Memory," *Communication*, 11, no. 2 (1989): 85–88.

5. There are numerous examples of the resurgence of the language of nullification and secession in contemporary conservative discourse. See for example Daniel Bice, "Proposed GOP Resolution Assert's State's Right to Nullify Federal Laws," *Milwaukee Journal Sentinel*, April 30, 2014, accessed July 12, 2014, http://www.jsonline.com/watchdog/noquarter/proposed-gop-resolution-asserts-states-right-to-nullify-laws-secede-b99259782z1-257427991.html; Alexander Mooney, "Texas Governor Says Secession Possible," CNN.com, April 16, 2009, accessed July 12, 2014, http://politicalticker.blogs.cnn.com/2009/04/16/texas-governor-says-secession-possible/. For a sampling of political rhetoric featuring references to

various policies as "slavery" see Jonathan Capeheart, "Herman Cain Flogs Slavery Theme to Push his Flawed 9-9-9 Plan," *Washington Post*, November 28, 2011, accessed July 14, 2014, http://www.washingtonpost.com/blogs/post-partisan/post/herman-cain-flogs-slavery-theme-to-push-his-flawed-9-9-9-plan/2011/03/04/gIQAmTgo5N_blog.html; Rikki Klaus, "West Says Obama Wants Americans to 'Be His Slave' at Port St. Lucie Rally," WPTV.com, July 2, 2012, accessed July 14, 2014, http://www.tcpalm.com/news/west-says-obama-wants-americans-be-his-slave-port; Tonya Somanader, "Bachmann Responds to Slavery Controversy with Another Slavery Analogy," ThinkProgress.org, July 11, 2011, accessed July 14, 2014, http://thinkprogress.org/politics/2011/07/11/265142/bachmann-responds-to-slavery-controversy/. For more on political discourse utilizing plantation metaphors, see Elspeth Reeve, "Parties Fight Over Who Gets to Talk About Slavery," *The Wire*, August 31, 2011, accessed July 14, 2014, http://www.thewire.com/politics/2011/08/parties-fight-over-who-gets-talk-about-slavery/41949/.

6. Charles Blow, "A Rancher's Romantic Revisionism," *New York Times*, April 26, 2014, accessed April 26, 2014, http://www.nytimes.com/2014/04/26/opinion/blow-a-ranchers-romantic-revisionism.html?hpandrref=opinionand_r=0.

7. Matt Patterson, "Union Invasion: UAW Targets Tennessee," Workplace-Choice, June 4, 2013, accessed January 21, 2014, http://workplacechoice.org/2013/06/04/union-invasion-uaw-targets-tennessee/; Lee Fang, "Anti-UAW Consultant: Defeat 'Invading Union Force' at VW Plant Like Our Confederate Ancestors," *The Nation*, January 18, 2014, accessed July 20, 2014, http://www.thenation.com/blog/177162/anti-uaw-consultant-defeat-invading-union-force-vw-plant-our-confederate-ancestors.

8. August Brown, "Lynyrd Skynyrd Denounces Confederate Flag, Angering Some Fans," *Los Angeles Times*, September 21, 2012, accessed December 21, 2012, http://articles.latimes.com/2012/sep/21/entertainment/la-et-ms-lynyrd-skynrd-denounces-confederate-flag-angering-some-fans-20120920; Gayle Thompson, "Lynyrd Skynyrd Confederate Flag Waves On," *The Boot*, September 25, 2012, accessed June 26, 2014, http://theboot.com/lynyrd-skynyrd-confederate-flag/.

9. See for example Orville Lloyd Douglas, "Why I Won't be Watching 'The Butler' and '12 Years a Slave.'" *Guardian*, September 12, 2013, accessed November 15, 2013, http://www.theguardian.com/commentisfree/2013/sep/12/why-im-not-watching-the-butler-12-years-a-slave; Kristen West Savali, "Why the Black Backlash Against '12 Years a Slave'?" *The Grio*, October 31, 2013, accessed November 18, 2013, http://thegrio.com/2013/10/31/why-the-black-backlash-against-12-years-a-slave/; Demetria Lucas, "'12 Years a Slave': Black Audiences Need More Than Slave Narratives," *The Grio*, October 31, 2014, accessed November 18, 2013, http://thegrio.com/2013/10/31/12-years-a-slave-loved-the-movie-tired-of-the-theme/; "Nick Cannon Says He's Tired of Seeing Movies about Slaves." *Clutch Magazine*, November 18, 2013, accessed November 18, 2013, http://www.clutchmagonline.com/2013/11/nick-cannon-says-hes-sick-seeing-movies-slaves/. For critiques on the film's shortcomings in its depiction of the breadth and depth of black resistance, see Carol Boyce Davies, "'12 Years a Slave' Fails to Represent Black Resistance to Enslavement," *Guardian*, January 10, 2014, accessed January 31, 2014,

http://www.theguardian.com/world/2014/jan/10/12-years-a-slave-fails-to-show
-resistence and Glenn David Brasher, "'Glenn David Brasher: A Historian's Take
on '12 Years a Slave,'" *UNC Press Blog*, November 26, 2013, accessed December 12,
2013, http://uncpressblog.com/2013/11/26/glenn-david-brasher-a-historians
-take-on-12-years-a-slave/.

10. *Django Unchained*, a much different film released in 2012, also inspired conversations about its depiction of the era, for both similar and different reasons. The
film, a fictional "Spaghetti Western" set in 1858, was criticized for its historical in-
accuracies and deployment of stereotypical racial tropes, including the erasure of
narratives foregrounding black resistance to slavery.

11. See the DuSable Museum website at http://www.dusablemuseum.org
/events/details/civil-war-re-enactment-on-the-dusable-museum-lawn.

12. For more on the Slave Mart Museum, along with a discussion of Charleston's transformation in terms of displaying its significance as a slave port, see
"City of Charleston Opens Old Slave Mart Museum," accessed June 30, 2014,
http://www.charlestoncvb.com/visitors/events_news/charleston-news/city_of
_charleston_opens_old_slave_mart_museum-787. See also Anne McQuary, "Emancipating History," *New York Times*, March 12, 2011, accessed January 29, 2014,
http://www.nytimes.com/2011/03/12/arts/design/charlestons-museums-finally
-chronicle-history-of-slavery.html?pagewanted=all. For a discussion of the planned
slavery museum that is set to open in the same city in 2018, see Bruce Smith,
"Charleston to Build Black History Museum Near Slave Trade Site," *Huffington
Post*, October 23, 2013, accessed December 29, 2013, http://www.huffingtonpost.
com/2013/10/24/charleston-black-history-museum_n_4151800.html.

13. David Amsden, "Building the First Slavery Museum in America," *New
York Times*, February 26, 2015, accessed March 1, 2015, http://www.nytimes.com
/2015/03/01/magazine/building-the-first-slave-museum-in-america.html.

14. See for example Grimm, "In Florida, When It Comes to Race and the
Confederacy, the Past Is Never Past" and Doug Stanglin, "Memphis Changes
Names of 3 Confederate-Themed Parks," *USA Today*, February 6, 2013, accessed
January 15, 2014, http://www.usatoday.com/story/news/nation/2013/02/06
/memphis-parks-confederate-ku-klux-klan/1895549/.

15. Campbell Robertson, "Before the Battles and the Protests, the Chains," *New
York Times*, 12/9/13, accessed 1/15/14, http://www.nytimes.com/2013/12/10/
us/before-the-battles-and-the-protests-the-chains.html.

16. For more detail on the events surrounding the removal of the flag, see
Richard Fausset and Alan Blinder, "South Carolina Settles Its Decades-Old Dispute over a Confederate Flag," *New York Times*, July 9, 2015, accessed July 17,
2015, http://www.nytimes.com/2015/07/10/us/relief-and-resentment-after
-confederate-flag-vote-in-south-carolina.html; Richard Fausset and Alan Blinder,
"South Carolina House Votes to Remove Confederate Flag," *New York Times*,
July 9, 2015, accessed July 17, 2015, http://www.nytimes.com/2015/07/10/us
/confederate-flag-south-carolina.html; Richard Fausset and Alan Blinder, "Era
Ends as South Carolina Lowers Confederate Flag," *New York Times*, July 10, 2015,
accessed July 17, 2015, http://www.nytimes.com/2015/07/11/us/south-carolina
-confederate-flag.html.

17. "Virginia Must Lead on Racial Truth and Reconciliation," *Richmond Times-Dispatch,* July 11, 2015, accessed July 19, 2015, http://www.richmond.com /opinion/our-opinion/article_5fca16bd-63ec-5b64–9216–47b445b438b0.html.

18. Luanne Rife, "W&L Will Remove Flags from Chapel," *Roanoke Times,* July 9, 2014, A1.

19. It is also important to note that the lowering of the flag in South Carolina inspired calls for the removal of Confederate monuments and street names in other parts of the South. One of the more dramatic of these calls involved a city council vote in Memphis for the removal of a statue of General Nathan Bedford Forrest from a state park, along with the removal of both his and his wife's graves. For more, see Marius Payton, "Debate Continues to Swirl around Nathan Bedford Forrest Statue," July 14, 2015, accessed July 17, 2015, http://www .myfoxmemphis.com/story/29495406/city-council-passes-ordinance-to-remove -nathan-bedford-forrest-statue.

20. While the battlefield at Olustee is an exception, all of the historic sites I have detailed here, including Monticello, are witnesses to processes of dialogue that have occurred between private interests and a public armed with increasing demands for more comprehensive interpretations.

21. The city of Hampton is considered a partner in the development of Fort Monroe, as it operates two facilities on the site. For more on this partnership, as well as on the development of Fort Monroe as a historic site under federal purview, see the Fort Monroe website at http://www.nps.gov/fomr/parkmgmt /index.htm.

22. Adam Goodheart, *1861: The Civil War Awakening* (New York: Knopf, 2012); James McPherson, *Battle Cry of Freedom,* 355; Kim O'Brien Root, "Panel: Fort Monroe Should Become a Museum," *Daily Press,* January 5, 2008, accessed June 22, 2014, http://www.dailypress.com/news/hampton/dpnews_monroe _0105jan05,0,5202832.story. Also see "African American Citizens for a Fort Monroe National Park," *Citizens for a Fort Monroe National Park,* accessed June 28, 2014, http://fortmonroecitizens.org/2–2/african-american/. It is also notable that during the immediate postwar era, missionaries and educators from the North arrived at the site to help the contrabands. One of the fruits of this project was the founding of Hampton Institute, now known as Hampton University.

23. See the website of the Fort Monroe Authority at http://wwwfmauthority .com/about/fort-monroe/history/ and http://www.fmauthority.com/visit /casemate-museum/. Though Davis's imprisonment in the provisional cell within the museum was brief, the entire length of his containment on the premises at Fort Monroe lasted two years. He was bonded out on May 13, 1867. For a more detailed timeline, see the *Encyclopedia Virginia,* accessed July 18, 2014, http:// encyclopediavirginia.org/Fort_Monroe_During_the_Civil_War#start_entry.

24. Chief Black Hawk was the first "political" prisoner held at Fort Monroe, following his defeat in the 1832 Black Hawk War. He was imprisoned there from 1832 to 1833. Another interesting aspect of the report is its discussion of the controversy over the use of the term "contraband." Though historically accurate, the term invites critical scrutiny from contemporary audiences uncomfortable with its dehumanizing connotation. For more on both of these issues, along with details of the committee's work and recommendations, see the work-

ing group's report, "Fort Monroe Area Development Authority African American Culture Working Group Final Report," December 23, 2009, accessed July 24, 2014, http://www.fmauthority.com/wp-content/uploads/AACWGfinalreportDec-09_formatted_12-23-09.pdf. For more on Black Hawk's imprisonment at Fort Monroe, see John Quarstein and Dennis Mroczkowski, *Ft. Monroe: The Key to the South* (Mount Pleasant, SC: Arcadia Publishing, 2000).

25. In late 2014, a copy of the letter could be found at https://www.google.com/url?sa=t&rct=j&q=&esrc=s&source=web&cd=2&cad=rja&uact=8&ved=0ahUKEwj5seDzpZHMAhVENSYKHYqzBxgQFgghMAE&url=https%3A%2F%2Fxa.yimg.com%2Fkq%2Fgroups%2F19331772%2F680139438%2Fname%2F2009-10-31TownHallLetterforSonsandFriends.doc&usg=AFQjCNFauKb7WXOEgxsFHMe1laoQds_3SQ&bvm=bv.119745492,d.eWE.

References

Alderman, Derek H. "Introduction to the Special Issue: African Americans and Tourism." *Tourism Geographies* 15, no. 3 (2013): 375–79.
———. "Surrogation and the Politics of Remembering Slavery in Savannah, Georgia." *Journal of Historical Geography* 36 (2010): 90–101.
Alderman, Derek H., and Rachel M. Campbell. "Symbolic Excavation and Artifact Politics of Remembering Slavery in the American South." *Southeastern Geographer* 48 (2008): 338–55.
Alexander, Bryant Keith. "Passing, Cultural Performance, and Individual Agency: Performative Reflections on Black Masculine Identity." *Cultural Studies <=> Critical Methodologies* 4, no. 3 (2004): 377–404.
Alexander, Jeffrey C., Ron Eyerman, Bernard Giesen, Neil J. Smelser, and Piotr Sztompka, eds. *Cultural Trauma and Collective Identity*. Berkeley: University of California Press, 2004.
Alexander, Jeffrey C. "Toward a Theory of Cultural Trauma." In *Cultural Trauma and Collective Identity*. Edited by Jeffrey C. Alexander, Ron Eyerman, Bernard Giesen, Neil J. Smelser, and Piotr Sztompka, 1–30. Berkeley: University of California Press, 2004.
Alvarez, Lizette. "Blue and Gray Still in Conflict at a Battle Site." *New York Times*, January 16, 2014. Accessed January 17, 2014. http://www.nytimes.com/2014/01/17/us/blue-and-gray-still-in-conflict-at-a-battle-site.html.
Amsden, David. "Building the First Slavery Museum in America." *New York Times*, February 26, 2015. Accessed March 1, 2015. http://www.nytimes.com/2015/03/01/magazine/building-the-first-slave-museum-in- america.html.
Anderson, Jay. "Living History: Simulating Everyday Life in Living Museums." *American Quarterly* 34, no. 3 (1982): 290–306.
Andrews, William L. *African American Autobiography: A Collection of Critical Essays*. Englewood Cliffs, NJ: Prentice Hall, 1993.

Annis, Sheldon. "The Museum as a Staging Ground for Symbolic Action." *Museum* 151 (1987): 168–71.

Atwater, Deborah F., and Sandra L. Herndon. "Cultural Space and Race: The National Civil Rights Museum and MuseumAfrica." *Howard Journal of Communication* 14, no. 1 (2003): 15–28.

Aubrecht, Michael. "Race and Remembrance: Thomas Jefferson's Monticello." Accessed July 15, 2014. http://www.pinstripepress.net/MonticelloPAR-1-10.pdf.

Back, Les. "Home from 'Home': Youth, Belonging, and Place." In *Making Race Matter: Bodies, Space and Identity*. Edited by Claire Alexander and Caroline Knowles, 19–41. New York: Palgrave Macmillan, 2005.

Baker, Houston. *Blues, Ideology, and Afro-American Literature: A Vernacular Theory*. Chicago: University of Chicago Press, 1987.

———. Preface to *The Black Public Sphere: A Public Culture Book*. Edited by The Black Public Sphere Collective, 1–4. Chicago: University of Chicago Press, 1995.

Bakhtin, Mikhail M. *The Dialogic Imagination: Four Essays*. Austin: University of Texas Press, 1981.

———. *Rabelais and His World*. Bloomington: Indiana University Press, 1984.

Banks, Adam. *Race, Rhetoric, and Technology: Searching for Higher Ground*. London: Routledge, 2006.

Banks, William M. *Black Intellectuals: Race and Responsibility in American Life*. W. W. Norton and Company, 1996.

Barton, Craig E. "Foreword." In *Sites of Memory: Perspectives on Architecture and Race*. Edited by Craig E. Barton, xiv–xv. New York: Princeton Architectural Press, 2001.

Bauman, Richard. "Verbal Acts as Performance." *American Anthropologist* 77, no. 2 (1975): 290–311.

Beard, Rick. "Organizing Black Soldiers." *New York Times*, May 31, 2013. Accessed January 30, 2014. http://opinionator.blogs.nytimes.com/2013/05/31/organizing-black-soldiers/.

Bergeron Jr., Arthur W. "The Battle of Olustee." In *Black Soldiers in Blue: African American Troops in the Civil War Era*. Edited by John David Smith, 136–49. Chapel Hill: University of North Carolina Press, 2002.

Berlin, Ira. "Coming to Terms with Slavery in Twenty-First Century America." In *Slavery and Public History: The Tough Stuff of American Memory*. Edited by James Oliver Horton and Lois E. Horton, 1–18. Chapel Hill: University of North Carolina Press, 2008.

Bertram, Carel. "Housing the Symbolic Universe in Early Republican Turkey: Architecture, Memory, and the 'Felt Real.'" In *Memory and Architecture*. Edited by Eleni Bastea, 165–90. Albuquerque: University of New Mexico Press, 2004.

Bice, Daniel. "Proposed GOP Resolution Asserts State's Right to Nullify Federal Laws." *Milwaukee Journal Sentinel*, April 30, 2014. Accessed July 12, 2014. http://www.jsonline.com/watchdog/noquarter/proposed-gop-resolution-asserts-states-right-to-nullify-laws-secede-b99259782z1-257427991.html.

Blair, Carole. "Contemporary U.S. Memorial Sites as Exemplars of Rhetoric's Materiality." In *Rhetorical Bodies*. Edited by Jack Selzer and Sharon Crowley, 16–57. Madison: University of Wisconsin Press, 1999.

Blair, Carole, Greg Dickinson, and Brian L. Ott. "Introduction: Rhetoric/Memory/

Place." In *Places of Public Memory: The Rhetoric of Museums and Memorials*. Edited by Carole Blair, Greg Dickinson, and Brian L. Ott, 1–56. Tuscaloosa: University of Alabama Press, 2010.

Blair, Carole, Greg Dickinson, and Brian L. Ott, eds. *Places of Public Memory: The Rhetoric of Museums and Memorials*. Tuscaloosa: University of Alabama Press, 2010.

Blight, David W. *Beyond the Battlefield: Race Memory, and the American Civil War*. Amherst, MA: University of Massachusetts Press, 2002.

——. *Race and Reunion: The Civil War in American Memory*. Cambridge, MA: Belknap Press of Harvard University Press, 2001.

Blow, Charles. "A Rancher's Romantic Revisionism." *New York Times*, April 25, 2014. Accessed April 26, 2014. http://www.nytimes.com/2014/04/26/opinion/blow-a-ranchers-romantic-revisionism.html?hpandrref=opinionand_r=0.

Bodnar, John E. *Remaking America: Public Memory, Commemoration, and Patriotism in the Twentieth Century*. Princeton, NJ: Princeton University Press, 1992.

Bowman, Michael S. "Performing Southern History for the Tourist Gaze: Antebellum Home Tour Guide Performances." In *Exceptional Spaces: Essays in Performance and History*. Edited by Della Pollack, 142–60. Chapel Hill: University of North Carolina Press, 1998.

Brasher, Glenn David. "Glenn David Brasher: A Historian's Take on '12 Years a Slave.'" *UNC Press Blog*, November 26, 2013. Accessed December 12, 2013. http://uncpressblog.com/2013/11/26/glenn-david-brasher-a-historians-take-on-12-years-a-slave/.

Brown, August. "Lynyrd Skynyrd Denounces Confederate Flag, Angering Some Fans." *Los Angeles Times*, September 21, 2012. Accessed December 21, 2012. http://articles.latimes.com/2012/sep/21/entertainment/la-et-ms-lynyrd-skynrd-denounces-confederate-flag-angering-some-fans-20120920.

Brundage, W. Fitzhugh. *The Southern Past: A Clash of Race and Memory*. Cambridge: Belknap Press of Harvard University Press, 2005.

Buckley, Gail. *American Patriots: The Story of Blacks in the Military from the Revolution to Desert Storm*. New York: Random House, Inc., 2001.

Burkhalter, Byron. "Reading Race Online: Discovering Racial Identity in Usenet Discussions." In *Communities in Cyberspace*. Edited by Marc A. Smith and Peter Kollock, 60–75. London: Routledge, 1999.

Byrne, Dara. "Public Discourse, Community Concerns, and Civic Engagement: Exploring Black Social Networking Traditions on Blackplanet.com." *Journal of Computer-Mediated Communication* 13, no. 1 (2007): 16.

——. "The Future of (the) 'Race': Identity, Discourse, and the Rise of Computer-Mediated Public Spheres." In *Learning Race and Ethnicity: Youth and Digital Media*. Edited by Anna Everett, 15–38. Cambridge: Massachusetts Institute of Technology Press, 2008.

Calos, Katherine. "Civil War Center, Confederacy Museum Join Forces." *Richmond Times-Dispatch*, November 17, 2013. http://www.timesdispatch.com/news/local/civil-war-center-confederacy-museum-join-forces/article_0295cb9f-fd5a-5177-98e8-0e1f5f46a6c2.html.

Cameron, Fiona. "Digital Futures 1: Museum Collections, Digital Technologies, and the Cultural Construction of Knowledge." *Curator* 46 (2003): 325–40.

Cannon-Brookes, Peter. "The Nature of Museum Collections." In *Manual of Curatorship: A Guide to Museum Practice*. Edited by John M. A. Thompson and Douglas A. Bassett, 500–512. Boston: Butterworth-Heinemann, 1992.

Capeheart, Jonathan. "Herman Cain Flogs Slavery Theme to Push his Flawed 9-9-9 Plan." *Washington Post*, November 28, 2011. Accessed July 14, 2014. http://www.washingtonpost.com/blogs/post-partisan/post/herman-cain-flogs-slavery-theme-to-push-his-flawed-9-9-9-plan/2011/03/04/gIQAmTgo5N_blog.html.

Casey, Edward S. "Public Memory in Place and Time." In *Framing Public Memory*. Edited by Kendall R. Phillips, 17–44. Tuscaloosa: University of Alabama Press, 2004.

Chidester, David, and Edward T. Linenthal. "Introduction." In *American Sacred Space*. Edited by David Chidester and Edward T. Linenthal, 1–42. Bloomington: Indiana University Press, 1995.

Church, Lila Teresa. "Documenting African American Community Heritage: Archival Strategies and Practices in the United States." PhD diss., University of North Carolina, Chapel Hill, 2008.

Citizens for a Fort Monroe National Park. "African American Citizens for a Fort Monroe National Park." n.d. Accessed June 28, 2014, http://fortmonroecitizens.org/2–2/african-american/.

"City of Charleston Opens Old Slave Mart Museum." Accessed June 30, 2014. http://www.charlestoncvb.com/visitors/events_news/charleston-news/city_of_charleston_opens_old_slave_mart_museum-787.

"Civil War Sites Advisory Commission Report on the Nation's Civil War Battlefields, Technical Volume II: Battle Summaries." National Park Service, Heritage Preservation Services. Accessed October 29, 2008. http://www.nps.gov/history/hps/abpp/battles/tvii.htm-sites.

Clark, Gregory. "Rhetorical Experience and the National Jazz Museum in Harlem." In *Places of Public Memory: The Rhetoric of Museums and Memorials*. Edited by Carole Blair, Greg Dickinson, and Brian L. Ott, 113–39. Tuscaloosa: University of Alabam Press, 2010.

Clarke, Margaret Anne. "The Online Brazilian Museu da Pessoa." In *Save as ... Digital Memories*. Edited by Joanne Garde-Hansen, Andrew Hoskins, and Anna Reading, 151–66. New York: Palgrave Macmillan, 2009.

Clemons, Leigh. "Present Enacting Past: The Functions of Battle Reenacting in Historical Representation." In *Enacting History*. Edited by Scott Magelssen and Rhona Justice-Malloy, 10–21. Tuscaloosa: University of Alabama Press, 2011.

Clutch Magazine. "Nick Cannon Says He's Tired of Seeing Movies about Slaves." November 18, 2013. Accessed November 18, 2013. http://www.clutchmagonline.com/2013/11/nick-cannon-says-hes-sick-seeing-movies-slaves/.

Cobb, James C. *Away Down South: A History of Southern Identity*. New York: Oxford University Press, 2005.

Collins, Patricia Hill. *Black Sexual Politics: African Americans, Gender, and the New Racism*. New York: Routledge, 2005.

Connerton, Paul. "Seven Types of Forgetting." *Memory Studies* 1, no. 1 (2008): 59–71.

Conquergood, Dwight. "Ethnography, Rhetoric, and Performance." *Quarterly Journal of Speech* 78, no. 1 (1992): 80–97.

Cook, Rhonda. "Declare 'Confederate Southern American' on Census Forms, Group Says." *Atlanta Journal Constitution*, March 26, 2010.

Coski, John. *The Confederate Battle Flag: America's Most Embattled Emblem*. Cambridge: Harvard University Press, 2005.

Courtney, Kent. *Returning to the Civil War: Grand Reenactments of an Anguished Time*. Darby, PA: Diane Publishing Company, 1997.

Cox, Karen L. *Dixie's Daughters: The United Daughters of the Confederacy and the Preservation of Confederate Culture*. Gainesville: University Press of Florida, 2003.

———. "The Confederate Monument at Arlington: A Token of Reconciliation." In *Monuments to the Lost Cause: Women, Art, and the Landscape of Southern Memory*. Edited by Cynthia Mills and Pamela H. Simpson, 148–62. Knoxville: University of Tennessee Press, 2003.

Crew, Spencer R. "African Americans, History, and Museums: Preserving African American History in the Public Arena." In *Making Histories in Museums*. Edited by Gaynor Kavanagh, 80–91. New York: Leicester University Press, 1996.

Cromartie, John B., and Carol B. Stack. "Reinterpretation of Black Return and Non-Return Migration to the South, 1975–1980." *Geographical Review* 79, no. 3 (1989): 297–310.

Cronin, Gloria L., and Ben Siegel, eds. *Conversations with Robert Penn Warren*. Jackson: University Press of Mississippi, 2005.

Crooke, Elizabeth. "Museums, Communities, and the Politics of Heritage in Northern Ireland." In *Museums and Their Communities*. Edited by Sheila Watson, 300–12. New York: Routledge, 2007.

Crummell, Alexander. "The Need of New Ideas and New Aims for a New Era." In *Civilization and Black Progress: Selected Writings of Alexander Crummell on the South*. Edited by J. R. Oldfield, 120–33. Charlottesville: University of Virginia Press, 1969.

Cubitt, Geoffrey. "Atrocity Materials and the Representation of Transatlantic Slavery." In *Representing Enslavement and Abolition in Museums: Ambiguous Engagements*. Edited by Laurajane Smith, Geoffrey Cubitt, Kalliopi Fouseki, and Ross Wilson, 229–59. New York: Routledge, 2011.

Cubitt, Geoffrey, Laurajane Smith, and Ross Wilson. "Introduction: Anxiety and Ambiguity in the Representation of Dissonant History." In *Representing Enslavement and Abolition in Museums*. Edited by Laurajane Smith, Geoffrey Cubitt, Kalliopi Fouseki, and Ross Wilson, 1–22. New York: Routledge, 2011.

Cullen, Jim. *The Civil War in Popular Culture: A Reusable Past*. Washington, DC: Smithsonian Institution Scholarly Press, 1995.

Cummings, Neil, and Marysia Lewandowska. *The Value of Things*. Berlin: Birkhauser, 2000.

da Silva, Angela. "African American Heritage Tourism." *Preservation Issues* 7, no. 3 (1997). Accessed March 12, 2014. http://law.wustl.edu/staff/taylor/preserv/v7n3/afamtour.htm.

Davies, Carol Boyce. "'12 Years a Slave' Fails to Represent Black Resistance to Enslavement." *Guardian*, January 10, 2014. Accessed January 31, 2014. http://www.theguardian.com/world/2014/jan/10/12-years-a-slave-fails-to-show-resistence.

Davis, Elizabeth Lindsay. *Lifting as They Climb*. New York: G. K. Hall, 1996.

Davis, Patricia G. "The Other Southern Belles: Civil War Reenactment, African American Women, and the Performance of Idealized Femininity." *Text and Performance Quarterly* 32, no. 4 (2012): 308–31.

Davis, Thadious M. "Expanding the Limits: The Intersection of Race and Region." *Southern Literary Journal* 20, no. 2 (1988): 6–7.

Davis, William C., Brian C. Pohanka, and Don Troiani, eds. *Civil War Journal*. Vol. 2, *The Battles*. Nashville: Rutledge Hill Press, 1998.

———, eds. *Civil War Journal*. Vol. 3, *The Legacies*. Nashville: Rutledge Hill Press, 1999.

Detlefsen, Ellen Gay. "Where Am I to Go? Use of the Internet for Consumer Health Information by Two Vulnerable Communities." *Library Trends*, 53 no. 2 (2004): 283–300.

Dolan, Jill. *Utopia in Performance: Finding Hope at the Theater*. Ann Arbor: University of Michigan Press, 2005.

Douban, Gigi. "Fewer People Participate in Civil War Reenactments." NPR.org, July 4, 2011. Accessed February 11, 2014. http://www.npr.org/2011/07/04/137609367 /fewer-people-participate-in-civil-war-reenactments.

Douglas, Orville Lloyd. "Why I won't be Watching 'The Butler' and '12 Years a Slave.'" *Guardian*, September 12, 2013. Accessed November 15, 2013. http://www .theguardian.com/commentisfree/2013/sep/12/why-im-not-watching-the-butler -12-years-a-slave.

Douglass, Frederick. "I Denounce the So-Called Emancipation as a Stupendous Fraud." In *Frederick Douglass: Selected Speeches and Writings*. Edited by Phillip Sheldon Foner and Yuval Taylor, 711–23. Chicago: Lawrence Hill Books, 1999.

Du Bois, William Edward Burghardt. *Black Reconstruction in America 1860–1880*. New York: Simon and Schuster, 1935.

———. "Darkwater." In *The Oxford W. E. B. Du Bois Reader*. Edited by Eric J. Sundquist, 481–623. New York: Oxford University Press, 1996.

Durhams, Sharif. "America's Black Holocaust Museum Closing After 20 Years in Milwaukee." *Milwaukee Journal Sentinel Online*, July 30, 2008. Accessed May 15, 2014. http://www.jsonline.com/entertainment/29565784.html.

Durkheim, Emile. *The Elementary Forms of Religious Life*. Translated by Karen E. Fields. New York: Free Press, 1995.

Dwyer, Owen, and Derek H. Alderman. *Civil Rights Memorials and the Geography of Memory*. Athens: University of Georgia Press, 2008.

———. "Memorial Landscapes: Analytic Questions and Metaphors." *GeoJournal* 73, no. 3 (2008): 165–78.

Dwyer, Owen, David Bulter, and Perry Carter. "Commemorative Surrogation and the South's Changing Heritage Landscape." *Tourism Geographies* 15, no. 3 (2013): 424–43.

Eichstedt, Jennifer, and Stephen Small. *Representations of Slavery: Race and Ideology in Southern Plantation Museums*. Washington, DC: Smithsonian Institution Press, 2002.

Encyclopedia Virginia. Accessed July 18, 2014. http://encyclopediavirginia.org/Fort _Monroe_During_the_Civil_War#start_entry.

Escott, Paul D. *Slavery Remembered: A Record of Twentieth Century Slave Narratives*. Chapel Hill: University of North Carolina Press, 1979.

Evans, Susan. "Personal Beliefs and National Stories: Theater in Museums as a Tool for Exploring Historical Memory." *Curator: The Museum Journal* 56, no. 2 (2013): 189–90.

Everett, Anna. *Digital Diaspora: A Race for Cyberspace*. Albany: State University of New York Press, 2009.

Eyerman, Ron. *Cultural Trauma: Slavery and the Formation of African American Identity.* Cambridge: Cambridge University Press, 2001.

Falk, William W., Larry L. Hunt, and Matthew O. Hunt. "Return Migrations of African-Americans to the South: Reclaiming a Land of Promise, Going Home, or Both?" *Rural Sociology* 69, no. 4 (2004): 490–509.

Fang, Lee. "Anti-UAW Consultant: Defeat 'Invading Union Force' at VW Plant Like Our Confederate Ancestors." *The Nation*, November 14, 2013. Accessed November 18, 2013. http://www.thenation.com/blog/177162/anti-uaw-consultant-defeat -invading- union-force-vw-plant-our-confederate-ancestors.

Farmer, James Oscar. "Playing Rebels: Reenactment as Nostalgia and Defense of the Confederacy in the Battle of Aiken." *Southern Cultures* 11, no. 1 (2005): 46–73.

Fausset, Richard, and Alan Blinder. "Era Ends as South Carolina Lowers Confederate Flag." *New York Times*, July 10, 2015. Accessed July 17, 2015. http://www.nytimes .com/2015/07/11/us/south-carolina-confederate-flag.html.

———. "South Carolina Settles its Decades-Old Dispute Over a Confederate Flag." *New York Times*, July 9, 2015. Accessed July 17, 2015. http://www.nytimes .com/2015/07/10/us/relief-and-resentment-after-confederate-flag-vote-in-south -carolina.html.

———. "South Carolina House Votes to Remove Confederate Flag." *New York Times*, July 9, 2015. Accessed July 17, 2015. http://www.nytimes.com/2015/07/10/us /confederate-flag-south-carolina.html.

Fehrenbacher, Don E. *The Dred Scott Case: Its Significance in American Law and Politics.* New York: Oxford University Press, 2001.

Ferris, William R. "The War that Never Goes Away: An Interview with Civil War Historian James M. McPherson." *Humanities* 21, 2 (March/April 2000). Accessed May 13, 2014. http://www.neh.gov/humanities/2000/marchapril/conversation /the-war-never-goes-away.

Foner, Jack D. *Blacks and the Military in American History: A New Perspective.* Santa Barbara: Praeger Publishers, 1974.

Foster, Frances Smith. *Witnessing Slavery.* Madison, WI: University of Wisconsin Press, 1979.

Foster, Mary. "Civil War Museums Changing as View on War Changes." *The Grio*, January 9, 2012. Accessed January 18, 2014. http://thegrio.com/2012/01/09/civil -war-museums-changing-as-view-on-war-changes/.

Foucault, Michel. "Nietzsche, Genealogy, History." In *The Foucault Reader.* Edited by Paul Rabinow, 76–100. New York: Pantheon, 1984.

———. *The Archeology of Knowledge.* Translated by A. M. Sheridan Smith. New York: Pantheon, 1972.

Fraser, Nancy. "Rethinking the Public Sphere: A Contribution to the Critique of Actually Existing Democracy." In *Habermas and the Public Sphere.* Edited by Craig Calhoun, 109–42. Cambridge: Massachusetts Institute of Technology Press, 1992.

Fredrickson, George M. *The Black Image in the White Mind: The Debate on Afro-American Character and Destiny, 1817–1914.* New York: Harper and Row, 1971.

Frey, William H. *The New Great Migration: Black Americans' Return to the South, 1965–2000.* Center on Urban and Metropolitan Policy, The Brookings Institution, May 2004. Accessed September 12, 2008. http://www.frey-demographer.org/reports /R-2004-3_NewGreatMigration.pdf.

Friend, Craig Thompson, and Lorri Glover, eds. *Southern Manhood: Perspectives on Masculinity in the Old South*. Athens: University of Georgia Press, 2004.

Fulton, DoVeanna. *Speaking Power: Black Feminist Orality in Women's Narratives of Slavery*. Albany: State University of New York Press, 2006.

Fuoss, Kirk W. "Performance as Contestation: An Agonistic Perspective on the Insurgent Assembly." In *Exceptional Spaces: Essays in Performance and History*. Edited by Della Pollack, 98–120. Chapel Hill: The University of North Carolina Press, 1998.

Gable, Eric. "The City, Race, and the Creation of a Common History at the Virginia Historical Society." In *Museums and Communities: Curators, Collections, and Collaboration*. Edited by Viv Golding and Wayne Modest, 32–47. London: Bloomsbury, 2013.

Gallagher, Victoria, and Margaret LaWare. "Sparring with Public Memory: The Rhetorical Embodiment of Race, Power, and Conflict in the Monument to Joe Louis." In *Places of Public Memory: The Rhetoric of Museums and Memorials*. Edited by Carole Blair, Greg Dickinson, and Brian L. Ott, 87–112. Tuscaloosa: University of Alabama Press, 2010.

Giddens, Anthony. *Modernity and Self-Identity: Self and Society in the Late Modern Age*. Palo Alto: Stanford University Press, 1991.

Glassberg, David. "Public History and the Study of Memory." *Public Historian* 18, no. 2 (1996): 7–23.

Goldfield, David R. *Still Fighting the Civil War: The American South and Southern History*. Baton Rouge: Louisiana State University Press, 2013.

Goodheart, Adam *1861: The Civil War Awakening*, New York: Knopf, 2012.

Gosse, Van. "Beyond 'Glory.'" *New York Times*, November 29, 2011. Accessed February 10, 2014. http://opinionator.blogs.nytimes.com/2011/11/29/beyond-glory/?_r=0.

Graham, Maryemma, ed. *The Complete Poems of Frances E.W. Harper*. Oxford, UK: Oxford University Press, 1988.

Gramsci, Antonio. "Observations on Folklore." In *An Antonio Gramsci Reader: Selected Writings, 1916–1935*. Edited by David Forgacs, 360–69. New York: Schocken Books Inc., 1988.

Griffin, Larry J., Ranae Jo Evenson, and Ashley B. Thompson. "Southerners, All?" *Southern Cultures* 11, no. 1 (2005): 6–25.

Grimm, Fred. "In Florida, When It Comes to Race and the Confederacy, the Past Is Never Past." *Miami Herald*, December 31, 2013. Accessed January 10, 2014. http://www.miamiherald.com/2013/12/31/v-print/3831619/in-florida-when-it-comes-to-race-and-the-confederacy-the-past-is-never-past/.

Guerrero, Ed. *Framing Blackness: The African American Image in Film*. Philadelphia: Temple University Press, 1993.

Gusdorf, Georges. "Conditions and Limits of Autobiography." In *Autobiography: Essays Theoretical and Critical*. Edited by James Olney, 28–48. Princeton: Princeton University Press, 1980.

Haden, Robert Lee. *Reliving the Civil War: A Reenactor's Handbook*. Mechanicsburg, PA: Stackpole Books, 1999.

Hagan, William T. "Archival Captive—The American Indian." *American Archivist* 41, no. 2. (1978): 135–42.

Halbwachs, Maurice. *On Collective Memory*. Chicago: University of Chicago Press, 1992.

Hall, Stuart. "Cultural Identity and Diaspora." In *Identity: Community, Culture, Difference*. Edited by Jonathan Rutherford, 222–37. London: Lawrence and Wishart, 2003.

Ham, F. Gerald. "The Archival Edge." *American Archivist* 38, no. 1 (1975): 5–13.

Hancock, Scott, and Alexandra Milano. "The Real Rebels of the Civil War." *New York Times*, October 15, 2013. Accessed January 30, 2014. http://opinionator.blogs.nytimes.com/2013/10/15/the-real-rebels-of-the-civil-war/.

Hanna, Stephen P. "A Slavery Museum: Race, Memory, and Landscape in Fredericksburg, Virginia." *Southeastern Geographer* 48, no. 3 (2008): 316–37.

Harris, Fredrick. "The Rise of Respectability Politics." *Dissent*, Winter 2014. Accessed August 12, 2014. http://www.dissentmagazine.org/article/the-rise-of-respectability-politics.

Harris, Verne. "The Archival Sliver: Power, Memory, and Archives in South Africa." *Archival Science* 2, nos. 1–2 (2002): 63–86.

Harvey, David. *The Condition of Postmodernity: An Enquiry into the Origins of Cultural Change*. Malden: Wiley-Blackwell, 1989.

Hauser, Gerard A. *Vernacular Voices: The Rhetoric of Publics and Public Spheres*. Columbia: University of South Carolina Press, 1999.

Hayden, Dolores. *The Power of Place: Urban Landscapes as Public History*. Cambridge: Massachusetts Institute of Technology Press, 1999.

Heatherington, Keith. "Manchester's Urbis: Urban Regeneration, Museums, and Symbolic Economies." *Cultural Studies* 21, nos. 4–5 (2007): 630–49.

Hesford, Wendy S. *Framing Identities: Autobiography and the Politics of Pedagogy*. Minneapolis: University of Minnesota Press, 1999.

Hess, Aaron. "In Digital Remembrance: Vernacular Memory and the Rhetorical Construction of Web Memorials." *Media, Culture and Society* 29, no. 5 (2007): 812–30.

Hoelscher, Richard H. "The White-Pillared Past: Landscapes of Memory and Race in the American South." In *Race and Landscape in America*. Edited by Richard Schein, 1–22. New York: Routledge, 2006.

Hoeslcher, Steven, and Derek Alderman. "Memory and Place: Geographies of a Critical Relationship." *Social and Cultural Geography* 5, no. 3 (2004): 347–55.

hooks, bell. *Talking Back: Thinking Feminist, Thinking Black*. Brooklyn: South End Press, 1989.

Hooper-Greenhill, Eileen. *Museums and the Shaping of Knowledge*. London: Routledge, 1992.

———, ed. *Museums, Media, Message*. New York: Routledge, 1995.

Hopson, Mark L. *Notes from the Talking Drum: Exploring Black Communication and Critical Memory in Intercultural Communication Contexts*. Cresskill, NJ: Hampton Press, 2011.

Horton, James Oliver. "Slavery in American History: An Uncomfortable National Dialogue." In *Slavery and Public History: The Tough Stuff of American Memory*. Edited by James Oliver Horton and Lois E. Horton, 35–56. Chapel Hill: University of North Carolina Press, 2008.

Horton, James Oliver, and Spencer R. Crew. "Afro-Americans and Museums: Towards a Policy of Inclusion." In *History Museums in the United States: A Critical Assessment*. Edited by Warren Leon and Roy Rosenzweig, 215–36. Champaign: University of Illinois Press, 1998.

Horwitz, Tony. *Confederates in the Attic: Dispatches from the Unfinished Civil War*. New York: Vintage, 1999.

Hoskins, Andrew. "The Mediatisation of Memory." In *Save as . . . Digital Memories*. Edited by Joanne Garde-Hansen, Andrew Hoskins, and Anna Reading. New York: Palgrave-Macmillan, 2009.

Hunter, Tera W. "A Mother's Letter to Lincoln." *New York Times*, August 1, 2013. Accessed January 30, 2014. http://opinionator.blogs.nytimes.com/2013/08/01/a-mothers-letter-to-lincoln/.

Irwin-Zarecka, Iwona. *Frames of Remembrance: The Dynamics of Collective Memory*. New Brunswick: Transaction Publishers, 1994.

Jackson II, Ronald L. *Scripting the Black Masculine Body: Identity, Discourse, and Racial Politics in Popular Media*. Albany: State University of New York Press, 2006.

Jameson, Fredric. *Postmodernism or the Cultural Logic of Late Capitalism*. Durham: Duke University Press, 1992.

Jenkins, Henry. "Confronting the Challenges of Participatory Culture: Media Education for the Twenty-First Century." The John D. and Catherine T. MacArthur Foundation Reports on Digital Media and Learning. Cambridge: Massachusetts Institute of Technology Press, 2006.

Johnson, Carrie. "Put Lee on Floodwall, Panel Says, General's Image Is Revised, El-Amin's Opposition." *Richmond Times Dispatch*, July 1, 1999.

Johnson, Carrie. "Tested in Year, Preserving the Past; Tredegar Iron Works to Play Another Role in History." *Richmond Times Dispatch*, April 20, 2000, B-1.

Johnson, E. Patrick. " 'Quare' Studies, or (Almost) Everything I Know About Queer Studies I Learned from My Grandmother." *Text and Performance Quarterly* 21, no. 1 (2001): 1–25.

Jones, Terry L. "The Free Men of Color Go to War." In *New York Times*, October 19, 2012. Accessed January 15, 2014. http://opinionator.blogs.nytimes.com/2012/10/19/the-free-men-of-color-go-to-war/.

Jordan Jr., Ervin L. *Black Confederates and Afro-Yankees in Civil War Virginia*. Nation Divided: New Studies in Civil War History. Charlottesville: University of Virginia Press, 1995.

Jorgensen, Marianne, and Louise J. Phillips. *Discourse Analysis as Theory and Method*. Thousand Oaks: SAGE Publications, 2002.

Kaplan, Flora. "Exhibitions as Communicative Media." In *Museums, Media, Message*. Edited by Eilean Hooper-Greenhill, 37–58. New York: Routledge, 1995.

Karp, Ivan. "Introduction: Museums and Communities: The Politics of Public Culture." In *Museums and Communities: The Politics of Public Culture*. Edited by Ivan Karp, Christine Mullen Kreamer, and Steven Levine, 1–18. Washington, DC: Smithsonian Institution Press, 1992.

Katriel, Tamar. "Our Future Is Where Our Past Is: Studying Heritage Museums as Ideological and Performative Arenas." *Communication Monographs* 60, no. 1 (1993): 69–75.

Katriel, Tamar, and Aliza Shenhar. "Tower and Stockade: Dialogic Narration in Israeli Settlement Ethos." *Quarterly Journal of Speech* 76, no. 4 (1990): 359–80.

Kaufman, Will. *The Civil War in American Culture*. Baas Paperbacks. Edinburgh: Edinburgh University Press, 2006.

Kavanagh, Gaynor. *Dream Spaces: Memory and the Museum*. New York: Leicester University Press, 2002.

Kilkenny, Salome. "Travel and Tourism." *The Network Journal: Black Professionals and Small Business News*, May 2011. Accessed March 12, 2014. http://www.tnj.com/departments/industry-focus/travel-and-tourism-1.

Killian, Lewis M. *White Southerners*. Amherst: University of Massachusetts Press, 1985.

Klaus, Rikki. "West Says Obama Wants Americans to 'Be His Slave,' at Port St. Lu-

cie Rally." WPTV.com, July 2, 2012. Accessed July 14, 2014. http://www.tcpalm
.com/news/west-says-obama-wants-americans-be-his-slave-port.
Krautler, Hadwig. "Observations on Semiotic Aspects of the Museum Work of Otto
Neurath: Reflections on the 'Bildpadagogische Schriften' (Writings on Visual Edu-
cation)." In *Museum, Media, Message*. Edited by Eilean Hooper-Greenhill, 59–71.
New York: Routledge, 1995.
Lefebvre, Henri. *The Production of Space*. Malden: Blackwell Publishing, 1991.
Legg, Stephen. "Sites of Counter-Memory: The Refusal to Forget and the Nationalist
Struggle in Colonial Delhi." *Historical Geography* 33 (2005): 180–201.
Leib, Jonathon. "Separate Times, Shared Spaces: Arthur Ashe, Monument Avenue, and
the Politics of Richmond, Virginia's Symbolic Landscape." *Cultural Geographies* 9,
no. 3 (2002): 286–312.
Leinhardt, Gaea, and Karen Knutson. *Listening In on Museum Conversations*. Walnut
Creek: AltaMira Press, 2004.
Lévi-Strauss, Claude. "Introduction à l'œuvre de Marcel Mauss." In *Sociologie et an-
thropologie: Précédé d'une introduction à l'œuvre de Marcel Mauss*. Marcel Mauss, Paris:
Presses Universitaires de France, 1950, 1–2.
Levine, Bruce. *Confederate Emancipation: Southern Plans to Free and Arm Slaves During the
Civil War*. New York: Oxford University Press, 2007.
———. "In Search of a Usable Past: Neo-Confederates and Black Confederates." In
Slavery and Public History: The Tough Stuff of American Memory. Edited by James Hor-
ton and Lois Horton, 187–212. New York: The New Press, 2006.
Linenthal, Edward T. *Sacred Ground: Americans and Their Battlefields*. Champaign: Uni-
versity of Illinois Press, 1993.
Logan, Rayford. *The Negro in American Life and Thought: The Nadir, 1877–1901*. New
York: Dial Press, 1954.
Lucas, Demetria. "'12 Years a Slave': Black Audiences Need More Than Slave Narra-
tives." *The Grio*, October 31, 2013. Accessed November 18, 2013. http://thegrio
.com/2013/10/31/12-years-a-slave-loved-the-movie-tired-of-the-theme/.
Mackun, Paul, and Steven Wilson. "Population Distribution and Change: 2000–2010."
2010 Census Briefs. United States Census Bureau, March 2011. Accessed July 14,
2013. https://www.census.gov/prod/cen2010/briefs/c2010br-01.pdf.
Magelssen, Scott. "Living History Museums and the Construction of the Real through
Performance." *Theater Survey* 45, no. 1 (2004): 61–74.
Marty, Paul, and Katherine Burton Jones. *Museum Informatics: People, Information, and
Technologies in Museums*. London: Routledge, 2008.
Marty, Paul. "Museum Informatics." In *Encyclopedia of Library and Information Science*.
3rd ed. Edited by M. J. Bates and M. N. Maack, 3717–25. New York: Taylor and
Francis, 2010.
———. "Museum Websites and Museum Visitors: Digital Museum Resources and their
Use." *Museum Management and Curatorship* 23, no. 1, (2008): 81–99.
McKay, Nellie Y. "The Journals of Charlotte L. Forten-Grimke: *Les Lieux de Memoire*
in African-American Women's Autobiography." In *History and Memory in African
American Culture*. Edited by Genevieve Fabre and Robert O'Meally, 261–71. New
York: Oxford University Press, 1994.
McPhail, Mark Lawrence. "A Question of Character: Re(-)signing the Racial Con-
tract." *Rhetoric and Public Affairs* 7, no. 3 (2004): 397–98.

———. "Dessentializing Difference: Transformative Visions in Contemporary Black Thought." *Howard Journal of Communication* 13, no. 1 (2002): 77–95.

McPherson James. *Battle Cry of Freedom: The Civil War Era.* New York: Oxford University Press, 1988.

———. *Marching Toward Freedom: Blacks in the Civil War 1861–1865.* Library of American History. New York: Facts on File, 1991.

———. *The Negro's Civil War: How American Blacks Felt and Acted during the War for the Union.* New York: Vintage, 2003.

———. "Was Blood Thicker Than Water? Ethnic and Civic Nationalism in the American Civil War." *Proceedings of the American Philosophical Society* 143, no. 1 (1999): 102–8.

McPherson, Tara. "I'll take My Stand in Dixie-Net: White Guys, the South, and Cyberspace." In *Race in Cyberspace.* Edited by Beth E. Kolko, Lisa Nakamura, and Gilbert B. Rodman, 117–32. New York: Routledge, 2000.

McQuary, Anne. "Emancipating History." *New York Times,* March 12, 2011. Accessed January 29, 2014. http://www.nytimes.com/2011/03/12/arts/design/charlestons -museums-finally-chronicle-history-of-slavery.html?pagewanted=all.

Menzel, Margie. "Civil War Passions Still Run Deep as Union Supporters Propose Monument on Confederate Site." *Miami Herald,* December 3, 2013. Accessed January 23, 2014. http://miamiherald.typepad.com/nakedpolitics/2013/12.civil-war -passions-still-run-deep-as-union-supporters/propose-monument-on-confederate -site/.

———. "House Bill Would Give Lawmakers Final Say on Park Monuments," *News Service of Florida,* March 24, 2014. Accessed April 2, 2014. http://www.news4jax .com/politics/house-bill-would-give-lawmakers-final-say-on-park-monuments /25146156.

Milloy, Courtland. "African American Civil War Museum Dedication Honors Black Soldiers." In *Washington Post,* July 17, 2011. Accessed March 15, 2014. www.washingtonpost.com/local/african-american-civil-war-museum-dedication-honors-black-soldiers/2011/07/17/gIQA5IAZKI_story.html.

Mitchell, Don. *Cultural Geography: A Critical Introduction.* Malden, MA: Blackwell Publishers, 2000.

Mirzoeff, Nicholas. "On Visuality." *Journal of Visual Culture* 5, no. 1 (2006): 53–79.

Montgomery Jr., Elvin. *Collecting African American History: A Celebration of America's Black Heritage Through Documents, Artifacts, and Collectibles.* New York: Stewart, Tabori and Chang, 2001.

Mooney, Alexander. "Texas Governor Says Secession Possible." CNN.com, April 16, 2009. Accessed July 12, 2014. http://politicalticker.blogs.cnn.com/2009/04/16 /texas-governor-says-secession-possible/.

Morrison, Toni. "The Site of Memory." In *Inventing the Truth: The Art and Craft of Memoir.* Edited by William Zinssler Boston, 103–24. New York: Houghton Mifflin, 1987.

"Nathan Bedford Forrest Monument—Selma, Alabama." ExploreSouthernHistory.com. Accessed April 26, 2014. http://www.exploresouthernhistory.com/selmaforrest .html.

National Museum of American History. "U.S Civil War Colored Troops Medal." http://americanhistory.si.edu/collections/search/object/nmah_1060806.

Nerone, Michael, and Ellen Wartella. "Introduction: Studying Social Memory." *Communication,* 11, no. 2 (1989): 85–88.

Nietzsche, Friedrich Wilhelm. *The Use and Abuse of History.* New York: Cosimo, Inc., 2006.

Ochs, Elinor. "Constructing Social Identity: A Language Socialization Perspective." *Research on Language and Social Interaction* 26, no. 3 (1993): 287–306.

Ono, Kent A., and John M. Sloop. "The Critique of Vernacular Discourse." *Communications Monographs* 62, no. 1 (1995): 19–46.

Ott, Brian L., and Greg Dickinson. "Visual Rhetoric and/as Critical Pegagogy." In *The Sage Handbook of Rhetorical Studies.* Edited by Andrea A. Lunsford, Kirt H. Wilson, and Rosa A. Eberly, 391–406. Los Angeles: SAGE Publications, 2009.

Owen, A. Susan, and Peter Ehrenhaus. "The Moore's Ford Lynching Reenactment: Affective Memory and Race Trauma." *Text and Performance Quarterly* 34, no. 1 (2014): 72–90.

Palmer, Daniel. "Emotional Archives: Online Photo Sharing and the Cultivation of the Self." *Photographies* 3, no. 2, (2010): 155–71.

Palmer, Joy. "Archives 2.0: If We Build It, Will They Come?" *Ariadne* 60 (2009). Accessed April 22, 2014. http://www.ariadne.ac.uk/issue60/palmer.

Patterson, Matt. "Union Invasion: UAW Targets Tennessee." WorkplaceChoice, June 4, 2013. Accessed January 21, 2014. http://workplacechoice.org/2013/06/04/union -invasion-uaw-targets-tennessee/.

Payton, Marius. "Debate Continues to Swirl Around Nathan Bedford Forrest Statue." MyFoxMemphis.com, July 8, 2015. Accessed July 17, 2015. http://www .myfoxmemphis.com/story/29495406/city-council-passes-ordinance-to-remove -nathan-bedford-forrest-statue.

Peers, Laura, and Alison K. Brown. "Museums and Source Communities." In *Museums and Their Communities.* Edited by Sheila Watson, 519–37. New York: Routledge, 2007.

Pew Research Center. "Civil War at 150: Still Relevant, Still Divisive." Pew Research Center, April 8, 2011. U.S. Politics and Policy. Accessed July 26, 2013. http://www .people-press.org/2011/04/08/civil-war-at-150-still-relevant-still-divisive/.

Pitcaithley, Dwight T. "'A Cosmic Threat': The National Park Service Addresses the Causes of the American Civil War." In *Slavery and Public History: The Tough Stuff of American Memory.* Edited by James Horton and Lois Horton, 169–86. New York: New Press, 2006.

Ponse, Barbara. *Identities in the Lesbian World: The Social Construction of Self.* Westport, CT: Greenwood Press, 1978.

Pollock, Della. Introduction to *Exceptional Spaces: Essays in Performance and History.* Edited by Della Pollock, 1–46. Chapel Hill: University of North Carolina Press, 1998.

Punday, Daniel. *Narrative Bodies: Toward a Corporeal Narratology.* New York: Palgrave MacMillan, 2003.

Prince, K. Michael. "Neo-Confederates in the Basement: The League of the South and the Crusade against Southern Emasculation." In *White Masculinity in the Recent South.* Making the Modern South. Edited by Trent Watts, 146–71. Baton Rouge: Louisiana State University Press, 2008.

"Proposal to Rename Edmund Pettus Bridge Dies in House." *Montgomery Advertiser.* Accessed November 1, 2015. http://www.montgomeryadvertiser.com/story/news /politics/southunionstreet/2015/06/05/proposal-rename-edmund-pettus-bridge -dies-house/28537757/.

Quarstein, John and Dennis Mroczkowski. *Ft. Monroe: The Key to the South*. Mount Pleasant, SC: Arcadia Publishing, 2000.

Radley, Alan. "Artefacts, Memory, and a Sense of the Past." In *Collective Remembering*. Edited by David Middleton and Derek Edwards, 46–59. Thousand Oaks: SAGE Publications, 1990.

Rastorgi, Sonya, Tallese D. Johnson, Elizabeth M. Hoeffel, and Malcolm P. Drewery Jr. "The Black Population: 2010." 2010 Census Briefs. United States Census Bureau, September 2011. Accessed July 14, 2013. https://www.census.gov/prod/cen2010 /briefs/c2010br-06.pdf.

Redkey, Edwin S. "Henry Mcneal Turner: Black Chaplain in the Union Army." In *Black Soldiers in Blue: African American Troops in the Civil War Era*. Edited by John David Smith, 336–60. Chapel Hill: University of North Carolina Press, 2002.

Reeve, Elspeth. "Parties Fight Over Who Gets to Talk About Slavery." *The Wire*, August 31, 2011. Accessed July 14, 2014. http://www.thewire.com/politics/2011/08 /parties-fight-over-who-gets-talk-about-slavery/41949/.

Reid, Richard M. *Freedom for Themselves: North Carolina's Black Soldiers in the Civil War Era*. Chapel Hill: University of North Carolina Press, 2008.

Reidy, Joseph P. "The African American Struggle for Citizenship Rights in the Northern United States During the Civil War." In *Civil War Citizens: Race, Ethnicity, and Identity in America's Bloodiest Conflict*. Edited by Susannah J. Ural, 213–36. New York: New York University Press, 2010.

Richardson, Riché. *Black Masculinity and the U.S. South: From Uncle Tom to Gangsta*. The New Southern Studies. Athens: University of Georgia Press, 2007.

Rife, Luanne. "W&L Will Remove Flags from Lee Chapel." *Roanoke Times*, July 8, 2014. A1.

Ritchie, Bruce. "Bill Prompted by Outcry against Union Monument on Civil War Battlefield Narrowly Passes." The FloridaCurrent.com, March 24, 2014. Accessed April 2, 2014. http://www.thefloridacurrent.com/article.cfm?id=36958041.

Richmond Times-Dispatch. "Virginia Must Lead on Racial Truth and Reconciliation." July 11, 2015. Accessed July 19, 2015. http://www.richmond.com/opinion/our -opinion/article_5fca16bd-63ec-5b64-9216-47b445b438b0.html.

Robertson, Campbell. "Before the Battles and the Protests, the Chains." *New York Times*, December 9, 2013. Accessed January 15, 2014. www.nytimes.com/2013/12/10/us /before-the-battles-and-the-protests-the-chains.

Robertson, William G. "From the Crater to New Market Heights: A Tale of Two Divisions." In *Black Soldiers in Blue: African American Troops in the Civil War Era*. Edited by John David Smith, 169–99. Chapel Hill: University of North Carolina Press, 2002.

Romano, Renee C., and Leigh Raiford, eds. *The Civil Rights Movement in American Memory*. Athens: University of Georgia Press, 2006.

Root, Kim O'Brien. "Panel: Fort Monroe Should Become a Museum." *Daily Press*, January 5, 2008. Accessed June 22, 2014. http://www.dailypress.com/news/hampton /dpnews_monroe_0105jan05,0,5202832.story.

Rosenzweig, Roy, and David Thelen. *The Presence of the Past: Popular Uses of History in American Life*. New York: Columbia University Press, 1998.

Rothstein, Edward. "Emancipating History." *New York Times*, March 11, 2011. Accessed January 29, 2014. http://www.nytimes.com/2011/03/12/arts/design/ charlestons-museums-finally-chronicle-history-of-slavery.html?pagewanted=all.

Sandell, Richard. *Museums, Prejudice, and the Reframing of Difference*. New York: Routledge, 2006.

Sandell, Richard, ed. *Museums, Society, Inequality*. New York: Routledge, 2002.

Savage, Kirk. *Standing Soldiers, Kneeling Slaves: Race, War, and Monument in 19th Century America*. Princeton: Princeton University Press, 1997.

Savali, Kristen West. "Why the Black Backlash Against '12 Years a Slave?'" *The Grio*, October 31, 2013. Accessed November 18, 2013. http://thegrio.com/2013/10/31/why-the-black-backlash-against-12-years-a-slave/.

Scheub, Harold. "Performance of Oral Narrative." In *Frontiers of Folklore*. Edited by William Russell Bascom, 69–73. Boulder: Westview Press, 1977.

Schivelbusch, Wolfgang. *The Culture of Defeat: On National Trauma, Mourning, and Recovery*. New York: Picador, 2004.

Schwartz, Barry. *Abraham Lincoln and the Forge of National Memory*. Chicago: University of Chicago Press, 2003.

Schwartz, Joan M., and Terry Cook. "Archives, Records, and Power: The Making of Modern Memory," *Archival Science* 2, nos. 1–2 (2002): 1–19.

Scott, David. "Introduction: On the Archaeologies of Black Memory." *Small Axe* 12, no. 2 (2008): v–xvi.

"Selma Ordnance and Naval Foundry." In *Encyclopedia of Alabama*. Accessed April 18, 2014. http://www.encyclopediaofalabama.org/face/Article.jsp?id=h-2331.

Selzer, Jack, and Sharon Crowley, eds. *Rhetorical Bodies*. Madison: University of Wisconsin Press, 1999.

Shackel, Paul A. *Memory in Black and White: Memory, Commemoration, and the Post-Bellum Landscape*. Lanham: AltaMita Press, 2003.

Sherman, Joan R. *The Black Bard of North Carolina: George Moses Horton and His Poetry*. Chapel Hill: University of North Carolina Press, 1997.

Shilton, Katie and Srinivasan, Ramesh. "Participatory Appraisal and Arrangement for Multicultural Archival Collections." *Archivaria* 63 (2007): 87–101.

Slotkin, Richard. *No Quarter: The Battle of the Crater, 1864*. New York: Random House, 2009.

Small, Stephen. "Still Back of the Big House: Slave Cabins and Slavery in Southern Heritage Tourism." *Tourism Geographies* 15, no. 3 (2013): 405–23.

Smith, Bruce. "Charleston to Build Black History Museum Near Slave Trade Site." *Huffington Post*, October 23, 2013. Accessed December 29, 2013. http://www.huffingtonpost.com/2013/10/24/charleston-black-history-museum_n_4151800.html.

Smith, John David. "Let Us All be Grateful That We Have Colored Troops That Will Fight." In *Black Soldiers in Blue: African American Troops in the Civil War Era*. Edited by John David Smith, 1–77. Chapel Hill: University of North Carolina Press, 2002.

Smith, Jonathan Z. *Map Is Not Territory: Studies in the History of Religions*. Chicago: University of Chicago Press, 1995.

Smith, Sidonie, and Julia Watson, eds. *Getting a Life: Everyday Uses of Autobiography*. Minneapolis: University of Minnesota Press, 1996.

Somanader, Tonya. "Bachmann responds to Slavery Controversy with Another Slavery Analogy." *ThinkProgress.org*, July 11, 2011. Accessed July 14, 2014. http://thinkprogress.org/politics/2011/07/11/265142/bachmann-responds-to-slavery-controversy/.

Spielvogel, J. Christian. *Interpreting Sacred Ground: The Rhetoric of National Civil War Parks and Battlefields.* Tuscaloosa: University of Alabama Press, 2013.

Stanglin, Doug. "Memphis Changes Names of 3 Confederate-Themed Parks." *USA Today,* February 6, 2013. Accessed January 15, 2014. http://www.usatoday.com/story /news/nation/2013/02/06/memphis-parks-confederate-ku-klux-klan/1895549/.

Stanton, Cathy, and Stephen Belyea. "Their Time Will Yet Come: The African American Presence in Civil War Reenactment." In *Hope and Glory: Essays on the Legacy of the 54th Massachusetts Regiment.* Edited by Martin Blatt, Tom Brown, and Donald Yacovone, 253–74. Amherst: University of Massachusetts Press, 2001.

Starling, Marion. "The Slave Narrative: Its Place in American Literary History." PhD diss., New York University, 1946.

Stein, Leigh. "I Would Have Followed Them into Battle: Female Reenactors Portray Women Who Passed as Men to Fight." Slate.com, April 27, 2014. Accessed April 29, 2014. http://www.slate.com/articles/news_and_politics/history/2014/04/female _civil_war_re_enactors_portray_women_who_passed_as_men_to_fight.html.

Stein, Robert. "Chiming in on Museums and Participatory Culture." *Curator: The Museum Journal* 55, no. 2 (2012): 215–26.

Stewart, Jeffrey, and Faith Davis Ruffins. "A Faithful Witness: Afro-American History in Historical Perspective, 1828–1994." In *Presenting the Past: Essays on History and the Public.* Edited by Susan Porter Benson, Stephen Brier, and Roy Rosenzweig, 307–38. Philadelphia: Temple University Press, 1986.

"The Stonewall of Forks Road." Cape Fear Historical Institute Papers. Accessed January 15, 2014. http://www.cfhi.net/TheBattleofForksRoad.php.

Stover, Johnnie M. *Rhetoric and Resistance in Black Women's Autobiography.* Gainesville: University Press of Florida, 2003.

Strauss, Mitchell D. "Identity Construction among Confederate Civil War Reenactors: A Study of Dress, Stage Props, and Discourse." *Clothing and Textiles Research Journal* 21, no. 4, (2003): 149–61.

Sturken, Marita. *Tangled Memories: The Vietnam War, the AIDS Epidemic, and the Politics of Remembering.* Berkeley: University of California Press, 1997.

Suitts, Steve. "Voting Rights, the Supreme Court, and the Persistence of Southern History." *Southern Spaces,* June 4, 2013. Accessed February 20, 2014. http://southernspaces .org/2013/voting-rights-supreme-court-and-persistence-southern-history#sthash .qBGrR5Gf.dpuf.

Taylor, Diana. *The Archive and the Repertoire: Performing Cultural Memory in the Americas.* Durham: Duke University Press, 2003.

"Text of Letter to President Obama." *ABC News.* Accessed April 30, 2014. http:// abcnews.go.com/US/Story?id=7658404&page=1.

Thompson, Ashley B., and Melissa M. Sloan. "Race as Region, Region as Race: How Black and White Southerners Understand Their Regional Identities." *Southern Cultures* 18, no. 4 (2012): 72–95.

Thompson, Gayle. "Lynyrd Skynyrd Confederate Flag Waves On." *The Boot,* September 25, 2012. Accessed June 26, 2014. http://theboot.com/lynyrd-skynyrd -confederate-flag/.

Thompson, Paul. *The Voice of the Past: Oral History.* New York, NY: Oxford University Press, 1978.

Towns, W. Stuart. *Enduring Legacy: Rhetoric and Ritual of the Lost Cause.* Tuscaloosa: University of Alabama Press, 2012.

Trescott, Jacqueline. "African American Civil War Museum Celebrates Reopening in Larger Location." *Washington Post*, July 8, 2011. Accessed May 13, 2013. http://www.washingtonpost.com/lifestyle/style/african-american-civil-war-museum-celebrates-reopening-in-larger-location/2011/06/30/gIQApPjb1H_story.html.

Trudeau, Noah Andre. *Like Men of War: Black Troops in the Civil War, 1862–1865*. New York: Little Brown and Company, 1998.

———. "Proven Themselves in Every Respect to Be Men: Black Cavalry in the Civil War." In *Black Soldiers in Blue: African American Troops in the Civil War Era*. Edited by John David Smith, 276–305. Chapel Hill: University of North Carolina Press, 2003.

Tullos, Allen. "Selma Bridge: Always under Construction," *Southern Spaces*, July 28, 2008. Accessed May 4, 2014. http://southernspaces.org/2008/selma-bridge-always-under-construction.

Turkle, Sherry. *Life on the Screen: Identity in the Age of the Internet*. New York: Simon and Shuster, 1995.

Turner, Victor. *The Ritual Process: Structure and Anti-Structure*. Chicago: Aldine Transaction, 1995.

Tyler-McGraw, Marie. "Southern Comfort Levels: Race, Heritage Tourism, and the Civil War in Richmond." In *Slavery and Public History: The Tough Stuff of American Memory*. Edited by James Oliver Horton and Lois E. Horton, 151–68. Chapel Hill: University of North Carolina Press, 2006.

United States Census Bureau. "American Fact Finder." Accessed March 12, 2014. http://factfinder2.census.gov/faces/tableservices/jsf/pages/productview.xhtml?pid=ACS_12_5YR_DP05.

Valtysson, Bjarki. "Access Culture: Web 2.0 and Cultural Participation." *International Journal of Cultural Policy* 16, no. 2 (2010): 200–214.

Vander Wal, Thomas. "Folksonomy" Vanderwal.net, February 7, 2007. Accessed May 5, 2014. http://www.vanderwal.net/folksonomy.html.

Vlach, John Michale. "The Last Great Taboo Subject: Exhibiting Slavery at the Library of Congress." In *Slavery and Public History: The Tough Stuff of American Memory*. Edited by James Oliver Horton and Lois E. Horton, 57–74. Chapel Hill: University of North Carolina Press, 2006.

Ward Jr., Thomas J. "The Plight of the Black POW." *The New York Times*, August 27, 2013. Accessed January 30, 2014. http://opinionator.blogs.nytimes.com/2013/08/27/the-plight-of-the-black-p-o-w/.

Warshauer, Mark. "Language, Identity, and the Internet." In *Race in Cyberspace*. Edited by Beth E. Kolko, Lisa Nakamura, and Gilbert B. Rodman, 151–70. New York: Routledge, 2000.

Watson, Sheila. "Introduction to Part Three." In *Museums and Their Communities*. Edited by Sheila Watson, 269–75. New York: Routledge, 2007.

Watts, Eric King. "Cultivating a Black Public Voice: W. E. B. Du Bois and the 'Criteria of Negro Art.'" *Rhetoric and Public Affairs* 4, no. 2, (2001): 181–201.

Watts, Rebecca Bridges. *Contemporary Southern Identity: Community Through Controversy*. Jackson: University Press of Mississippi, 2007.

Wilder, L. Douglas. "Wilder: Locate the Slavery Museum in Shockoe." *Richmond Times-Dispatch*, February 26, 2014. Accessed March 27, 2014. http://www.timesdispatch.com/opinion/their-opinion/columnists-blogs/guest-columnists/wilder-locate

-the-slavery-museum-in-shockoe/article_fcbe76a9–586c–5d13–8b98–95b8f7579876
.html.

Williams, Chad L. *Torchbearers of Democracy: African American Soldiers in the World War I Era*. Chapel Hill: University of North Carolina Press, 2010.

Wills, Garry. *Lincoln at Gettysburg: The Words That Remade America*. New York: Simon and Schuster, 1992.

Wilson, Charles Reagan. *Judgment and Grace in Dixie: Southern Faiths from Folklore to Elvis*. Athens: University of Georgia Press, 2007.

Wilson, Kirt. "The Racial Politics of Imitation in the Nineteenth Century." *Quarterly Journal of Speech* 89, no. 2, (2003): 89–188.

Woodward, C. Vann. "Look Away, Look Away." *The Journal of Southern History* 59, no. 3 (1993): 487–504.

Woodward, William E. *Meet General Grant*. Whitefish, MT: Kessinger, 2003.

Yetman, Norman R., ed. *Voices from Slavery: 100 Authentic Slave Narratives*. Mineola, New York: Courier Dover Publications: 2000.

Yoneyama, Lisa. "For Transformative Knowledge and Postnationalist Public Spheres: The Smithsonian Enola Gay Controversy." In *Perilous Memories: The Asia-Pacific War(s)*. Edited by T. Fujitani, Geoffrey M. White, and Lisa Yoneyama, 323–46. Durham and London: Duke University Press, 2001.

Zagacki, Kenneth, and Victoria Gallagher. "Rhetoric and Materiality in the Museum Park at the North Carolina Museum of Art." *Quarterly Journal of Speech* 95, no. 2 (2009): 171–91.

Index

African American Civil War Memorial Freedom Foundation, 77

African American Civil War Museum and Freedom Foundation (AACWM): black civil rights, 105; black identity, 110; black memory, 110; civil rights movement, 105; Civil War-era on display, 105; Civil War-era history, 105; hegemonic memories (disruptive of), 121; history (community-specific), 99; performance (interactive), 102; place, use of, 99; presentations, 102; rhetorical approach, 99; spatial features, 94; social space, 102; Washington, DC, 75–77, 98

African American history museums: resistant memories constructed through, 74

African American reenactors, 15, 18, 20–21, 25–38, 43–70, 83, 134

African American/s, 2, 152, 154; activists, 119; actors, 14; agency, 13–15, 18; alternative narratives, 33; as in audience, 139; caricatures, 7; Civil War history (notions of), 151; Civil War memory, 46; communicative practices, 5; concerns, 80, 87; consumers, 124; contributions, 33; critiques of power, 35; discourse, 25; dominant notions, 11; experiences, 7; hegemonic history (intervening critically in), 53; his-

torical agency (sense of), 33; historical consumers, 14; historical endurance, 145; historical experiences (demanding recognition of), 150; historical experiences (in the war), 95; historical objects, 14; historical producers, 14; historical representation, 80; historical subjects, 14; ideological access, 30; identity (struggles over), 35; memories (recovery of), 5; narrative traditions of, 126; national community (position within), 40; population, 12; power, 150; source communities, 124; South, the (identification with), 5; South, the (migration out of), 12; South, the (return migration to), 4; southerners (likely to identify as), 16; symbolic annihilation, 7, 11, 16; transformation from objects to subjects, 53; trauma, 5; unique needs of, 133–34, 139; veterans, 36. *See also* agency, battle reenactments; Civil War; narratives; *12 Years a Slave*

African American southern identity: analysis of, 17; belonging (ideal of), 15; Civil War memory (definition of), 4; Civil War memory (role of), 4; contemporary inequalities (transhistorical nature of), 14; representation (practices of), 4; sectional identification (acknowledgment), 15;